W9-AAE-616

Sex and the American Teenager

Seeing through the Myths and Confronting the Issues

R. Murray Thomas

Rowman & Littlefield Education
Lanham • New York • Toronto • Plymouth, UK

Published in the United States of America
by Rowman & Littlefield Education
A Division of Rowman & Littlefield Publishers, Inc.
A wholly owned subsidiary of The Rowman & Littlefield Publishing Group, Inc.
4501 Forbes Boulevard, Suite 200, Lanham, Maryland 20706
www.rowmaneducation.com

Estover Road
Plymouth PL6 7PY
United Kingdom

British Cataloging in Publication Information Available

Library of Congress Cataloging-in-Publication Data

Thomas, R. Murray (Robert Murray), 1921–
Sex and the American teenager : seeing through the myths and confronting the issues / R. Murray Thomas.
p. cm.
Includes bibliographical references and index.
ISBN-13: 978-1-60709-016-8 (cloth : alk. paper)
ISBN-10: 1-60709-016-3 (cloth : alk. paper)
ISBN-13: 978-1-60709-018-2 (electronic)
ISBN-10: 1-60709-018-X (electronic)
1. Students—Sexual behavior—United States. 2. Sexual harassment in education—United States. 3. Sex instruction—United States. I. Title.
HQ27.T448 2009
371.7'140973—dc22 2008041596

∞™ The paper used in this publication meets the minimum requirements of American National Standard for Information Sciences—Permanence of Paper for Printed Library Materials, ANSI/NISO Z39.48-1992.
Manufactured in the United States of America.

Contents

Chapter 1

Decisions about Sex in Schools

Statistics compiled in recent years suggest why American schools cannot easily ignore students' sex lives.

- Around half of all Americans ages 15 to 19 have had vaginal intercourse, and more than half have had oral sex. Whereas by age 15 only 13 percent of teens have ever had sex, 70 percent have engaged in sexual intercourse by the time they reach age 19.
- Every year 3 million teens—about 1 in 4 sexually active youths—get a sexually transmitted disease, with chlamydia and gonorrhea more common among teens aged 15 to 19 than in any other age group. Each year, hundreds of adolescents also become infected with HIV (human immunodeficiency virus), which can destroy their body's protection against serious infections.
- Between 1990 and 2004, the pregnancy rate for America's 15- to 19-year-olds decreased by an average of 3 percent a year; an estimated 11.7 percent of teenage girls were pregnant in 1990 compared with 7.6 percent in 2002. By 2004, about 31 percent of teenage girls had become pregnant before they were 20 years old. A sexually active teenage girl who did not use contraceptives had a 90 percent chance of becoming pregnant within a year. By the mid-1990s, the rate in the United States had become the highest of any of the world's industrialized democracies—twice as high as that of England, France, and Canada, and nine times as high as the Netherlands and Japan (Bailey & Piercy, 1997). The decline in teen pregnancies from 1990 to 2005 reversed in 2006 when the teen birth rate began to rise, and unmarried childbearing increased significantly (Ventura, 2007).

- About one quarter of Americans have been victims of some form of child sexual abuse, ranging from unwanted touching to sexual intercourse. Some of the abuse has occurred in schools.

Such numbers reflect conditions that impose on students and school personnel the need to decide what to do about matters of sex in schools. Typical kinds of decisions are illustrated in the following sampling of incidents that students and school personnel can face.

STUDENTS' DECISIONS

Among sexual episodes that require student decisions, some concern (a) joining the crowd, (b) interrupting schoolmates' sex acts, (c) serving as a lookout for classmates who engage in sexual behavior, (d) objecting to condoms, and (e) avoiding embarrassment.

Joining the Crowd

The Incident

In a suburban high school, 16-year-old Lucinda's classmates urged her to join them in "ditching school next Friday for a hooky party at Lance's house. Everybody who's anybody is cutting school that day to be at Lance's. His parents will be away at Palm Springs all next week."

Lucinda had never been to a hooky party, so it was only by hearsay that she knew the day would be devoted to drinking and having sex. If she didn't go to the party, she suspected that her refusal could alienate her closest school friends and acquaintances—both girls and boys. And she knew for sure that her parents would "raise hell" if they learned of the escapade.

Lucinda's Decision

Should she go to the hooky party? And if she did go, how could she keep her parents from learning about it? What would she say to her parents if they found out? But if she did not go, how would she explain to her classmates why she had turned down their invitation? And if she did not go, should she tell her parents about the hooky-party plan and explain to them that she had refused her classmates' offer? Should she tip off school authorities about the party plan—perhaps by sending an anonymous note to the principal?

Interrupting Couples

The Incident

Even though students had been warned to stay out of the high-school auditorium when no programs were being held there, teenagers who yearned to try illicit lovemaking during school hours often found the temptation irresistible. Other students who simply wanted to doze would also occasionally slip into the darkened hall. On one such occasion, Mark—a 17-year-old linebacker on the high-school football team—had crept into the auditorium for a short nap when he discovered an 18-year-old team member engaged in oral sex with a freshman girl whose parents were close friends of Mark's father and mother.

Mark's Decision

Should Mark interrupt the couple and tell them to stop, or should he just ignore them? Should he tell his parents about the episode? Should he tell any other students? Should he inform anyone on the school staff?

Becoming a Lookout

The Incident

The fifth-grade teacher in a small rural school was called from the classroom to help with a medical emergency on the playground. While she was away, two 11-year-old girls and two 12-year-old boys pulled down their pants to engage in intercourse on the floor while their classmates watched. They told a fellow student, Michael, to stand outside the classroom door and warn them if any adults were coming.

Michael's Decision

Should Michael agree to be the sentinel? Should he tell the quartet of miscreants to abandon their plan? Should he later report the incident to his parents or to school personnel?

Objecting to Condoms

The Incident

In order to join the high school's junior-varsity volleyball team, 16-year-old Jessie was required to take a physical examination to ensure that she was fit to play. The woman physician who conducted the exam discovered that Jessie had chlamydia and thus should take antibiotics to clear up the infection. During the interview, the physician asked when Jessie had last engaged in intercourse. Jessie said it had been two weeks earlier with her steady boyfriend, an 18-year-old schoolmate. When the physician asked why Jessie's boyfriend didn't use a condom, Jessie said her boyfriend told her a condom "was a bother and took the fun out of it." When the physician asked why Jessie didn't insist on his using a condom, Jessie said, "He said he wouldn't love me any more and he'd get another girlfriend, and I couldn't stand that. I'll take a birth-control pill instead." But the doctor informed her that the pill would not protect her from getting chlamydia again. "There are only two ways you can avoid having him reinfect you. Either you stop having sex with him, or he uses a condom."

Jessie's Decision

Jessie faced a variety of options in deciding what to do in the future. She could insist that her lover use a condom. Or she could insist that he cure his case of chlamydia by taking antibiotics before she had intercourse with him again. Or she could refuse to engage in sex again and thereby risk losing her boyfriend. Or she could continue their sex sessions in the hope that, if she did become reinfected, she could again take antibiotics to rid herself of the disease.

Avoiding Embarrassment

The Incident

At the close of the health-education class, 16-year-old Shawn stopped to talk with Mr. Lopez, the basketball coach who also served as the high-school's health-education teacher. Larry asked, "If I needed a condom, isn't there some way to get it without having to buy it in a drug store?"

MR. LOPEZ: You don't feel comfortable buying condoms there?

SHAWN: The checkout clerk there is a woman who knows our family.

MR. LOPEZ: So it's embarrassing?

SHAWN: Well, yeah. I don't want people spreading it around that I've been . . . well, you know.

MR. LOPEZ: I understand. Yes, there are other ways to get condoms. One is through the Internet. Enter the words "buy condom" into Google or some other search engine and you'll find places that will mail condoms to you. Or have a friend buy them at a drugstore. Or look for a store with one of those dispensers on the wall. You put your money in, and the package comes out. No need to face a checkout clerk.

Shawn's Decision

The choices Shawn had in mind for solving his dilemma include (a) abstaining from sexual encounters, (b) substituting oral sex for intercourse, (c) removing his penis from the girl's vagina before he ejaculates, (d) buying condoms at a drugstore where no one knows him, (e) buying over the Internet but facing the problem of having the condoms delivered at his home where his parents might receive them, (f) locating a dispenser, or (g) asking a friend to buy the condoms.

SCHOOLS' DECISIONS

Among problems faced by school personnel are ones that involve (a) releasing news of student sexual behavior, (b) dismissing a sex abuser, (c) designing sex education, (d) banning library books, and (e) limiting students' Internet access.

Releasing News of Student Sexual Behavior

The Incident

In a middle school's woodwork and metalwork shop, two sixth-graders—a boy and a girl—performed sexual intercourse behind the lumber-storage area while the instructor was helping another student operate a lathe in the front of the room. Several class members witnessed the sex act. One of them served as a lookout to warn the erotic pair if the instructor appeared. The instructor did appear and stopped the act.

The Principal's Decision

The school principal faced several options for coping with the episode. Should she announce the incident to the press and then expect clamor from a shocked public? Should she send a letter home to parents, explaining what had occurred and what action had been taken in response to the event? Or should she warn the school staff to keep the matter quiet so as not to upset parents? When news of the incident finally leaks out—as it might well do, because other students had witnessed the episode—should the principal issue a statement to the press and parents that "Two students were involved in inappropriate conduct in a lab class last semester. We have investigated the matter and have taken appropriate action. The school staff considers the matter closed and will have no further comment"?

The Superintendent's Decision

When the news of the event does spread, should the district superintendent hold a meeting that parents can attend in order to air the incident? Then, following the meeting, should the superintendent send a letter to parents that reads:

> I would like to thank the many parents who attended the meeting last night. The majority of comments favored the way the school has responded to this incident and were very supportive of the good work being done by the middle-school staff. I also heard the comments of those who disagreed with our actions, and I respect their right to differ with our approach.
>
> My major concern, however, is how we move forward from this point. While we would all like to think that similar misconduct will not occur again, I do not think this is a realistic view. Accordingly, if sexual misconduct occurs at our schools, we will proceed as we did in this situation following these steps: (1) we will notify law enforcement and child protective services so they can determine if criminal or child abuse charges need to be pursued; (2) we will investigate the situation and determine if our staff acted properly in supervising the students and addressing the behavior; (3) we will discipline the students following the requirements of due process and informing and involving parents in that process; (4) if other students witness the behavior, we will advise their parents of the circumstances so they may counsel with their students.
>
> Absent unusual circumstances, we will not advise other students or parents of the incident. Instead, we will deal with these issues in a way that respects and protects the confidentiality of the students in abiding by relevant state and/or federal requirements. We believe this approach has the support of a wide majority of our parents. (Warren Township, 2007)

Dismissing a Sex Abuser

The Incident

Three members of the high-school girls' softball team accused their coach of unwanted sexual overtures. According to the girls, he had patted each of them on the bottom, put his arm around their shoulders, remarked how attractive he found their figures, and told "off-color" jokes. On one occasion he had offered to drive one player home, and then said they could stop by his house on the way in order to have a drink or two. The girl had rejected the offer.

When the girls' parents brought the accusations to the high-school principal and threatened a lawsuit if the coach was allowed to continue on the job, the principal agreed to investigate the charges. His interviews with the three girls and their teammates convinced him that the coach had indeed violated the school district's sexual harassment policies.

The Administrator's Decision

The principal considered four choices for settling the dispute. He could dismiss the staff member as coach of the softball team but not remove him from his other role at the school as a biology teacher. Or he could fire the coach and also request the state department of education to revoke the coach's license to teach, an action that could result in the teachers' union fighting the revocation request by means of a costly, protracted lawsuit. Or he could fire the coach from the school staff but not ask the department of education to revoke the coach's teaching license, thereby enabling the coach to teach in a different school. Or, if the coach agreed to resign quietly from the school, the principal would offer to write a favorable recommendation letter for him to use when seeking work elsewhere.

Designing Sex Education

The Incident

For the past 8 years, a middle school's health-education course had included several sex-education lessons. The lessons were aimed at convincing students that the only acceptable way they could avoid pregnancy and sexually transmitted infections was to abstain from vaginal intercourse, oral sex, and anal sex. School officials, by agreeing to adopt an abstinence-only approach to sex education, received funds from the federal government. However, research evidence in recent years had revealed that a sizable number of youths who signed an abstinence pledge often broke the pledge by having sexual encounters while still in their teens. Furthermore, during those encounters the youngsters had often failed to use any method of protection against pregnancy and disease. In light of such evidence, health officials urged the inclusion of information about condoms and birth-control pills in sex-education programs so that youths who did not abstain would know how to protect themselves from unwanted pregnancies and infections. Within the middle school's own student population, there continued to be unplanned pregnancies and sexually transmitted diseases despite the abstinence-only lessons.

The problem the school's faculty now faced was that of deciding whether to expand sex-education lessons to include information about methods, other than abstinence, for avoiding pregnancy and disease.

The Faculty's Decision

Faculty members weighed the following options in their attempt to design a satisfactory sex-education program. The school could:

- Retain the present *abstinence-only* program and thereby continue receiving government funds for sex education.
- Adopt an *abstinence-plus* program, thereby teaching abstinence as the surest way to prevent unwanted pregnancy and disease but also including information about such protective devices as males' and females' condoms and females' birth-control pills. However, by adding information about protective measures, the school would not only lose the federal funds but would also alienate religious groups and parents who were strong advocates of abstinence-only programs.
- Change to an abstinence-plus approach and then appeal to philanthropic foundations or health-education organizations for money to compensate for the loss of government funds.
- Prepare the public—and particularly parents—for the transition to abstinence-plus by mounting a publicity campaign to explain the reasons for the change. The campaign would include press releases, letters to parents, and public meetings.

Banning Library Books

The Incident

At an elementary school's monthly Parent Teacher Association meeting, a husband and wife demanded that school officials remove from the school library a book titled *And Tango Makes Three*. The couple, whose son and daughter attended the school, portrayed themselves as evangelical Christians who objected to the school's advocating homosexuality as an acceptable lifestyle. They said that *And Tango Makes Three* "clearly valorizes homosexuality, tacitly urging children to become homosexual." Several additional parents at the meeting spoke in support of the couple's complaint, whereas others questioned the wisdom of censuring any library books, especially without a thorough understanding of the books' virtues and vices. The school principal, in response to the debate, said she would investigate the book-banning proposal and report her decision at the next PTA meeting.

The Principal's Decision

In judging the worth of the parents' complaint, the principal (a) read the book, (b) consulted published reviews of the book, (c) asked the school librarian's opinion, and (d) invited several parents to a meeting with three teachers to discuss banning the book. The principal ended up with four options from which she could choose for settling the controversy.

Read the book. The principal discovered that *And Tango Makes Three* was a children's book about Roy and Silo, a pair of male penguins in New York City's Central Park Zoo. Over a 6-year period, the two were inseparable—engaging in such ecstatic behavior as entwining their necks, vocalizing, and having sex. Zookeepers failed in their attempts to get the pair interested in female penguins. Then Roy and Silo displayed a parenting instinct by trying to hatch a stone. When sympathetic zookeepers replaced the stone with an abandoned penguin egg, Roy and Silo hatched the egg and adopted the resulting female penguin as their child—Tango. The result was an unconventional family—a child with a pair of gay male parents.

Consulted reviews. When the book was first published in 2005, it was lauded by some readers and condemned by others. It received several prestigious awards—a 2006 American Library Association Notable Children's Book citation and the Gustavus Myer Outstanding Book Award. It was a *Nick Jr. Family Magazine* Best Book of the Year and a Bank Street Best Book of the Year. At the same time, *And Tango Makes Three* was the most challenged book of 2006 for portraying homosexuality and a nontraditional family structure as acceptable lifestyles. The book was condemned by critics as especially unsuitable for young children.

Consulted the librarian. The librarian suggested that the book be retained with the understanding that students could read it if their parents gave permission.

Chaired a meeting. Two parents who had objected to the book at the PTA meeting and two who had objected to censoring the book were invited to a meeting with three teachers (first grade, fourth grade, sixth grade). The meeting, led by the principal, gave all members an opportunity to voice their opinion of the book.

The resulting options. The four alternative actions from which the principal would choose her solution were those of

- Permanently removing *And Tango Make Three* from the school library.
- Retaining the book, but permitting only pupils in grades 5 and 6 to borrow it.
- Retaining the book, but allowing children to read it only if their parents gave written permission.
- Removing the book from the library, but allowing teachers to use it in the classroom where they could guide the interpretation that pupils might draw from the story.

Limiting Internet Access

The Incidents

The Internet and its World Wide Web provide students entry to millions of web pages that have sexual content, including pornography, deviant sexual behavior, and sex predators. A high school's faculty members were distressed about students using school computers to access such websites. Not only was such a practice deemed damaging to students' moral development, but it wasted time that should be invested in constructive learning. The problem the faculty faced was that of controlling what students viewed on the Internet without curtailing their access to the host of valuable learning resources available on the World Wide Web.

The Faculty's Decision

The following are options the high-school staff members considered when deciding how they would cope with the problem of eroticism on the Internet. The school could:

- Provide no access to the Internet from school computers—but then the web pages that were considered educationally valuable would no longer be available to either students or teachers
- Install web filters on school computers to block out selected sites that had undesirable sexual content
- Retain unrestricted access to Internet websites but instruct students to avoid sexual material
- Assign faculty members to periodically (a) observe which sites students visited and (b) open students' computer files to discover if the files contained pornographic content

Summary

It should be apparent that the foregoing 10 types of decisions are not the only kinds of controversies over sex in schools. Thus, our sample of 10 has been intended only to illustrate the varied nature of controversies but not to expose the entire range of conflicts that confront students and school personnel. Other sorts of decisions are described in later chapters.

THIS BOOK'S VANTAGE POINTS

Every discussion of such topics as sex in schools is conducted from one or more perspectives. As the opening pages of this chapter have illustrated, one such perspective is that of *decision making*—the decisions students and schools face about matters of sex. That perspective is reflected throughout the book's remaining chapters. But decision making is not the only lens through which matters of sex can be viewed. Therefore, I have also adopted five additional vantage points that I believe enrich the understanding of sex in schools. The purpose of the following discussion is to explain the five so that readers will be prepared when those vantage points appear in later chapters.

But before describing those perspectives, I should note that discussions of sex can focus on either one of two aspects of sexual matters. The first aspect concerns *eroticism,* defined here as (a) people's physical and emotional arousal to sexually stimulating events and (b) people's behavior that results from such arousal. The second aspect concerns *gender,* defined as the anatomical, psychological, and social characteristics that distinguish males from females. This book focuses on both youthful eroticism and gender.

Issues addressed throughout the book are suggested by the following questions.

How does human eroticism develop over the first two decades of life, and how do different patterns of development affect children's and adolescents' schooling?

What kinds of behaviors qualify as *erotic acts,* which of those acts do children and adolescents perform, and with what results?

How do the young learn about eroticism? In other words, where do children and adolescents get their knowledge of eroticism? What role do schools play in sex education?

How often and why does sexual development go awry, resulting in such outcomes as unwanted seduction, emotional distress, rape, teenage pregnancy, and disease? What significance do such events hold for schools?

In American culture, which personal traits and activities have been considered feminine and which have been considered masculine?

How does a young person's preference for a particular gender develop when the available preferences include heterosexual, homosexual, and bisexual lifestyles? Why is a child's or teenager's gender-role preference significant for schools?

At the outset, it is important to recognize that there is no universal agreement about which answers are best for such questions. In other words, which answers represent "the truth" about sex is a highly controversial issue, as the chapters of this volume demonstrate.

Finally, the book's contents are a combination of facts and interpretations. The facts consist of descriptive information that has been collected about eroticism and gender. The interpretations are what those facts mean when analyzed from six perspectives that bear the labels (a) decisions by students and school personnel, (b) heredity and environment, (c) *could-be, is,* and *should-be,* (d) sources of evidence, (e) power and authority, and (f) implications for schools.

Each perspective serves as a mental lens or filter that gives a distinct meaning to eroticism and gender. At the outset of this chapter, the first of the perspectives—decision making—was illustrated. The purpose of the following description is to introduce the additional five vantage points and to explain how each has guided the task of choosing and interpreting the facts that populate the book. It will be obvious that the five involve concepts already familiar to readers. Therefore, my intent is not to propose that the five are novel notions; rather, the purpose is to illustrate how the five can be combined to yield the book's interpretation of sexual matters in schools.

HEREDITY AND ENVIRONMENT

All scientific attempts to explain people's development and behavior basically concern the interaction of heredity and environment. Each person's *heredity* derives from the biological genetic material carried by a sperm cell from the father and by an ovum cell from the mother that merge to form the beginning of a new human. The term *environment* encompasses all of the surroundings that affect this new human from the time of initial conception in the mother's womb until this person eventually dies, usually around eight or nine decades later.

One important function of heredity is to establish the range of possibilities for the newborn human's development. The expression *range of possibilities* means that how a person develops—physically, sexually, intellectually, socially, emotionally—is not precisely set by one's genes. Instead, the genes establish boundaries within which a person's actual development will occur. Such fanciful advice as "You can become anything you want to be if you try hard enough" is obviously nonsense. People do not have unlimited potential for what they can become. Instead, genetic inheritance offers a range of potentiality. Where within that range a person actually develops depends on the individual's encounters with a succession of environments throughout the lifespan.

A second function of heredity is that of determining when during people's lifetimes they can be influenced by certain environmental encounters. In effect, the genes that people inherit operate like a clock that establishes when individuals will profit from certain kinds of experiences.

The clock performs a readiness function. For instance, in intellectual development, the genetic timing mechanism equips the average child to profit from being taught to read at around age 6. In sexual development, puberty (the ripening of eroticism and gender characteristics) normally occurs in a series of five stages that begin between ages 8 and 13 among girls and ages 9 and 14 among boys. As a result, postpubescent young people are newly ready—at least physically—to engage in sexual intercourse that can result in the birth of an infant.

So it is that the environments with which a youngster interacts become determinants of the actual development that the growing child or adolescent displays within a genetically set range of potentials. In other words, individuals' sex characteristics and beliefs at a particular time in their life have been fashioned by environmental influences, including types of diet, modes of exercise, accidents and illnesses suffered, ways of being treated by family members and companions, television shows watched, websites visited on the Internet, books read, lessons learned at school, religious experiences, and more.

Because no two individuals—except identical twins—have inherited the same pattern of genes, and because even identical twins have not had identical environmental encounters, no two people are precisely alike in their eroticism and gender traits. And those differences among individuals in their sex characteristics and beliefs confront schools with a host of challenges.

In summary, a basic question to be asked about sexual development is: How have children's and teenagers' genetic inheritance interacted with the environments that the young have experienced to produce their individual present sex characteristics?

COULD-BE, IS, AND *SHOULD-BE*

Conflicts over matters of sex in schools typically result from disagreements among people about what youngsters' sexual development *could-be, is,* and *should-be.*

Could-be is a person's idea of what is genetically and environmentally possible for a young person's eroticism and gender development at a given time of life. For each of us, our *could-be* beliefs consist of our convictions about (a) the genetically set range within which a child's or youth's sexual characteristics can develop and (b) the possible environments with which that child or youth might interact. Therefore, *could-be* is our best guess about *what is possible* for a child's or teenager's sexual development. It's apparent, however, that no one knows precisely the genetically established range of sex-development potential for either an age group of youngsters or a particular child. Nor does anyone know for sure how past and current environmental encounters have affected a youngster's past and present eroticism and gender condition. Therefore, because the science of human development is still unable to offer exact answers about such matters, we are obliged to depend on our best guess. And because one person's best estimate can differ from another's, people often disagree about what a child's sexual development *could be*.

Is is a description (apparently factual) of a youngster's present sexual characteristics—the youngster's appearance, feelings, thoughts, and actions relating to eroticism and gender matters.

Should-be is a person's belief about what a particular youngster's sexual characteristics and behavior *ought to be* at present and in the future. *Should-be* is a set of values that enables us to distinguish between good and bad or proper and improper sexual thoughts, feelings, and actions.

The importance of recognizing how *could-be, is,* and *should-be* relate to each other is found in the fact that if we identify—or at least estimate—people's beliefs about *could-be, is,* and *should be,* we can better understand why people act as they do regarding children's and teenagers' sexual behavior. This point is illustrated in the following seven hypothetical incidents. In each case, an event is first described and then interpreted by estimating the *could-be, is,* and *should-be* beliefs of a key participant in the event. The estimate is derived from answering this question: In light of the way the person has acted, what does logic suggest about that person's underlying *could-be, is,* and *should-be* beliefs?

Incident 1

While a young mother was bathing her 10-month-old son, the infant often touched his penis. Each time, the mother slapped the infant's hand to teach him to stop fondling his genitals.

Could-be. Apparently the mother believes that her son is already intellectually mature enough (a) to distinguish between touching his penis and touching any other part of his body and (b) to understand that touching his penis is forbidden. Perhaps the mother also believes that newborns are naturally (genetically) prone to sexual misconduct and that they are also capable of reforming that conduct, so parents are wise to dissuade their young as early as possible from such an improper innate sexual bent.

Is. The infant appears to enjoy fondling his genitals. His desire to do so seems strong, because he continues to fondle even after being slapped a few times.

Should-be. The mother is convinced that children should not manipulate their private parts. Not only is it wicked, but other people will think such a child is a pervert and that his parents have failed to raise him properly.

Incident 2

During the high-school junior prom, an assistant principal who supervises the event warns a pair of 16-year-olds that the way they are dancing is prohibited. To support his warning, he mentions a passage from the school's student-behavior handbook, which notifies students that "School rules outlaw 'grinding dancing' in which the girl leans forward and the boy, while standing behind her, holds onto her hips, puts his pelvis against her backside, and thrusts."

Could-be. The assistant principal believes it is natural for postpubescent youths to have strong, genetically inherited eroticism instincts that mature at the time of puberty. He also believes that the pair of dancers—as a result of the socializing function of their past environments—is capable of suppressing their eroticism instincts on such occasions as the prom. In other words, the pair is not forced by genetic nature to dance in such a manner. Instead, the two have intentionally chosen that option from among a variety of ways that teenagers dance.

Is. The two young people have strong sex drives that override traditional social customs that would deter them from openly indulging their eroticism instincts at a high-school dance. Either the two have been socialized by families or by peers who tolerate grinding dancing—so that the couple "doesn't know any better" than to dance that way—or else they are rebels who intentionally challenge school customs.

Should-be. Schools are one of society's institutions for socializing the young. The term *socializing* means initiating the young into the culture's traditions—language, skills, occupations, arts, pastimes, etiquette, and values. Those traditions are ones that older generations cherish, so the content and standards of schooling are usually more conservative than teenagers might like. Whereas dancing in a grinding fashion might be approved by a significant proportion of teens, it is not acceptable to the people who determine schools' behavior standards. Hence, the assistant principal in this episode believes that students should adhere to the school's traditional conservative standards. As he would tell the grinding pair, "Maybe you can get away with your vulgar dancing someplace, but not here."

Incident 3

A 14-year-old ninth-grade girl in a middle school used a computer in the school library to add personal information to her MySpace page on the Internet. In her description, she portrayed herself as a 17-year-old high-school cheerleader and homecoming queen who was interested in corresponding with boys, either high-school seniors or college students. A librarian who was passing behind the girl glanced at the computer screen, saw what the girl was writing, ordered her to erase the information, and reported the incident to the principal, who then phoned the girl's mother to inform her of the episode.

Could-be. In the librarian's opinion (which was probably shared by the principal), the interaction of the ninth-grader's genetic time clock with her past and present environments equipped her with active postpubescent sexual drives that she might attempt to express in various ways.

Is. The 14-year-old hopes to engage in erotic experiences (actual or vicarious). That hope is a typical desire of postpubescent teenage girls. But according to social custom, her ambition is more suitable for older girls. She also wishes that she were more glamorous, attractive, and world-wise than is actually the case.

Should-be. The librarian believes that the girl is playing a dangerous game by trying to attract older youths through the Internet. Sex predators of all ages search Internet chat groups and such social-networking sites as MySpace, Facebook, Friendster, iShoals, Yahoo! 360°, Hi5, Bebo, and YouTube in the hope of finding naïve girls with whom they can arrange sexual liaisons. This 14-year-old should not place personal information (either factual or fictitious) on the Internet. And she certainly should not be inviting assignations with strangers who might do her harm.

Incident 4

A 19-year-old college freshman attended a fraternity party at which potential initiates could meet the organization's members. After the party, the current members of the fraternity met to discuss the potential initiates in order to decide which ones should be invited to join the fraternity. When the 19-year-old's name came up, one of the members said, "There's no way we're going to pledge guys who want to be faggots. He's obviously gay. Look at the way he acted. This frat is for men, not fairies."

Could-be. In saying "guys who *want to be* faggots," the outspoken fraternity member revealed that he thinks people are born with the genetic potential to select whichever gender role they wish to adopt—heterosexual, homosexual, or some combination of the two. In other words, gender preference is not genetically determined. The fraternity man also believes that people's appearance, manner of speaking, gestures, and interests indicate their gender preference. He thinks that any observant person can recognize the differences between masculine and feminine mannerisms, personality traits, and interests. A male who displays feminine traits is obviously homosexual. Likewise, a female who displays masculine traits is undoubtedly homosexual.

Is. The 19-year-old wore a pastel-colored jacket and shirt to the fraternity party. He explained that he was majoring in theater arts. He spoke in a rather high-pitched voice, expressed his opinions in sophisticated phrases, and accompanied his comments with dramatic gestures. Therefore, he was, in the opinion of the outspoken fraternity member, an effeminate homosexual.

Should-be. The outspoken member believed that individuals born with the physical equipment of males ought to display traditional masculine attributes throughout their lives and should have sexual relationships exclusively with females. In like manner, individuals born with the physical equipment of females ought to display feminine traits throughout their lives and should have eroticism relations exclusively with males. Male organizations—such as fraternities and athletic teams—should not include homosexuals as members.

Incident 5

When 8-year-old Marty's third-grade teacher phoned Marty's home, the boy's father answered. The teacher introduced herself and then explained, "The trouble began after I had shown the class a movie about the life of gorillas in an African jungle. I asked each pupil to draw a picture showing what he or she had learned from the movie. I had also told them a bit about the Tarzan stories—about a boy supposedly growing up with apes."

FATHER: So what's the trouble?

TEACHER: It's the picture Marty drew—a naked boy with gorillas in a jungle.

FATHER: So?

TEACHER: He drew the naked boy's private parts very prominently. I told him to redraw it without the boy being naked. The picture he next drew had a naked girl instead of a boy, with the girl's private parts very obvious. Marty showed the drawing to a girl in the class and told her that's the way she would look if she took off her clothes. When the girl reported the matter to her mother, the mother phoned me to find out what kind of class I was running.

FATHER: So why are you telling me this?

TEACHER: Because your son is out of control. He has to stop this sex business—this drawing naked people and making lewd comments to classmates.

FATHER: What's the big deal? I don't see that he did anything wrong. A kid in the jungle with gorillas would probably be naked. And obviously the girl classmate would look naked if she took off her clothes.

TEACHER: But your son has to stop this sort of thing. He seems obsessed with sex.

FATHER: Oh, come on! All kids are curious about their bodies. It's normal. So what? Eight-year-olds are on their way to puberty. Some get there faster than others. Marty is probably developing early. Kids' interest in naked people is nothing to be shocked about. It's natural.

Could-be. Marty's father believes that (a) children's curiosity about sexual organs is a natural (innate) interest and (b) the genetic clock that determines when such interest comes to the fore can differ from one child to another, thereby making some children earlier developers than others.

Is. Marty shows an interest in nakedness and is willing to express his interest publicly.

Should-be. Marty's father believes that people—including children—should openly express their interest in their genetically determined characteristics. In effect, because such attributes are part of human nature, they should not be a cause of shame. The father also believes it's all right for children to express such interests at school.

Incident 6

When the father of an 11-year-old girl suddenly opened the door to his daughter's bedroom to tell her that dinner was ready, he was shocked to discover her masturbating with a plastic toothbrush case. He shouted, "What on earth do you think you are doing? Self-abuse is a sin that'll land you in hell! Shame . . . shame on you."

Could-be. Likely this father subscribes to a fundamentalist Christian belief that Adam and Eve committed "the original sin" when they disobeyed

God's command that they not eat the forbidden fruit in the Garden of Eden. Ever since that event—according to many doctrinaire Jews, Christians, and Muslims—original sin has been inherited by all subsequent generations of humans. Although people are born with the potential to act in either good ways or bad ways, they are burdened with original sin and thus naturally do evil things unless constantly corrected. Stimulating one's own genitals is a sin, an expression of humans' innate evil tendency, so masturbation requires correction.

Is. The fact that the 11-year-old has succumbed to the influence of original sin is evident from her act of genital stimulation.

Should-be. The father believes that in order for his daughter to save herself from an afterlife in hell, the girl should suppress her erotic yearnings, beg forgiveness, and sincerely vow never to repeat the evil act.

Incident 7

The angry mother of 16-year-old Chelsea came to the high school to complain to the dean of girls about her daughter's being sent for half a day to the school's detention room for bringing to her English class a book to read that was on the school's banned-reading-matter list. The book was from the *Gossip Girl* series that had been banned because of the plots' homosexuality, sexual content, alcohol, drugs, and offensive language. The series—consisting of 12 volumes published from 2002 through 2007—follows high-society teenagers in New York City's glamorous, sophisticated Upper East Side. The central characters are rich girls who shop, party, drink, and cope with issues of sex, drugs, and relationships. A blurb on the back of the copy that the girl had brought to school suggested the series' central theme: "Welcome to New York City's Upper East Side, where my friends and I live, go to school, play, and sleep—sometimes with each other."

The 16-year-old's mother demanded to know why her daughter had been disciplined. In answer, the dean of girls explained, "Chelsea knew that series was prohibited, so she intentionally disobeyed the rule."

Chelsea's mother responded, "I've looked through the Gossip Girl books, and I don't see why they should be banned. I was a teenager in the late 1960s and early '70s, and we did a lot of those things the Gossip Girls do in the books. It did us no harm. It's just young people's ways of spreading their wings, trying new things. The teen years are a phase of life that soon passes. Banning such books stifles teenagers' chance to learn about life."

Could-be. Chelsea's mother believes that a variety of sexual behaviors are natural (genetically determined), and that the timing of adolescents' erotic development has readied them for learning about and practicing those behaviors.

Is. Chelsea, according to her mother's account, is currently experiencing—at least vicariously through books—diverse forms of heterosexual and homosexual behavior that are often linked to the use of alcohol and drugs.

Should-be. Youths should be free to indulge in all sorts of sexual experiences that appeal to them. Schools should permit—even encourage—teenagers to read about and discuss those matters because eroticism is such an important aspect of life.

In summary, the two-part proposition illustrated in the foregoing examples is that (a) underlying the conflicts between individuals over sexual matters are those individuals' *could-be, is,* and *should-be* beliefs, and (b) our understanding of such conflicts can be improved through our estimating the nature of those beliefs by analyzing what people say and do.

SOURCES OF EVIDENCE

An important reason that people differ in their *could-be, is,* and *should-be* beliefs is that they differ in the sources of evidence on which they base those beliefs.

Could-Be Sources

For convenience of discussion, *could-be* sources can be divided into customary and scientific types.

The term *customary* refers to beliefs handed down from one generation to the next, often in the form of folk beliefs or religious lore. An example of a customary version of *could-be* is the range of eroticism behaviors and gender roles implied in passages of Jewish and Christian Bibles, as supplemented by theologians' interpretations and embellishments of those passages. Another example of a customary type is the sexual content of American Indian legends that have been passed orally from generation to generation.

Scientific refers to multiple observations of animals' and humans' sexual structures and behavior, with the observations summarized as theories of sexual development. Charles Darwin's theory of evolution (*The Origin of Species*, 1859) qualifies as a scientific *could-be* source, as does Sigmund Freud's *Outline of Psychoanalysis* (1938) and Alfred Kinsey's *Sexual Behavior in the Human Male* (1948) and *Sexual Behavior in the Human Female* (1953).

Is Sources

As explained earlier, *is* beliefs are what an observer thinks a student's erotic or gender status is at the present time. Four conditions that can influence an observer's impression are (a) the opportunity to directly witness the student's behavior, (b) aspects of the student's appearance or actions that can be interpreted as signs of eroticism or gender, (c) how open the student is to express sexual thoughts, and (d) how trustworthy other people's reports are about the student's sex status.

Opportunities to Observe

Rarely do teachers have a chance to observe pupils beyond the classroom, school corridor, lunchroom, or playground. Rarely do parents see how their children or teenagers act outside the home. Seldom does a counselor witness a youth's behavior outside the counselor's office. Consequently, people's impressions of a youngster's current eroticism and gender status that is gained from direct observation is necessarily a restricted version, biased by the limited opportunity to see the student in various environments.

Among our earlier samples of sexual incidents, the assistant principal at the prom based his beliefs about the grinding couple's eroticism beliefs on their style of dancing. The third-grade teacher drew her impression of Marty's current eroticism mainly on the boy's drawings. In the case of Chelsea, the dean of girls based much of her understanding of Chelsea's eroticism and gender beliefs on Chelsea's reading a banned book.

Signs of Eroticism and Gender

Among the ideas about sexual development that the Viennese psychiatrist Sigmund Freud (1956–1939) brought to public attention was the notion that people's sexual thoughts are often masked behind symbols that have no apparent eroticism meaning. For example, when analyzing clients' dreams, Freud interpreted any elongated object (spear, tower, tree) as indicative of a person's thoughts about a penis, and any container-like object (basket, barrel, bowl) as symbolizing a vagina. Likewise, a person's preference for the female gender might be masked behind behavior typically associated with maleness, and vice versa. Therefore, an observer's impression of a youngster's present sexual condition can be affected by what the observer believes the youngster's appearance and actions might symbolize. But there is always the possibility that the observer is wrong and that the ostensible symbol (spear, bowl) was not a sign of erotic thoughts at all.

The Person's Openness

A particularly influential constraint on an observer's discovering a youth's eroticism status is the youth's willingness to talk about such matters. Such willingness extends from the extremely loquacious ("She's never had an unexpressed thought") to the extremely reticent ("You never know what she's really thinking"). At school, a teenage boy may, when he is with close companions, describe at length his sexual thoughts, but he will never mention such matters when speaking with a teacher or counselor.

In one of the seven incidents described earlier, a student's comments were interpreted as indicators of the student's eroticism or gender status. That occurred in the case of the outspoken fraternity member judging that the 19-year-old at the party expressed himself in a fashion that suggested he was gay. In three of the episodes, the remarks of parents suggested the beliefs they currently held about sexual matters. Those were the cases in which a father chastened his daughter for masturbating, Chelsea's mother defended her daughter's reading interests, and Marty's father defended the boy's drawings.

Others' Reports

Frequently a teacher's impressions of a student's sex thoughts and behavior are based on what other teachers, counselors, or the student's parents and companions say. But this brings up a question about how accurate and unbiased such reports are. And how well do the described incidents represent the student's usual appearance or behavior rather than a unique event?

In the Marty episode, a third-grade girl reported to both her teacher and her mother what Marty had said to her about taking off her clothes. But there remains the question of whether the boy's remark was an indicator of his eroticism intent or was simply a description of an obvious way to distinguish between female and male genders.

In summary, the impression that school personnel gain about a student's current eroticism and gender condition depends on opportunities to observe the student, on possible symbols of sexual thoughts, on the student's willingness to reveal sexual concerns, and on other people's reports.

Should-Be Sources

The sources of *should-be* beliefs can be either adopted ones or ones that are self-devised.

Adopted sources are philosophical convictions about eroticism or gender that a person learns about and embraces. Such sources are frequently religious doctrines in written form, such as the Jewish/Christian Bible. Other examples are the Muslim Quran, the Hindu Manu Smriti, the Confucian Analects, the Buddhist Theravada canon, the Book of Mormon of the Church of Jesus Christ of Latter Day Saints, and Scientology's *Dianetics* and *Pain and Sex*. Adopted nonreligious sources include Marx and Engel's *Communist Manifesto*, the American Humanist Association's *Humanist Manifesto II*, and writings about sex by naturalists, realists, atheists, and feminists.

Self-devised sources are conceptions of proper eroticism and gender beliefs that individuals create by themselves from their own observations of others' behavior and from the consequences of that behavior. Frequently, self-devised sources are variants of adopted sources. An example of self-devised beliefs about proper erotic behavior are the hedonistic sexual standards advocated by a portion of America's youths during the 1960s—the portion made up of hippies, beatniks, and flower children who lived by such mottos as "If it feels good, do it" and "Enjoy the madness of it all." The effects of the hippie generation linger into the present day, as suggested by the remarks of Chelsea's mother in the earlier banned-book episode.

POWER AND AUTHORITY

The expression *exercise of power* means the extent to which the behavior of one person (or group) influences the beliefs or behavior of another person (or group). For example, if Person A thinks or acts differently because of Person B's presence (bodily or symbolic), then Person B has power over Person A. But if Person A thinks or acts just the same, whether or not Person B is present, then B has no power over A. The amount of power B exerts over A is indicated by how drastically or inevitably A's beliefs and behavior are altered by the presence of B. So, one vantage point from which controversies about sex in schools are viewed throughout this book is that of who wields power, by what means, and with what success.

The word *authority* refers to the official power—the legal right to influence decisions—held by an individual or a group. People holding different amounts of authority over matters of sex in schools include school-board members, administrators, teachers, coaches, counselors, bus drivers, security officers, the police, district attorneys, juvenile-court officials, and criminal-court judges. People in positions of authority typically enjoy a greater advantage in affecting decisions about matters of sex than do people without official power. Students, parents, and ordinary citizens have no authority—or at least they have less authority than do officials.

People can attempt various methods for exerting power in controversies over sex issues. They can (a) adduce a persuasive line of reasoning, (b) cite a law or a school regulation that bears on sexual behavior, (c) be accompanied by a host of supporters at a hearing or trial about an eroticism incident, (d) file a lawsuit against their adversary in a sex-issue dispute (such an adversary as a school system, teacher, administrator, parent, student organization), (e) bribe or threaten someone (school superintendent, juvenile-court social worker, school principal) who holds the authority to dictate which side triumphs in a dispute, or (f) attack the opposition in the public press.

IMPLICATIONS FOR SCHOOLS

Finally we arrive at this book's last perspective. It's apparent that human sexual development and behavior can be viewed in terms of their implications for any of society's institutions and functions—the family, the justice system, businesses, the vocational structure, the financial system, welfare organizations, medical services, and more. This book focuses on the implications that children's and youths' eroticism and gender-role development hold for America's schools.

CONCLUSION

The dual purpose of the nine chapters that follow this introduction is to (a) describe ways that individuals' sex characteristics develop throughout the first two decades of life and (b) analyze conflicts that arise in schools over young people's sexual thoughts and actions. The conflicts are interpreted from the perspectives of (a) decision making; (b) the interaction of heredity and environment in determining youngsters' sexual development; (c) people's *could-be, is,* and *should-be* beliefs about sexual development; (d) sources of those beliefs; (e) how people exercise power to promote their beliefs; and (f) the implications that the outcomes of the first five perspectives hold for school practice.

Chapter 2

The Course of Sexual Development

To furnish a three-dimensional view of sexual development over the first two decades of life, this chapter describes children's and youths' sexual progress from physical, psychological, and social perspectives. The term *physical* refers to observations of changes in young people's bodies—changes that bear on eroticism and gender. *Psychological* means how young people think and feel about their sexual selves as they grow up. *Social* refers to ways the young act toward others in situations that people regard as sexual.

The chapter is divided into two major sections. The first section is factual—a description of what sex development *is* rather than what it *could be* or *should be*. The second section offers suggestions about school practice that are implied by the content of the first section.

BASIC PATTERNS OF DEVELOPMENT

The purpose of the following discussion is to identify principal characteristics of human sexual development from the moment of conception until young adulthood. The description focuses mainly on the average person but also notes how individuals can deviate from average or typical growth. Throughout the discussion, it will become apparent that the physical and social facts of sexual development are better understood and more generally agreed on than are the psychological.

Physical Features of Sexual Development

As students discover when they study biology, a new human normally begins when, during sexual intercourse between a male and female, a spermatozoa cell from the male merges with an egg cell (ovum) of the female. This merging (*conception* or *fertilization*) forms a zygote, which is a single cell that multiplies rapidly, developing first into an embryo, then into a fetus, and, after about 9 months, into a newborn infant.

At conception, the merging produces the newly conceived individual's *genome*, which is formed half from the father's spermatozoon and half from the mother's ovum. The genome is a container holding a descending series of three other containers—*chromosomes*, *genes*, and *DNA* (*deoxyribonucleic acid*). In effect, chromosomes carry genes that are composed of the chemical DNA. As the embryo, fetus, infant, child, youth, and adult develop, each additional cell in the evolving human (except mature red blood cells) will include a nucleus that contains a copy of the genome.

A human's genome consists of 46 chromosomes arranged as 23 pairs, with most human cells including all 46. But male spermatozoa and female ova are different. They contain half of each pair—23 chromosomes—so that when a sperm and ovum merge, the new combination totals 46, half from the mother and half from the father. One pair in the 46 is known as the sex pair, which comes in two types, X and Y. In females, both of the pair are of the X variety. In males, one of the pair is an X, the other a Y. At the time of sexual intercourse between a father and mother, the father normally ejects 200 to 600 million sperm cells into the mother's uterus and fallopian tube where a ripe ovum awaits fertilization. Half of the sperms carry an X sex chromosome and half a Y chromosome. Which spermatozoon happens to arrive first to merge with the ovum determines whether the newly conceived human will have the physical attributes of a female or a male. If a male X sex chromosome pairs up with one of the mother's X chromosomes, the resulting genome will contain an XX pair of sex chromosome, so a female child results. But if a sperm carrying a Y chromosome fertilizes the ovum, the resulting offspring will be an XY male.

The genes that are lined up along chromosomes are the architectural designers of (a) the features that children and youths inherit from their parents and (b) the basic time of life in which those features will appear or change. Genes are composed of the chemical deoxyribonucleic acid (DNA), which is the source of information about how to construct a developing human. So the patterning of a person's DNA dictates the basic sex characteristics that the person will display over his or her lifespan. No two people, except identical twins, have the same DNA pattern, a fact that accounts for the basic individual differences in sex characteristics among students. (Identical twins are formed when one fertilized ovum splits so the twins have the same genome with identical DNA. Fraternal twins are formed when two different eggs are fertilized, so those twins have different genomes and DNA patterns).

> DNA is a very large molecule, made up of smaller units called nucleotides that are strung together in a row, making a DNA molecule thousands of times longer than it is wide. . . . A DNA molecule is a double helix, a structure that looks much like a ladder twisted into a spiral. The sides of the ladder are made of alternating sugar and phosphate molecules, the sugar of one nucleotide linked to the phosphate of the next. The bases found in DNA come in four varieties: adenine, cytosine, guanine, and thymine—often abbreviated as A, C, G, and T, the letters of the genetic alphabet. (DeWeerdt, 2003)

At the time of birth, the most obvious sexual differences between girls and boys are in their genitals—girls with a vagina, boys with a penis. These characteristics will be the only readily observed physical differences between female and male from birth until the arrival of puberty at around ages 8 or 10 or 12. However, during childhood there are significant internal differences between the genders, principally in such sex hormones as estrogens (chiefly in females) and androgens (chiefly in males) that affect a child's erotic feelings and the onset of puberty. Whereas males and females have both estrogens and androgens (such as testosterone) in their systems, adult males usually have 10 times the amount of testosterone as females, and females usually have 10 times the amount of estrogens (such as estradiol) as males. Significant deviations from these ratios result in girls displaying more male-like characteristics and boys showing more female-like attributes.

Guided by a genetically set time schedule, the hormones direct puberty's development of physical traits for girls and boys. Over the past century, puberty has appeared at increasingly earlier years in children's lives, particularly as a result of improved nutrition.

Puberty

As the years of childhood advance, changes in children's external and internal sexual characteristics change dramatically with the onset of puberty—the stage of growth that equips teenagers to engage in sexual intercourse that can produce a new human. Puberty, on the average, arrives a year or so earlier for girls than for boys and is completed in a shorter time for girls than for boys. However, there are marked differences among individuals in the age at which puberty begins and ends. For girls, the beginning of normal pubescent growth is between ages 9 and 14, and for boys is between ages 10 and 17. A girl usually completes the series of pubertal changes within about 4 years, whereas a boy finishes the pattern in around 6 years.

The usual sequence of external and internal physical changes that girls experience progresses in the following order, with the average age for each change shown in parentheses along with the usual age range within which that change appears.

- *Height and weight increase.* Girls' growth spurt usually starts between ages 8 and 12 and continues for 3 or 4 years. From the beginning of the growth spurt until its end, the percentage of girls' weight that is body fat increases from an average of about 15 percent to around 27 percent. (Average beginning, 9 years.)
- *Breast development.* The pigmented region around the nipple (areola) begins to darken and enlarge. Over the next 6 years, breasts expand to adult size. (Average beginning, 9 years; range for beginning, 8–12 years.)
- *Hair growth.* Pubic hair gradually appears and becomes curly and coarse over the following 5 years. Armpit hair begins to grow, usually reaching its final form by age 18 or 20. (Average beginning of pubic-hair growth, 9 years; range for beginning, 8–12 years.)
- *Menarche.* Girls experience the menarche—their first menstrual period—when the lining of the uterus is shed and flows from the vagina as a bloodlike fluid. Menarche is a signal that the girl has reached an age at which she soon could conceive a child. (Average age, 12.5 years; usual range, 11–14 years. Over the decades, menarche for American girls has come increasingly early. A century ago menarche arrived on the average at age 16.) Within a year or two after menarche, menstruation will become a regular monthly event that usually lasts from 3 to 7 days on each occasion. During menstruation, an ovum descends into a fallopian tube, ready to be fertilized by a male sperm. If no sperm merges with the ovum, the lining of the uterus—which has been prepared to nourish a fertilized egg—sloughs off as fluid. The entire supply of ova for all of the years of a woman's ability to conceive has existed in her ovaries since birth. Girls' rapid growth in height ends shortly after the menarche.
- *Skin oil glands become more active.* As a result, teenage girls can develop skin blemishes (acne) that may last into adulthood. (Range, 11–20 years.)

For boys, the typical sequence of pubertal changes advances in the following fashion:

- *Hair growth.* Sparse pubic hair starts to grow below the penis, then pubic hair spreads to the thighs; hair begins to appear on various parts of the body—armpits, abdomen, chest, arms, legs, and buttocks—up

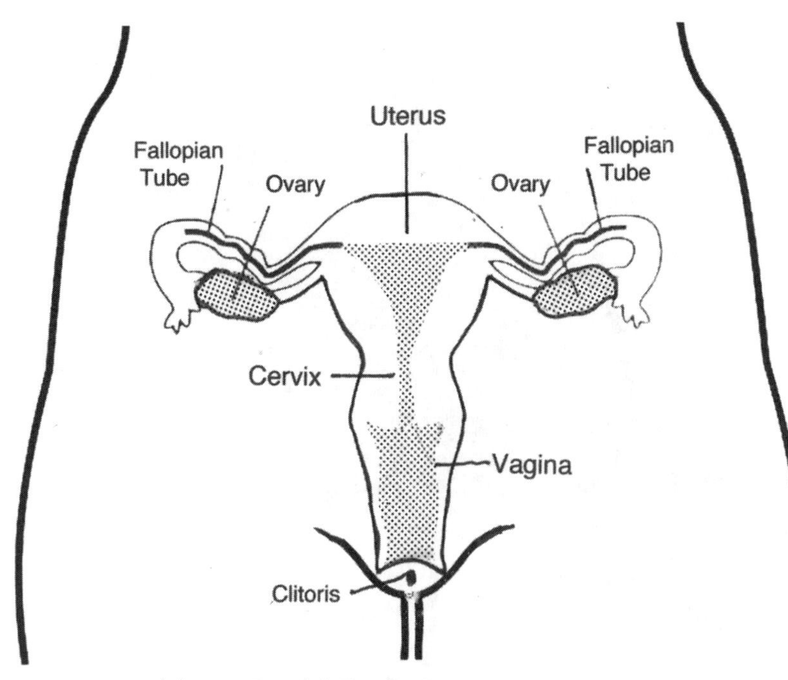

Figure 2.1. Adolescent Female's Sex Organs

to age 20. (Average beginning age, 12.4 years; range for beginning, 10–15 years.)

- *Voice change.* Vocal cords lengthen and thicken, causing the voice pitch to lower. (Average, 13.5 years; range, 11–15 years.)
- *Height and weight increase.* Rapid height and weight growth begins. Bones lengthen and thicken, and muscle mass increases, especially in the upper chest and shoulders. The growth spurt continues about 2 years longer in boys than in girls. (Average beginning, 12.5 years; range, 10–17 years.)
- *Genitalia growth.* Penis and scrotum begin to enlarge, reaching adult size 3 or 4 years later. (Average beginning, 14 years; range 13–16 years.)
- *Sperm production.* Whereas all of a female's ova are present at birth, a male's spermatozoa are continually produced at a rapid pace in the testes throughout the years of an individual's active sexual life—eventually totaling 12 trillion or more sperm.
- *Ejaculation.* Early in puberty, the boy's penis tissues periodically fill with blood, causing the penis to become stiff and large. If the penis is then stimulated, it will eject *semen,* a fluid containing sperm cells. As puberty advances, the number of sperm emitted during a single

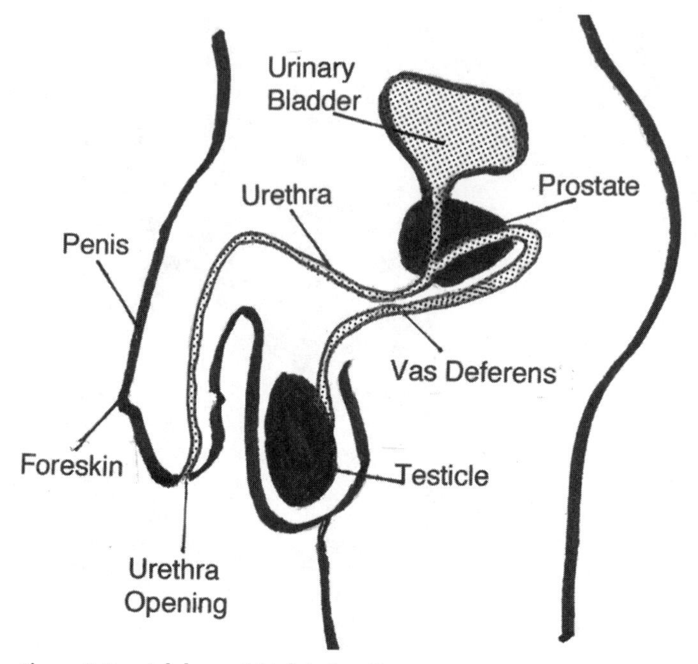

Figure 2.2. Adolescent Male's Sex Organs

ejaculation can be from 400 to 500 million. Ejaculation is usually accompanied by a momentary pleasurable sensation known as *orgasm*. Ejaculation may also occur spontaneously during sleep, producing a *nocturnal emission* or *wet dream*.

- *Skin oil glands become more active*. Like girls, teenage boys can suffer from acne. (Range, 11–20 years.)

With the completion of puberty, girls and boys achieve adult sexual status, capable of conceiving a new human being unless something has gone wrong with the normal development of their reproductive mechanisms.

Deviations from the Average

As already noted, the timing of pubertal changes can vary markedly from one adolescent to another, with the timing a result of both genetic and environmental factors. Therefore, the basic time schedule set by the genes can be significantly affected by a variety of factors in the maturing child's surroundings and lifestyle.

The most powerful environmental influence is diet. A higher intake of calories brings on earlier puberty and a faster advance through the phases of puberty. A higher percentage of animal protein and lower percentage of fibrous vegetables also hastens the onset and progress of puberty.

Other conditions that affect when and how pubertal changes occur include:

- *Exercise.* Particularly in girls, a high level of physical activity that reduces the proportion of body fat slows the pubertal process.
- *Chronic illness.* Diseases that inflame the lower digestive tract, including long-term parasitic infections, retard normal pubertal development.
- *Family stress.* Noticeable, but less important to the timing of puberty, is anxiety that can result from troubled family conditions. Girls in households marked with continuing stress may experience menarche earlier than ones in more peaceful family settings.

Body-Fat Effects

Two special features of physical development affecting American students' erotic appeal in recent decades have been the *female slim image* and *obesity.*

Female slim image. Since the mid-20th century, the trendsetters in the world of fashionable female clothing have portrayed the ideal female figure as extremely thin. Girls and women hired to model clothing have invariably been skinny. This image has become envisioned by a substantial segment of the nation's teenage girls as an ideal to emulate, an ideal whose pursuit can cause adolescents—particularly girls—to try losing weight and, at the extreme, to become anorexic.

> Teen anorexia, or anorexia nervosa, is one of the most common eating disorders among teens. Anorexia means that a troubled teen is starving her or himself. . . . Anorexic troubled teens hardly eat anything, and have a distorted view of themselves so that they always think they are fat even if they become dangerously thin. Teen anorexia can cause serious health problems or death, so troubled teens with anorexia need to get medical treatment to recover from their eating disorder. Teen anorexia is most common among teen girls, but about 10 percent of troubled teens with anorexia are boys, and teen boys with eating disorders often go undiagnosed and untreated. Between 5 and 20 percent of teens with anorexia will die because of the disorder. (Anorexic teens, 2005)

Obesity. A rapidly increasing percentage of America's youngsters have grown overweight, especially as a result of "junk foods." (The term *junk foods* refers to salty French fries, beef burgers, fried chicken, and pizzas with a thick cheese covering that appeal to the Western palate by being fatty, low in fiber and nutrients, and high in salt. Such items are often served with sugar-laden soft drinks or creamy milkshakes full of empty calories or fat.) In addition to unhealthy diets, weight gain results from a lack of exercise among the nation's increasingly sedentary youngsters who are addicted to television and computer video games. Those who watch television 4 hours a day are more likely to be overweight than those who watch 2 hours or less (Gavin, 2005).

Studies reveal that by 2007 approximately one third of American youths were overweight or obese, a tripling of excess weight since the 1960s and 1970s (LaFontaine, 2008). In addition to overweight causing medical problems for youngsters, increased weight yields psychological and social problems by rendering plump girls and boys less erotically attractive to their peers. The contrast between the ideal teenage body image and a youth's actual obesity often leads psychologically to a damaged self-concept and socially to peers avoiding and ridiculing "the fat kid."

Summary

In children's and adolescents' eroticism development, the most significant physical changes occur during puberty—changes that include increased sex hormones (female estrogens, male androgens) that initiate such visible physical transformations as a spurt in height and weight, altered body contours, growth of body hair, acne, the female menarche, and the male production of sperm.

Psychological Features of Eroticism Development

The term *psychological* refers to what youngsters think and feel about how their eroticism develops over the first two decades of their lives. As the result of scientific advances, reports of physical sex changes during childhood and adolescence (what physical eroticism development *is*) are clear and trustworthy. But such is not the case with the psychological aspects of sexual development because the task of one person understanding another person's erotic thoughts and emotions is fraught with difficulties.

Problems in Understanding the Youthful Psyche

For several reasons, trying to comprehend someone else's sexual thoughts is a daunting venture. First, the person's thoughts may not be well formed or readily cast into words. This is particularly true with young children, whose vocabularies and ability to analyze their beliefs are still in a primitive state. Second, social conventions that ban open discussion of sexual notions can hamper people's willingness to say what they think about sex. Third, among a person's erotic thoughts, some may have been relegated to an unconscious portion of the mind, so those beliefs are not available to report.

The questionable reliability of students' reports of their sexual activities was observed in a survey of more than 13,000 teens who ranged from grades 7 through 12. On two occasions, 1 year apart, students were asked the same series of questions about their sex life. Among the questions was one about whether they had already engaged in intercourse, and another was, "Have you taken a public or written pledge to remain a virgin until marriage?"

> In the first survey, about 13 percent of the students said they had taken a pledge of virginity. In the second survey more than half of that group denied having taken [such a pledge]. Those who reported having sexual relations for the first time in the second survey were three times as likely to retract a virginity pledge as those who did report having had sex then. About a third of the students said in the first survey that they had had sex, but about 10 percent of them denied it when asked the second time. Those who had newly made a pledge were four times as likely to retract reports of sexual activity. (Nagourney, 2006)

In an effort to account for such inconsistencies, the researchers surmised, "Survey respondents typically reconcile their memories with their present beliefs. Respondents may recall only memories consistent with their current beliefs or report actions that did not occur but are consistent with their current beliefs" (Nagourney, 2006).

However difficult it is for us to understand others' sexual thoughts, that task is far easier than understanding others' erotic emotions. How people feel about sexual matters must be inferred from their words and actions, but feelings do not translate adequately into words since language and emotions are distinctly different phenomena. When a participant in a Sexual Emotions Survey tells the investigator that "I hate being touched by men" or "The orgasm wasn't really great, only so-so," investigators are obliged to imagine how they themselves would feel in a similar circumstance. Then the investigators—from the perspective of their own unique eroticism—are expected to transpose that feeling into words. In sum, the task of understanding the psychological dimension of human eroticism is elusive and imprecise.

Facets of the Youthful Psyche

Four psychological phenomena often associated with people's eroticism are individuals' sexual self-concepts, erotic satisfaction, guilt, and fear. The term *self-concept* refers to children's and teenagers' beliefs about their own sexual attractiveness and their ability to perform sex acts successfully. *Erotic satisfaction* means the extent of pleasure youngsters derive from sex activity. *Guilt* means the shame and blame the young feel about their sexual thoughts and behavior. One type of *fear* is girls' expectations that they could become pregnant. Or boys can expect they might impregnate a sexual partner. Fear can also result from the prospect that, by engaging in erotic liaisons, adolescents could contract a sexually transmitted disease (especially HIV/AIDS), disappoint their parents, or suffer social disgrace.

The professional literature about sex is replete with empirical studies and opinions bearing on self-concept, erotic satisfaction, guilt, and fear. However, in surveying the literature, I failed to find anything substantial about how youths' status regarding those four attributes has changed over recent decades. Thus, I am left to estimate likely changes in such feelings on the basis of the following general trends in sexual behavior during the past half century. Ever since the "sexual revolution" of the 1960s, candid displays of all manner of erotic acts have appeared at an expanding rate in television shows, movies, videos, popular magazines, and on the Internet. More youngsters have engaged in sexual intercourse at younger ages than before. More couples have openly lived together outside of marriage. More sex-education programs have offered information about how youths can avoid pregnancy or disease. More schools' and colleges' health clinics have distributed condoms and diaphragms to students. In addition, earlier laws designed to punish people who engaged in erotic acts outside of marriage have been rescinded or are no longer enforced. Therefore, I estimate that such trends have produced the following outcomes for youngsters' self-concepts, erotic satisfaction, guilt, and fear.

First are youths' sexual self-concepts. I assume that youngsters' beliefs about their sexual attractiveness and prowess are strongly influenced by (a) their popularity among their peers—especially what peers say about teenagers' appearance—and (b) their impression of others' sexual prowess. Individuals' opportunities to estimate others' prowess have been greatly expanded in recent decades by revealing displays of erotic acts in public communication media—television, movies, videos, magazines, and the Internet. The Internet, in particular, has provided an endless variety of images of people engaged in all sorts of sex acts with which students can compare their own potential and actual erotic performances.

Next is erotic satisfaction. I would propose that three dimensions of erotic satisfaction are frequency of erotic events, types of sex acts, and intensity of emotion. Different people can be satisfied with different frequencies of acts, types of acts, and intensities of emotion. The first two—frequency and type of act—can be objectively described and conveyed from one person to another. The third—intensity—is a sensation whose nature cannot be communicated accurately. It is not possible to precisely convey the sensual feeling of an erotic encounter by use of such verbal expressions as *WOW, phenomenal, out of this world, not bad, pretty dull, disappointing, blah,* or *ugh*. Nevertheless, teens can get an overall impression about other people's sense of intensity by what those people report. So, the opportunity for teens to compare the level of satisfaction (frequency, types of acts, intensity) of their own sexual experiences with other people's levels has been dramatically increased over recent decades by the mass-communication media, especially by the Internet offering millions of websites on which people describe their sexual encounters.

Then there is guilt. The Christian religion on which American culture's sexual ideals were founded has traditionally portrayed sexual acts as sinful. Certainly all acts outside of marriage are forbidden, along with any acts within marriage that fail to produce a baby. So eroticism that is intended simply to give pleasure is viewed as ungodly and thus warrants punishment. Even thinking about potential sexual acts (like "coveting" a neighbor's wife, as condemned in the Bible's Ten Commandments) invites censure. Consequently, among youngsters reared in such a biblical tradition, we might assume that the farther their sexual thoughts and behavior deviate from those ideals, the more guilt they suffer. But I assume that societal trends of recent decades have resulted in present-day youths feeling less guilt and shame over their eroticism than did youths in the distant past. Public standards of acceptable sexual thoughts and behavior have been changing so drastically that present-day students can easily believe it's quite okay to entertain salacious thoughts and to dabble in premarital sex that yields immediate orgasmic delight.

Finally, there is fear. I imagine that two ways children's and adolescents' fears have been affected by the past half century's trends are these: (a) youths' dread of infection has been heightened as they have gained more information about the kinds and incidences of sexually transmitted diseases, and (b) their fear of pregnancy and disease has been diminished by their learning methods of protecting themselves from infections when engaging in sex acts.

In summary, I have suggested that changes in public attitudes and mass-communication developments since the mid-20th century have affected American youngsters' sexual self-concepts, erotic satisfaction, guilt, and fear.

With the foregoing observations in mind, we turn now to ways that eroticism's psychological development can be viewed from the perspectives of (a) heredity and environment, (b) *could-be, is,* and *should-be* beliefs, (c) sources of beliefs, and (d) authority and power.

Heredity and Environment

Two ways that children's genetic inheritance appears to influence their erotic thoughts and emotions are by the genes setting a time schedule (a) for intellectual development that gradually improves youngsters' ability to understand language, recognize cause-and-effect relationships, and predict the likely consequences of different kinds of behaviors and (b) for the release of hormones that increase erotic urges and heighten interest in erotic acts, particularly at the time of puberty. In effect, genetic timing prepares youngsters to be influenced differently by environmental encounters at different stages of their development. For example, we could expect girls' and boys' thoughts and feelings to be affected differently at age 6 than at age 16 by such encounters as:

- Hearing a lecturer explain the menarche
- Seeing a pornographic video portraying a young woman and young man engaged in a variety of sexual acts
- Being fondled in the pubic region by an adult relative
- Being kissed on the lips by a sibling
- Watching a television program about the spread of AIDS (acquired immune deficiency syndrome)
- Being hugged by a 26-year-old woman teacher
- Being hugged by a 54-year-old man teacher
- Hearing a joke about orgasm
- Hearing that masturbating can drive a person insane
- Witnessing a demonstration of how to use a condom safely

The psychological aspects of eroticism are influenced far more by environments than are the physical aspects. In other words, youngsters' thoughts and feelings about sexual matters are more strongly affected by parents, teachers, companions, and communication media (books, magazines, television, Internet websites) than is youngsters' physical sex development.

Could-Be, Is, *and* Should-Be

As proposed in chapter 1, *could-be* is a person's idea of what is genetically and environmentally possible for a young person's eroticism development at a given time of life. *Is* is a description (apparently factual) of a youngster's present sexual characteristics—the youngster's appearance, feelings, thoughts, and actions relating to eroticism and gender. *Should-be* is a person's belief about what a particular youngster's sexual characteristics and behavior (including one's own) ought to be at present and in the future.

Throughout this book, I am assuming that all beliefs about *could-be, is,* and *should-be* are the result of environmental encounters. None are genetically inbred. All are the result of either (a) what youngsters have been told by others (parents, teachers, religious workers, mass-communication media) or (b) what the young have concluded on their own from events they have witnessed or heard about.

The following are examples of *could-be, is,* and *should-be* beliefs that people might hold.

Could-be beliefs concern potential developmental outcomes.

- 12-year-old girl—"If I had sex with Paul, I might get pregnant."
- Father—"Carl, now age 11, is shorter than average, so he'll still be shorter than average when he's a 20-year-old."
- 16-year-old boy—"Getting a good suntan will get rid of the pimples on my face."
- Mother—"I didn't start to menstruate until age 14. So Janie—now age 8—will also get to puberty late. Daughters mature the way their mothers did."
- 19-year-old boy—"There's no way I could turn straight. I was born to be gay."
- 13-year-old girl—"I'll have a better figure and be more appealing to boys when I get older . . . if I start eating right and exercising."
- School nurse—"Birth-control pills can prevent you from getting pregnant, but they won't protect you from getting herpes or gonorrhea."

People's *could-be* beliefs are not necessarily true, that is, not necessarily accurate predictions of potential outcomes. The father's estimate of his son's height at age 20 may be wrong. So also may be the mother's belief about when her daughter's menarche will arrive. But accurate or not, *could-be* beliefs are important because people act on those convictions. In other words, people base their behavior on what they believe is true, whether or not those beliefs are valid descriptions of reality.

Inaccurate *could-be* beliefs can do harm when they set unrealistic expectations for how a child or adolescent can develop, especially when the expectations establish impossible goals of physical attractiveness. All boys cannot become ideally tall, muscular, agile, and handsome. Nor can all girls become as slender and exotic looking as fashion models. In contrast, realistic *could-be* predictions can lead to constructive outcomes for the growing child by posing attainable goals for which to strive. For instance, a teenage girl who believes it can be both mentally healthful and socially acceptable to refrain from sexual intercourse will avoid the risk of becoming pregnant.

Is beliefs concern youngsters' present developmental status. Boys' and girls' descriptions of their own status can reflect both thoughts and feelings.

- 14-year-old boy—"I'm starting to grow a mustache—but just barely, so it's kind of embarrassing."
- 10-year-old girl—"Nearly every month now I menstruate, and that's when I feel sick and cranky."
- 16-year-old boy—"Some nights I have a wet dream. Even though it's fun, it's messy, and that's the part I don't like."
- 12-year-old girl—"When I was young, I didn't hunt for sexy stuff on the Internet, but now I do it a lot. It's real cool."
- 17-year-old boy—"Every time we go on a date, I feel her breasts and massage her snatch. Wow!"
- 11-year-old girl—"I didn't want to let him do it, but he said if I wouldn't let him put his thing in, he wouldn't love me anymore and he'd never want to see me again."
- 14-year-old boy—"I don't want to go to hell, so I'm not doing any sex before I get married."

Should-be beliefs describe what somebody thinks a child's or teenager's sexual-development status (including one's own) ought to be at present or in the future.

- 19-year-old girl—"I shouldn't still be having acne."
- 13-year-old boy—"Even some girls in our class are taller than I am. I shouldn't be this short."
- 15-year-old girl—"Of course I'm worried. I still haven't started menstruating."
- Father of 18-year-old boy—"By his age he ought to be screwing girls so he learns all the ways to do it."
- Mother of 18-year-old girl—"She should remain a virgin until she's wed."
- 16-year-old boy—"People in our family don't tell filthy jokes, so I stay away from guys who talk dirty about sex."

Sources of Beliefs

The young can acquire eroticism beliefs from a variety of sources, including parents, other family members (siblings, cousins, uncles, aunts), schoolmates, religious workers, teachers, counselors, school nurses, medical doctors, and such mass-communication media as books, magazines, movies, television, and the Internet.

Parents. Mothers and fathers have been among the most important of children's informants about sexual matters as a result of (a) parents' continuing intimate association with children from infancy onward and (b) the authority that the parental role has traditionally represented. However, as the years of early childhood pass and children enter school, parents' influence is rivaled by that of youngsters' peers and mass-communication media, particularly during adolescence.

One problem with parents as the source of students' eroticism beliefs is the inaccuracy of parents' information. For instance, in a telephone survey, 1,069 Wisconsin and Minnesota parents were asked their opinions of the effectiveness of condoms and birth-control pills when used by teenagers. The researchers then compared parents' opinions with data from the Centers for Disease Control and Prevention (CDC).

The CDC data showed that condoms were effective in preventing sexually transmitted diseases.

> The ability of latex condoms to prevent transmission of HIV has been scientifically established in "real life" studies of sexually active couples as well as in laboratory studies. . . . Latex condoms, when used consistently and correctly, can reduce the risk of transmission of gonorrhea, chlamydia, and trichomoniasis. . . . [When used consistently and correctly, condoms] can decrease the risk of genital herpes, syphilis, chancroid, and human papillomavirus (HPV) infection. (Eisenberg, Bearringer, Sieving, Swain & Resnick, 2004)

Furthermore,

> When used consistently and correctly, condoms prevent pregnancy 97 percent of the time, and the pill does so 99.9 percent of the time. In "typical use"—that is, when use is not consistent or always correct—the effectiveness rates for condoms and the pill are 86 percent and 95 percent, respectively. . . . [and] most teenagers who use condoms or the pill do so as effectively as older users. (Eisenberg et al., 2004)

In contrast to the CDC evidence, parents offered lower estimates of the success of condoms and the pill. Only 47 percent percent of parents thought condoms were very effective in preventing sexually transmitted diseases (STDs) and 55 percent believed condoms were only somewhat effective for pregnancy prevention.

> In general, men held more accurate views of condoms, while women held more accurate views of the pill. . . . Differences by race were also apparent: Nonwhite parents were significantly more likely than white parents to give [a less accurate] response on several questions. This disparity may in part reflect some minority groups' general mistrust of the medical community, or

suspicions that STDs are being used as genocidal agents. Historical experience, particularly for black Americans, may contribute to inaccurate views of condoms and the pill. Also, many nonwhite respondents may have been immigrants who had never learned about these methods. Because the survey did not ask about country of origin and length of time living in the United States, the extent of this potential influence is unknown. Finally, the more politically conservative a parent was, the less medically accurate his or her views typically were. (Eisenberg et al., 2004)

Companions. Teenagers' peers are usually an abundant store of eroticism beliefs that include folk myths passed from one generation of adolescents to the next—myths that are often at odds with reality. Consider, for example, the following items of bogus folk wisdom.

- You can't get pregnant if it's your first time.
- Jumping up and down immediately after intercourse will prevent conception.
- Douching with Coca-Cola or 7-Up will kill whatever sperm the process doesn't wash away.
- It's impossible to get pregnant if you have sex during your [menstrual] period.
- After intercourse, a hot bath or a heating pad on the stomach prevents conception.
- As long as neither party takes off their underpants, no babies will result.
- Taking 20 aspirin right after will halt conception from taking place.
- Provided you do it standing up or with the girl on top, the sperm will never reach the egg.
- As long as he pulls out before he ejaculates, no sperm will be loosed inside the girl.
- Sneezing after sex prevents pregnancy. (Impregnable defences, 2007)

For adolescents who are newly impelled by powerful hormones, the sex urge can be so strong that it overrides reason. Thus, when emotions are allowed to trump logic, hormone-driven teens are prone to accept folk myths as true.

School. Sex education—traditionally located in the home—has increasingly been assigned to schools, especially since the "free love" movement among youths in the 1960s. However, the public's disappointment with how well home and church taught youths about sex began well before the mid-20th century. The National Education Association (NEA) in 1912 had proposed adding sex education to teacher-training programs. In 1950 the U.S. Public Health Service, in reaction to increased teenage pregnancy and sexually transmitted diseases, called school sex education an "urgent need." In 1955, the American Medical Association joined the NEA in publishing five pamphlets on sex education for schools.

However, the present-day ubiquitous presence of sex education in American schools is mainly a development of the past four decades—a development accompanied by a continuing impassioned controversy over what the content of sex education should be and who should teach it. (See chapter 9.)

Books and magazines. Over the years, an increasing number of books and periodical articles have been designed to teach children and teenagers about the biology and eroticism aspects of sex. The publications range from expressing very restrictive religious attitudes to offering unrestrained portrayals of what eroticism *could be, is,* and *should be.* That range is illustrated by the following three examples of books intended for teenagers.

Near the restrictive, traditional end of the scale is *Sex, Love and You: Making the Right Decision* (Lickona, Lickona & Boudreau, 2003), which advocates an official Catholic Church position on sexual activity that emphasizes the desirability of abstaining from sexual acts until marriage. A reviewer who endorsed the book wrote that it was designed "for those who want to know why they should keep themselves pure for their future wife or husband. My wife was hooked reading the introduction and read the book straight through. We'll be using it with our kids" (Field, 2006). However, a critic condemned *Sex, Love and You: Making the Right Decision,* claiming that

> Most teenagers, Catholic or not, will not get into books such as this and the similar *Sex and the Teenager* book from the same publisher. The reason is that these moralistic books are irrelevant to the reality that most teenagers have and enjoy a variety of sex acts. This book is unhealthy and irresponsible in its message. Sex is part of all of us. We need to embrace it with commonsense, not see it as something to wait for. (Libby, 2006)

Next is a volume whose message is closer to the middle of the conservative-liberal scale—*101 Questions about Sex and Sexuality—With Answers for the Curious, Cautious, and Confused.* A reviewer in the *School Library Journal* described the book as intended for students in grade 6 and above.

> These questions were collected from middle school and high school students, and the answers offer readers solid information, organized into chapters that include "21 Questions Young Men Ask," "22 Questions Young Women Ask," and "22 Questions About Wrongs and Risks." [The author] emphasizes abstinence as the only sure way of avoiding STDs and pregnancies, but also gives detailed information on contraception. AIDS and HIV are mentioned, but cited as subjects too big for adequate treatment here. The matter-of-fact style is never condescending or alarmist in tone; the author

> emphasizes sexuality as an integral part of human life, and urges young adults to make wise choices, armed with the facts. Explicit black-and-white illustrations lend an almost clinical touch, further moving sexuality away from myths and mistakes. (Burner, 2003)

Near the unrestrained end of the conservative-liberal scale, the book titled *It's Perfectly Normal: Changing Bodies, Growing Up, Sex, and Sexual Health* presents a version of eroticism intended for readers between ages 10 and 14. *Publishers Weekly* described the book as

> intelligent, amiable, and carefully researched. [It] frankly explains the physical, psychological, emotional and social changes that occur during puberty . . . [with watercolor and pencil art that] reinforces the message that bodies come in all sizes, shapes and colors—and that each variation is "perfectly normal." (Harris, 1996)

However, a parent, whose review of *It's Perfectly Normal* appeared on Amazon.com's website, complained,

> I didn't have to read this book to know it was far too much for my 11-year-old daughter. If you believe that cartoon characters in explicit illustrations including people have missionary sex, oral sex, [masturbating], and wearing condoms is appropriate for your age 9–11 year old child, then I would recommend you buy the book. However, if you believe that the subject should be dealt with sensitivity and a bit more seriousness, I would most certainly not recommend this ridiculous book. I returned the book to Amazon.

In contrast, another Amazon customer wrote,

> I bought this book for my 13-year-old granddaughter because she had so many questions about boys and changes that were happening to her body. This book took very difficult subjects and put [them] into plain English that any child could understand. I have recommended this book over and over to parents and grandparents for their little ones. I am concerned with where our young people get their information and this was an excellent source for understanding some of the do's and do not's for adolescents.

In view of the wide differences in the content of books about sex, librarians and teachers are well advised—before accepting such books for the school library or classroom—to examine the books' contents to determine if they would be acceptable in the local community.

A 1982 U.S. Supreme Court decision gave school officials greater latitude for banning books from classrooms than from libraries. Justice William Brennan, in writing the Court's ruling, stated that school officials did have the authority to control the content of school curricula, but that authority was not absolute, so "students may not be regarded as closed-circuit recipients of only that which the State chooses to communicate."

> While [school boards] might rightfully claim absolute discretion in matters of curriculum by reliance upon their duty to inculcate community values in schools, [their] reliance upon that duty is misplaced where they attempt to extend their claim of absolute discretion beyond the compulsory environment of the classroom into the school library. . . . [School authorities] possess significant discretion to determine the content of their school libraries, but that discretion may not be exercised in a narrowly partisan or political manner. Whether [school officials'] removal of books from the libraries denied [students] their First Amendment rights depends upon the motivation behind the actions. Local school boards may not remove books from school libraries simply because they dislike the ideas contained in those books and seek by their removal to "prescribe what shall be orthodox in politics, nationalism, religion, or other matters of opinion." (Brennan, 1982)

Consequently, a book with a controversial treatment of sex might not be accepted as a classroom textbook but still might be included in a school's library collection. Then, to satisfy parents who might object to their children reading such books, the librarian can stipulate that parents' permission is required before youngsters are allowed access to those volumes.

Television and movies. Three issues addressed in debates about the effect of television and films on children concern: How much access do youngsters have to erotic TV programs and movies? How do such programs influence youths' sexual behavior? How can potential harm from television and movie viewing be minimized?

Youngsters' access to sex-focused TV and films is very great, indeed. One summary of studies over the years 1997–2001 reported that 75 percent of prime-time television included sexual content, 23 percent of couples in intercourse scenes appeared to be ages 18–24, sex material was in 87 percent of movies, premarital sex was referred to two or three times every hour in soap operas, and the average American adolescent would annually see nearly 14,000 references to sex on TV and in movies. In one survey, 66 percent of children ages 10 to 16 said their peers were influenced by television broadcasts (National Coalition, 2008). A study of network and cable programs showed that the number of sexual scenes in about 1,000 shows nearly doubled from 1,930 in 1998 to 3,780 in 2005. By 2005, 7 in 10 television programs watched by teens contained some form of sexual content, with each show including more sexual references than during the 1990s (Zwillich, 2005).

Explicit sex in motion pictures, as in TV programs, has also increased rapidly. Tim Dirks summarized the state of affairs in the following manner.

> Sexy and erotic images in film scenes can be displayed in many varieties and kinds of films. Sexual scenes may appear in art-house films, horror/slasher films, erotic dramas, foreign-language films and mainstream films. They may be "old-fashioned," risqué, blatant, mature, PG-13, excessive, suggestive, cheap, exploitative, outrageous, innovative, infantile, soft-hued and soft-focused, campy, voyeuristic, trashy, sensual, highly-charged, symbolic or visually metaphoric, carnal, highly-choreographed and artsy, prurient or soft-core. Erotic films, unlike pornography, do not have as their sole purpose the explicit and graphic display of sex and nudity. Erotica sometimes is explicit, but can often be teasing, intriguing, stylized, unique and imaginative. However, trends in recent art-house films (that are unrated) suggest that simulated sex is becoming more explicit, unsimulated sex—bordering on pornographic! Although most theatrical releases are often edited to obtain an [parental-guidance] R-rating, the DVD releases include the "director's cut," with unrated, explicit extra material. (Dirks, 2008)

In brief, not only are present-day television programs and movies heavily laden with eroticism, but the amount and intimacy of sex scenes have also been increasing.

What, then, is the effect of such entertainment choices on youngsters' sexual development? Two surveys in recent years have suggested that the more erotic the TV and film fare that teenagers consume, the earlier youths engage in sexual intercourse. In a study of 1,011 adolescents, ages 12 to 15, researchers noted that young viewers who see more TV and DVD sexual content "perceive greater support from the media for teen sexual behavior [and] report greater intentions to engage in sexual intercourse and more sexual activity" (Vanderheyden, 2006). The study team reported that

> the majority of the 264 media sources examined found sexually-charged situations were almost always between unmarried couples and usually portrayed sex as "risk-free." The [media were described] as a "sexual super peer" with an influence at least equal to religion or the relationship between the child and parents. (Vanderheyden, 2006)

A second survey was conducted through a pair of telephone interviews that were 1 year apart. The respondents were 1,792 adolescents who ranged in age from 12 to 17. Results showed that teenagers who had not yet engaged in sex acts at the time of the first interview were more likely to start during the following year if they watched TV shows that contained sexual content. Not only did seeing sexual encounters on TV affect the viewers, but people who were merely seen talking about sex also led to youths engaging earlier in erotic acts. The research team concluded that

> Watching sex on TV predicts and may hasten adolescent sexual initiation. Reducing the amount of sexual content in entertainment programming, reducing adolescent exposure to this content, or increasing references to and depictions of possible negative consequences of sexual activity could appreciably delay the initiation of coital and noncoital activities. Alternatively, parents may be able to reduce the effects of sexual content by watching TV with their teenaged children and discussing their own beliefs about sex and the behaviors portrayed. (Collins et al., 2004)

Finally, how can potential harm from television and movie viewing be minimized? The increase of sex and violence in movies during the 1960s was met with angry parent groups clamoring for government regulation of motion pictures' content. Moviemakers, fearing legislation that would curtail the sorts of films they produced, responded by introducing the Motion Picture Association of America's film-rating system in 1968. The most recent code letters and their meanings are as follows:

G—General Audiences—All ages admitted.
PG—Parental guidance suggested—Some material may not be suitable for children.
PG-13—Parents strongly cautioned—Some material may be inappropriate for children under age 13.
R—Restricted—Viewers under age 17 must be accompanied by a parent or adult guardian.
NC-17—No one age 17 and under admitted.
NR—Film is not rated.

The television-programming industry, following the passage of the federal government's Telecommunications Act of 1996, created its own rating system in collaboration with child-advocacy organizations. Like the film-rating scheme, it was a voluntary-participation system with no legal force but was adopted by most broadcast and cable networks. The system was designed to utilize the V-chip, a device built into all television sets that allowed parents and school officials to block certain categories of programs. Television networks often display the rating of a program by a symbol in the corner of the television screen. The symbols bear the following meanings.

TV-Y—Appropriate for all children
TV-Y7—Directed to older children; may not be suitable for children under age 7.
TV-Y7-FV—May not be suitable for children under 7; contains fantasy violence.

TV-G—General audience; for viewers of all ages.
TV-PG—Unsuitable for young children without the guidance of a parent.
TV-14—Parents strongly cautioned that content may be offensive.
TV-MA—For mature adult viewers only.

Several codes may be added to the TV-PG, TV-14, and TV-MA ratings—V = intense violence; S = intense sexual situations; L = strong, coarse language; D = intensely suggestive dialogue.

Schools have frequently used the movie and television rating schemes as guides to what sorts of films and TV programs will be permitted at different grade levels. However, both rating schemes have been criticized for inconsistency and secrecy in how the standards are implemented. A study of how the movie ratings were applied over the 1992–2003 decade exposed *ratings creep*. That is, film-industry raters gradually allowed more explicit sex within a rating category. The increases were particularly evident in the (a) sexual content of films rated PG, PG-13, and R and (b) profanity in films rated PG-13 and R (Thompson & Yokota, 2004).

Internet. Among the sources of eroticism beliefs, the one that is least subject to control by governments, parents, or schools is the Internet, with its millions of World Wide Web sites that the young can visit via their computers. The accelerating rate at which new sites were created is suggested by a report that 155, 230,051 websites were activated by December 2007, an increase of 50 million sites since December 2006. The three fastest-growing sites were ones on which individuals place personal information and opinions—MySpace, Live Spaces, and Blogger—designed to facilitate individuals communicating with each other (Web server survey, 2007). Additional personal-identity sites bear such names as Orkut, Friendster, iShoals, Yahoo! 360°, Hi5, Bebo, Facebook, and Xanga. One called YouTube specializes in members sharing videos.

Characteristics of personal-identity services can be illustrated with MySpace, which is one of the world's most frequently visited web sources. It attracts 80 percent of the social-networking traffic. Individuals who are at least age 14 can establish a MySpace account at no cost, then customize their profile with information about themselves and their friends.

However attractive Internet social-contact sites appear to be, they invite potential harm. The danger risked by people who place their profiles in a social network includes sexual abuse that can result when a visitor to a teenager's page seduces the teenager into a tragic encounter—unrequited affection, disgusting sexual acts, rape, pregnancy, or disease. For example, a 34-year-old man created a MySpace site in which he described himself as a 19-year-old North Carolina State University student and, through searching MySpace profiles, persuaded two boys, ages 14 and

15, to have sex with him, a ruse that landed him in prison. In December 2006, the operators of MySpace announced that new methods were being adopted to protect children from known sex offenders in the United States, but no details were given about what those methods would be. In February 2007, a U.S. district judge in Texas ruled that parents could not sue MySpace for negligence, fraud, and misrepresentation because their daughter had been sexually assaulted by a man she met through MySpace after she had misrepresented her age as 18 when she was actually only 13. The judge reasoned that the parents, not MySpace, had the responsibility for protecting the girl. In May 2007, MySpace began screening their millions of accounts worldwide for sex predators. Pressured by states' attorneys, the company released a list of 7,000 registered sex offenders who had MySpace profiles (North Carolina battling, 2007). During the same month, the North Carolina Senate passed a bill requiring youths below age 18 to have their parents' consent before they could sign up for a MySpace account (Weigl, 2007).

A particular source of eroticism beliefs is the Internet's enormous mine of pornography from which students can extract ideas about sex. Pornography on the Internet typically consists of pictures or descriptions of naked persons or of people engaged in sex acts. Child pornography—sometimes known as *kiddie porn*—is defined as

> visual depiction of minors (i.e., under 18) engaged in a sex act such as intercourse, oral sex, or masturbation as well as the lascivious depictions of the genitals. Various federal courts in the 1980s and 1990s concluded that "lewd" or "lascivious" depiction of the genitals does not require the genitals to be uncovered. Thus, for example, a video of underage teenage girls dancing erotically, with multiple close-up shots of their covered genitals, can be considered child porn. (Child pornography, 2005)

Although statistics on Internet pornography are difficult to compile, estimates that seem fairly reliable reflect the extent of tantalizing sexual content. Ropelato (2008) has reported 4.2 million websites offering 420 million pages of pornography. Explicit erotic content is distributed daily in 2.5 billion e-mails. An estimated 43 percent of Internet users view porn, while 34 percent receive unwanted pornography. More than 100 million websites display illegal child pornography, and sexual solicitations to young people appear in 89 percent of chat rooms. Internet pornography sales worldwide have been estimated at $4.9 billion. Thus, the likelihood is very great, indeed, that youngsters who visit the Internet without any sort of adult control will view explicit eroticism.

Summary. The amount and diversity of sources of students' beliefs about eroticism are greater today than at any time in the past. Furthermore, not only are youngsters tempted to believe that the increasingly explicit portrayals of sex on television, in movies, and on the Internet accurately represent what generally *is* human sexual behavior, but youngsters can also become convinced that—because so many people supposedly act in such ways—the media portrayals represent what *should be* the way they themselves act. This extension of a seemingly popular *is* to a personal *ought* may lead to unfortunate consequences. In effect, the kind of sexual *should-be* that will yield the most desirable present and future for a child or teenager depends on a variety of factors in that person's life. Those factors beg for a youngster's serious consideration when she or he is deciding how best to act under tempting erotic circumstances. In other words, will the thrill of this present erotic encounter be worth the consequences it might yield? Thus, a key aim of sex education in schools is to prepare students for making that *should-be* decision.

Authority and Power

As proposed in chapter 1, *power* is the ability of one individual or group to influence the behavior of another individual or group. *Authority* is the assignment of decision-making power to an individual or group, with people expected to honor that assignment. The assignment can be in the form of a written law or regulation, or it may be an unwritten custom passed down from one generation to the next. These concepts of power and authority are important for explaining matters of sex in schools, especially for explaining which beliefs about eroticism the school will promote and which the school will denounce or simply ignore.

Authority over sexual matters in schools can be viewed as a hierarchy of power levels descending from Congress, the president, and the U.S. Supreme Court at the federal level, down through state legislatures and school boards, and finally to classroom teachers.

An example of federal authority is the abstinence-only legislation passed by Congress in 1996 under the Clinton administration—legislation that channels millions of dollars to schools conducting sex-education programs that teach students that refraining from sexual intercourse until marriage is the only acceptable form of sexual behavior. Following the Clinton era, the Bush administration over the period 2002–2008 increased funding for the abstinence-only plan. But because the U.S. Constitution assigns the authority over education to the states rather than to the federal government, Congress could not order states to adopt the plan. Therefore, as the federal government's device for wielding power, federal officials offered states money if they would adopt the abstinence-only approach. Money did the trick. Virtually all states accepted the funds.

An instance of the U.S. Supreme Court's authority is the 1982 ruling (mentioned earlier in this chapter) that school boards' rights to ban books with sexual allusions from classrooms did not extend equally to banning books from school libraries. The reason that this ruling has been so important is that it applies to the entire nation. Such a decision in a state court would apply only to school boards within that state.

At the next lower level in the hierarchy, the authority of state legislatures was demonstrated when 15 states by 2008 rejected federal abstinence-only funds because the legislators preferred their own sex-education programs that included instruction in the use of birth-control and disease-prevention methods (such as condoms) in addition to abstinence.

States can then delegate their authority to the next lower stratum—school districts—as illustrated in the Mississippi legislature stipulating that

> abstinence education shall be the state standard for any sex-related education taught in the public schools, [and] any course containing sex education offered in the public schools shall include instruction in abstinence education. However, the local school board may authorize, by affirmative vote of a majority of the members, the teaching of sex education without instruction on abstinence. In such event, the curriculum offered in the schools relating to sex education must be approved by a majority of the school board members. (HIV, STD, 2007)

An example of a board ruling about sex education is the Montgomery County (Virginia) Board of Education's 2007 approval of lessons for 8th- and 10th-graders focusing on people's sexual orientations and what it means to be homosexual (de Vise, 2007).

Next, at the individual-school level, administrators have the authority to set standards for student behavior, with those standards often specified in handbooks distributed to students and their parents. For instance, a statement in the Norton (Ohio) High School handbook warns that

> Sexual harassment is prohibited. Sexual harassment is defined as unwanted sexual advances, which may be verbal, visual, or physical contact. The definition is very broad and could include propositioning, making threats of reprisals after a proposition is refused, making actual reprisals after a proposition is refused, displaying sexually suggestive objects, making sexual remarks or gestures, making sexual comments, displaying sexual pictures or cartoons, making derogatory comments or slurs based on sex, making sexual comments about a person's body, touching a person, blocking their exit, assaulting a person, or other acts adjudicated as harassment by the school administration. (Sexual harassment, 2007)

Finally, classroom teachers and other school personnel (counselors, bus drivers, athletic coaches) are authorized to supervise students' erotic behavior in accordance with school rules and a staff member's personal standards of proper sexual conduct.

Interactions between levels of this authority hierarchy are not always amicable but involve conflicts, marshaling the power tactics of people on one level against the tactics of people on another. Furthermore, at the school-district and individual-school levels, power struggles can develop between school personnel and parents, with parents bearing their own authority. Sometimes parental authority is cast in written law, but, if not, it is still powerful as long-established custom. And when the two sides in a dispute between parent and school are unyielding, with one side failing to admit defeat or accept a compromise, the conflict may need to be settled in court.

Although students lack formal authority, they are not without power. Students have the final power of decision over their own erotic behavior. They can violate school or parental policies if they are willing to risk the sanctions that the school or parent might invoke. Students' attempts to exert their power of decision cause many of the eroticism problems faced by schools and parents.

Summary

In the foregoing discussion, I have proposed that the psychological component of children's and teenagers erotic development is comprised of *could-be, is,* and *should-be* beliefs and of associated emotions. As children grow up, their thoughts about sex are accumulated through encounters with environments from which eroticism beliefs can be extracted. Over recent decades, the potential sources of beliefs have greatly expanded beyond the family, church, companions, and books to include schools' sex-education lessons and eroticism-loaded movies, television broadcasts, and Internet websites. Never before has the quantity of conflicting viewpoints about proper sexual behavior been as great as it is today.

The beliefs about eroticism taught in public schools are determined by people on different levels of an authority hierarchy that extends from the federal government at the top to classroom teachers at the bottom. Those beliefs have been a matter of continuing debate and negotiation, and they undoubtedly will continue to be contentious in the future.

Social Aspects of Erotic Development

In this chapter's physical, psychological, and social version of eroticism development, the term *social* refers to a person's sexual interaction with others. I am assuming that erotic acts result from a combination of a person's (a) present physical condition (the body's sexual equipment, including sex hormones) and (b) present psychological condition (emotions and beliefs about *could-be, is,* and *should-be*). Although it is obvious that

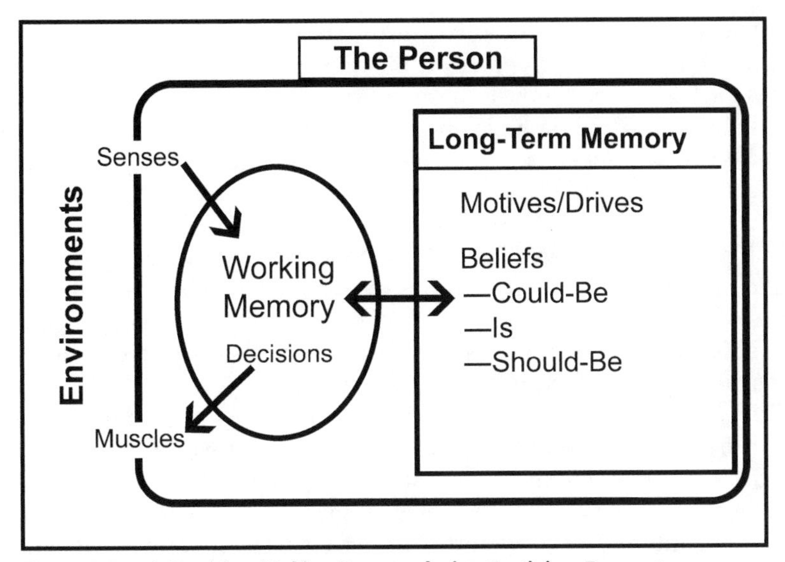

Figure 2.3. A Decision-Making Process during Eroticism Encounters

youngsters can perform sexual acts in solitude (as is typical of masturbation), even such private acts usually involve imaginary sex partners and thus, for present purposes, those acts qualify as social behavior.

How, then, does a student's decision making operate in social settings interpreted as erotic? In response, I would suggest that the decision-making process operates in the manner portrayed in figure 2.3. It is a process that repeats itself endlessly as children and adolescents encounter a never-ending succession of environments that are interpreted as sexual.

The simplified model in figure 2.3 portrays decision making as progressing through three phases that determine how a person will act in eroticism settings.

Phase 1: Readiness

Youngsters bring to an environment the motives, drives, or needs that influence which features of that environment will attract their attention. Figure 2.3 locates the source of motives in the person's long-term memory. This model of the mind assumes three types of needs that guide youngsters' behavior in eroticism settings.

- First is the drive to satisfy a hormonal sexual urge—to gain pleasure from expending the hormonal energy that matures during puberty. High-school students may express this condition as being "horny."

- Second is a need for emotional or social acceptance—to be welcomed and cherished by a person who is the object of one's desire.
- Third is a need for harm-avoidance—to avoid physical, psychological, or social damage. In sexual contexts, this is a desire to escape from such unwelcome outcomes as pregnancy, infection, or the social disgrace of "a bad reputation."

In figure 2.3, long-term memory is divided into a white portion and a shaded portion. The white signifies contents of memory that the person consciously recognizes and can "bring to mind." The shading signifies influential motives and needs of which the person is unaware but that, nevertheless, influence the person's behavior.

During students' eroticism decision making, the first two needs (erotic energy release and emotional/social acceptance) are often pitted against the third (harm-avoidance) so that decision making involves the question: "Is the enjoyment of a sexual encounter worth the risk of damage?" As British author G. K. Chesterton observed, "The first two facts which a healthy boy or girl feels about sex are these: first that it is beautiful and then that it is dangerous" (Chesterton, 2008). And Chesterton is said to have reminded his son that the pleasure of sexual intercourse was "Oh, so brief" and the potential consequences "Oh, so lasting."

Phase 2: Perception

The term *perception* refers to a person's interpreting the meaning of an environment as preparation for making a decision. The process of perception begins with the person using the senses (sight, hearing, touch, smell) to draw information from the environment into working memory. Working memory then compares those impressions with the contents of long-term memory so as to determine what the impressions mean in relation to the beliefs (*could-be, is,* and *should-be*) the person has gathered over the years. In effect, interpreting consists of answering the question, "How does the environmental information match my beliefs?"

On the basis of this comparison, working memory's second task is to reach a decision about how to act toward the environment so as best to satisfy the sexual drive and desire for emotional acceptance without violating deeply held *should-be* beliefs or risking pregnancy, infection, and social disgrace.

Phase 3: Action

Finally, working memory's decision is put into action by ordering the muscle system to act on the environment, thereby determining what the person will say or do in response to the environment's apparent erotic opportunity.

This three-phase decision-making process may be completed in an instant, or it may take hours or days, as suggested by such remarks as:

> "When she invited me to put my hand inside her bra, I said, 'No way.'"
> "You want me to meet you in the boy's locker room after school? I'll have to think about it and tell you later."
> "Three weeks ago he asked me to go with him to next Friday's party, but I know they'll all be drinking and on drugs and screwing, and I still can't decide what to do."

Environments vary in the sorts of erotic behaviors they can feasibly accommodate. Adjacent chairs in the busy school library permit a pair of students to unobtrusively hold hands and touch knees, but the library is not a reasonable setting for oral sex. A classroom permits students to furtively exchange amorous notes but not to engage in genital fondling. The empty, dark gymnasium in the evening may allow a pair of lovers to practice coitus but that setting is not conducive to examining pornographic photos.

A decision produced in working memory is not unalterable. Circumstances can force a change at any moment, as when an environment changes. That is, environments vary in their stability, with a stable environment being one that remains consistent throughout a sexual encounter. The less stable an environment, the greater the risk that a decision to engage in erotic activities will produce unsatisfactory results for the participants. Consider two examples of environmental conditions interrupting erotic behavior by altering the emotional atmosphere for liaisons. In the midst of intercourse, a 15-year-old girl's hormone-driven ardor suddenly vanishes when her 18-year-old partner announces, "I'm pulling out early so you won't get HIV." And the expected joy in a couple's act of coitus evaporates when a police officer's flashlight exposes their half-naked bodies in the backseat of a Chevrolet.

Not only may a change in an environment force the revision of a decision, but a change in a participant's mental state in the midst of an erotic episode can alter a decision as well. For instance, a girl's passion during a sexual act can suddenly freeze when her subconscious *should-be* belief about unwelcome pregnancy rushes into consciousness and she gasps, "Oh my god, what am I doing!"

The Resulting Beliefs

It is through the endless iterations of this readiness/perception/action process that students accumulate their storehouse of *could-be, is,* and *should-be* beliefs that guide their eroticism decisions when the consequences of their actions provide information that adds to and alters their convictions about what is true regarding sex.

Conclusion

This chapter has portrayed children's and teenagers' sexual development from three perspectives—physical, psychological, and social.

The basic pattern of young people's physical development is determined by the genetic material received from their parents at the time of conception. The design of physical development carried by the newborn's DNA structure establishes the basic pattern and pace of sexual development throughout the first two decades of life. Variations in that pattern and pace can result from such environmental influences as the growing child's diet and family emotional conditions.

Psychological development consists of the child's accumulating a growing store of beliefs about what one's sex life *could-be, is,* and *should-be*. The beliefs have accumulated over the past through encounters with environments that involved such sources as parents, companions, teachers, religious leaders, reading materials (books, magazines, newspapers), television programs, movies, and the Internet.

The social perspective concerns how people act in situations that are seen as sexual. Young people's behavior in such settings is determined by decisions reached through working memory's interpreting the present environment's erotic opportunities in relation to eroticism beliefs (*could-be, is, should be*) held in long-term memory.

SUGGESTIONS FOR SCHOOL PRACTICE

Throughout this book, suggestions are offered about constructive ways schools can respond to students' eroticism development. The suggestions in this chapter concern educators' (a) holding realistic development expectations, (b) coping with weight problems, (c) setting behavior standards, (d) providing timely information, and (e) monitoring students' access to information sources.

Holding Realistic Development Expectations

Some people—including school personnel—seem to believe that children should not entertain erotic thoughts or engage in erotic acts. But because eroticism is so obviously a normal and necessary human attribute, such beliefs are counterproductive. If parents and educators are to contribute most effectively to youngsters' welfare, they need to hold realistic expectations for children's and teenagers' sexual development. Such expectations can profitably include knowledge about (a) typical physical, psychological, and social aspects of eroticism's development and (b) significant differences among individual youngsters in how those aspects evolve.

This chapter, as an intended contribution to such knowledge, has sketched typical features of such development. Thus, teachers should not be amazed when a 9-year-old girl begins to menstruate, a 12-year-old boy's tight jeans reveal an erect penis, a 15-year-old boy's computer files include Internet photos of couples fornicating, or a 16-year-old girl becomes pregnant. It is also vital that school personnel recognize the wide range of individual ways that students advance through the stages of development as a result of their differences in genetic endowment and the environments they have encountered while growing up. School staff members should expect that no two children will develop in precisely the same way and at exactly the same pace.

Coping with Weight Problems

Two concerns about students' weight, as described earlier in this chapter, are teenagers (a) attempting to slim their bodies to an unrealistic and medically dangerous size and (b) becoming overweight as a result of unhealthy diets and lack of exercise.

First, consider the anorexia problem. Schools have sought to change students' beliefs about "skinny" being the only desirable female body shape by adopting such measures as teaching the dangers of extreme dieting, featuring photos in school publications of attractive students who represent a normal range of body sizes, and sponsoring fashion shows that use models in different body sizes.

Next is the problem of overweight youngsters. After the federal government's No Child Left Behind legislation in 2001 required schools to spend more time teaching reading and mathematics, many schools found that extra time by eliminating physical education and shortening recess periods. However, the rapid increase of child and adolescent obesity as the decade advanced prompted a growing number of schools to reinstate compulsory physical activities.

At the same time that more physical activity has been required, more schools have been banning junk food. In the beginning, the fast-food and snacks industry strongly resisted nutritionists' attempts to eliminate junk food from lunch menus and vending machines. But gradually purveyors of junk began introducing more healthful products. For instance, a September 2007 report from the beverage industry noted that significant progress had been made in removing nondiet sodas from schools. Consequently, the proportion of sugary drinks sold in schools declined from 47 percent in 2004 to 32 percent in 2007. The report predicted even more rapid replacement of nondiet drinks in the years ahead (Report, 2007). Thus, it appears that, as students' obesity increases and their fitness deteriorates, health-food proponents will gain further ground in eliminating sugar- and fat-laden foods and drinks in schools.

Setting Behavior Standards

Social chaos would obviously result if students were permitted to vent their hormonal sex urges in an unbridled fashion. Thus, it is necessary for schools to set limits on what sorts of sexual expressions are permissible in settings over which schools bear supervisory responsibility—on school premises, on school buses, at sporting events, at dramatic performances, during science or music excursions, and the like. Such limits are set for two reasons: (a) to enforce cultural conventions about sex and (b) to promote instructional efficiency by not allowing students' preoccupation with sexual interests to interfere with their studies.

Cultural conventions are a society's—or, more specifically, a community's—dominant beliefs about what kinds of erotic behaviors are appropriate—by whom, when, and where. Some conventions are laws or rules in printed form. Others are simply understood as traditional values passed informally from one generation to the next as "standards of common decency." Particularly since the freer expression of eroticism in the 1960s, those standards have been the focus of much controversy. And when standards are thus in transition, it becomes especially important for schools to state precisely which expressions of eroticism are not permitted in school settings so that students can predict the consequences of sexual acts they might contemplate. The typical form in which schools cast such regulations are as descriptions in school boards' policies, in handbooks supplied to students, in letters sent to parents, in rules posted on bulletin boards, and in articles in school newspapers. The following are examples of such regulations.

Banned Books

Most school districts permit the banning of books for use in the classroom on grounds of sexual inappropriateness, but the policies usually fail to specify what constitutes *inappropriateness*. Instead, school-board members and administrators tend to base their judgments on their personal conceptions of sex-related content unsuitable for students. However, some districts do offer guidelines in a slightly more specific form. For instance, the Bay County School Board (Florida) has assigned books to one of three categories: (1) works that contain no vulgarity or explicit sex and are thus suitable for classroom use, (2) works that contain a "sprinkling" of vulgarity and thus are likely inappropriate, and (3) books that include the curse word "goddamn" and "a lot of vulgarity" so they definitely should be excluded from classrooms (although they might be allowed in school libraries). Among the works placed in the school board's category 3 are Shakespeare's *Twelfth Night* and *The Merchant of Venice* along with such novels as Ernest Hemingway's *The Old Man and the Sea,* Thomas Heggen's *Mister Roberts,* Ray Bradbury's *Fahrenheit 451,* F. Scott Fitzgerald's *The Great Gatsby,* and Stephen Crane's *Red Badge of Courage* (Suit challenges, 1987).

To reduce confusion among teachers, administrators, students, and parents regarding what sorts of books are to be banned, schools can usefully produce a written policy describing their standards (and the reasons for such standards) in judging books' suitability for classrooms and libraries.

Dress Codes

Handbooks that explain school regulations often describe modes of dress and adornment that are banned because they are deemed sexually suggestive, offensive, or distracting. By way of illustration, consider the following descriptions of prohibited garb in the Stafford (Virginia) Public Schools student handbook:

- Clothing and accessories that contain vulgar, derogatory or suggestive diagrams, pictures, slogans, or words that may be interpreted as sexually offensive and which cause or are likely to cause a disruption within the school environment.
- Clothing, accessories and/or any words, pictures, diagrams, etc., thereon which are lewd, vulgar, indecent, plainly offensive, or which cause or are likely to cause a material disruption.
- Tank tops, tube tops, mesh tops, sheer tops, sleeveless tops, halters, or bare midriff tops. Shirts cannot have necklines that are lower than the straight line from top of underarm across to opposite underarm. Shirts must cover shoulders, must have sleeves, and must extend past the top of the pants. Display of cleavage is not permitted. Tops may not expose the midriff, and clothing must cover undergarments at all times. Note that at the elementary level, sleeveless tops and dresses are permitted providing they do not violate any other part of the dress code. (Student dress code, 2005)

Students receive their best guidance for what garb is acceptable at school when, as in the Stafford handbook, the requirements are specified in printed form and distributed to both students and their parents.

Speech and Writing

Some words relating to sex are prohibited in schools while others are not. In a health-education class, *coitus, copulation,* and *sexual intercourse* are typically acceptable while *fuck, screw, bang, lay, ride, root,* and *shag* are not. The words *vagina, clitoris,* and *cervix* are acceptable, whereas *cunt, snatch, twat, pussy,* and *poontang* are not. The terms *penis* and *male sex organ* are acceptable, but *cock, dick, dong, pecker, peter,* and *prick* are not. The expression *testicles* is permitted but *acorns, balls, bollocks, knackers, nuts, twiddle-diddies,* and *cojones* are not.

Jokes, rhymes, and ditties about people's sexually related body parts and about people's erotic behavior are usually considered offensive in school settings and are therefore censored.

Two awkward problems school personnel face in applying speech and writing standards are those of (a) informing students of what constitutes forbidden language and (b) adjusting to students' diverse backgrounds in language usage.

Identifying forbidden language. Students would understand most clearly which words are outlawed at school if they had received a list of those words, including terms that properly should replace the forbidden ones. However, such a solution has at least two drawbacks. It would fail to be definitive, because it's unlikely the list would include the entire array of unwelcome slang that students might use. But perhaps more important, the list would acquaint students with a host of additional offensive terms they had not known before. Therefore, schools typically solve this problem by vaguely phrasing their warnings about prohibited sexual terms—"Students are advised to avoid coarse sex language" or "Offensive remarks referring to sex will not be tolerated." Then applying such an imprecise language proscription depends on what individual teachers and other staff members consider improper, with teachers' judgments often affected by the situations in which forbidden language is used. Thus, a coach may ignore a frustrated quarterback's uttering an oath on the football field, and the woodshop instructor may overlook a girl's lewd outburst when the hammer hits her thumb.

Cultural-background adjustments. The sex-related terminology commonly used in students' homes and by students' companions is often not identical to the language acceptable in schools. Therefore, students may not be aware of which words and topics will be forbidden at school. Consequently, the first time students are caught saying or writing an objectionable word, they may require only an explanation of why that term is unacceptable at school rather than their needing to be punished for using it.

Providing Timely Information

Over the decades, the task of sex education has increasingly been imposed on schools because traditional sex educators—primarily parents and the church—have too often done a poor job of it. Many parents have either avoided the task out of neglect or embarrassment, or the information they have offered has been inaccurate or has arrived too late to be of much help for their confused and distressed offspring. Before a girl's menarche, she needs to know the nature of menstruation so she doesn't fear that she is bleeding from a loathsome disease. Boys need to know about a wet dream before they experience one and believe they have urinated in their bed or that they deserve punishment for being wicked. Both boys and girls, before they sprout embarrassing facial pimples, need to understand about acne and how it can be treated. In short, students need timely information about matters of sex.

If all youngsters started their pubertal changes at the same time and advanced through puberty at the same rate, the decision about when to introduce different sex topics in school (menstruation, nocturnal emissions, masturbation, pregnancy, sexually transmitted infections) would be simple. However, as noted earlier in this chapter, there are wide differences among individual children in the age at which different sexual changes occur. Therefore, educators are left to decide when to introduce learners to each eroticism topic—(a) soon enough, so that students will be on the brink of experiencing that developmental change in their own lives, but (b) not too early, so that students are puzzled and confused because they will not soon be experiencing such changes in their own lives. Sex education at school—unlike sex education at home—cannot be paced to suit each child's development rate, because pupils are taught in groups. Thus, the timing of topics will not be perfect for every student. But teachers can introduce topics at a time that will prepare most learners for changes they soon will experience. In the case of teaching girls about the menarche and menstruation, that time may well be in fifth or sixth grade, since the average age for the appearance of the menarche is 12.5 years. Teaching boys about nocturnal emissions might be assigned to sixth or seventh grade, since most boys will likely have their first wet dream at age 12 or 13. Many parents are concerned that their daughters' and sons' innocence about sexual matters not be dispelled too early during childhood, so that a school's decision about when different sex topics are introduced may be affected by influential parents and community members.

Monitoring Students' Internet Use

An important issue of recent origin is the question of what control, if any, should be wielded by schools over students' access to Internet websites. Should students be permitted to view the millions of web pages that feature pictures of people engaged in all manner of erotic acts? Should students be allowed to join chat groups and to advertise their own personal information on social-contact pages that can be visited by sex abusers?

The answer—from both school personnel and parents—has generally been that schools should, indeed, curtail students' Internet access. One way to do this is to install web-filter or web-blocker software on school computers. The following paragraphs explain what that entails.

Web Filters—Pro and Con

Computer users gain access to the Internet via an ISP—Internet service provider. The ISP may be a commercial provider—such as America Online, MSN, ATT-Yahoo, or Earthlink—or it may be an institution, such as a school system. It is possible to install a device (a *web proxy server*) between the ISP and the computers that students use at home or at school. A proxy server can be programmed to purge information from particular websites. Thus, parents and school personnel can prevent students from visiting websites that are considered harmful or are simply a waste of study time. Such proxy devices are known as *web filters* or *web blockers*.

A great variety of web filters on the market are designed for use on home and school computers. Consider this sample of filters advertised on the Internet: WebBlocker, WiseChoice, Kid Safe, Net Nanny, CYBERsitter, CyberPatrol, Cyber Centinel, McAfee Parental Controls, Norton Parental Controls, MaxProtect, FilterPak, Safe Eyes, K9 Web Protection, Block Web Site Buddy, Netmop, WebWatcher, SpectorPro 6.0, SpyAgent, IamBigBrother, Content Protect, 8e6 Technologies, Websense, SurfControl, Symantec, N2H2, CyBlock, Untangle, Predator Guard, and Barracuda.

Web blockers are distinguished from each other by such features as (a) the types of web materials they will screen out, (b) how easily they can be programmed, (c) cost, (d) reliability, and (e) flexibility (how different patterns of filtering can be suited to different types of users, such as young children versus teenagers).

Web-filter companies' advertising emphasizes qualities of their products that they consider particularly appealing to customers. For instance:

- *WebWatcher* is touted as providing administrators with the ability to (a) block access to inappropriate websites, (b) see each website a user has visited, (c) read every e-mail sent or received, and (d) see both sides of the conversation of every instant-message or chat in which a user participated.

- *CyberPatrol* is designed to block by (a) the particular individual using the computer, (b) groups of users (such as seventh graders), (c) the time of day that computers are used, (d) how long a user is online, (e) particular websites, and (d) specific kinds of banned material (pornography, racist, hate).
- *Sophos* blocks computer games that lure students into wasting study time or that feature violence and sexual content regarded as harmful.

In one study that assessed the comparative advantages of 12 commercially available web filters, the top three products were Net Nanny, CYBERsitter, and CyberPatrol. The systems were rated on such features as the sorts of Internet contents filtered, monitored, or blocked (chat groups, e-mail, pop-up ads, peer-to-peer connections, newsgroups), password controls, and how Internet users' profiles were displayed (Internet filter report, 2007).

Alorie Gilbert's and Stefanie Olsen's (2006) evaluation of filter programs offers suggestions for parents and school personnel.

> Consider your Internet provider. Filtering comes free with [such servers as] AOL, EarthLink or MSN. AOL and MSN both filtered effectively, but AOL blocked sites such as NewsMax, a conservative political site, and Operation Truth, an advocacy site for Iraq War veterans. In both cases, a parent could override the block.
>
> Weigh protection [of children] versus interference [with children's legitimate activities]. All filtering programs either overblock or underblock. For young children, look for maximum protection. For older children, look for filtering software that doesn't overly interfere [with what children should be allowed to do].
>
> [Select which activities you need to control.] Older children are more likely to engage in activities such as e-mail, instant messaging, and gaming.
>
> Decide how much customization you need. If your children aren't close in age, consider a program that can be customized by age. [Programs] that offer more filtering flexibility make fine-tuning [by age] easier but may not offer [the most reliable protection]. (Gilbert & Olsen, 2006)

Some filter programs have come under attack by critics who accuse them of blocking web pages that should be available to users. For example, operators of the website Peacefire are especially concerned about rights of free speech and open access to information.

> The site has conducted long battles against the most commonly used filter programs, including, most famously, Net Nanny, CyberPatrol, and Bess. In particular, Peacefire has demonstrated that the filter programs suppress

political speech and filter preferentially for corporate and conservative causes. In other cases, Peacefire has presented evidence that several filtering programs block some websites without having a human being review those sites first, despite the filtering companies' claims to the contrary. However, Peacefire is not usually active against filters that act in a more neutral way. (Peacefire, 2007)

In 1998, Internet expert Lawrence Lessig warned that web filters were poor devices for controlling people's access to harmful sites because "Filtering software is 'opaque' [and] necessarily relies on blunt, mechanistic key words and phrases to identify potentially troublesome material [so that] it censors far too much" (Heins, 2003). However, in 2000, Congress passed the Children's Internet Protection Act (CIPA), which was intended to shield minors from seeing sexually explicit material. The act required libraries and schools (those that received federal funds for Internet connections) to install filters on their computers whether the computers were used by minors or adults, including library staff members. When a lawsuit was filed in 2002 against the government by free-speech advocates, a three-judge federal court struck down the CIPA, citing problems of inaccuracy, overblocking, and secrecy that resulted in filters screening out "thousands of Web pages with no sexual content, on subjects ranging from religion to politics, careers to public health" (Heins, 2003). But when the case was appealed to the U.S. Supreme Court in 2003, the justices, in a 6-to-3 decision, reversed the lower court's ruling, thereby reinstating the CIPA.

So it is that the debate continues about which Internet sources to block, with the debate accompanied by computer buffs figuring out new ways to bypass filters and companies that sell filters inventing new ways to foil the bypassers.

Chapter 3

Erotic Acts and Protective Measures

Understanding matters of sex in schools includes recognizing the kinds of erotic acts students perform and ways students can protect themselves from such unwelcome consequences as unplanned pregnancy and sexually transmitted diseases. This chapter's first section offers a description of popular sexual acts, including an estimate of their incidence and the apparent advantages and disadvantages of each type. The second section reviews protective methods that youngsters can adopt and identifies those methods' effectiveness, popularity, strengths, and weaknesses.

A DIVERSITY OF EROTICISM ACTS

Sexual activities in which children and adolescents' engage include *masturbation, voyeurism, oral sex, coitus,* and *paraphilias*. Whereas the erotic drive that impels youngsters to seek sexual gratification derives from the maturation of their genetic inheritance, which acts they choose for expressing that drive are heavily influenced by the environments they encounter. Environments encourage them to adopt some acts and eschew others.

Masturbation

Masturbation is the most frequent eroticism practice at all age levels, from infancy to old age. Among toddlers—age 2 through ages 4 or 5—masturbation consists of their fondling their genitals or rubbing their genital area against a pillow or rug to achieve a pleasurable sensation.

A typical opinion of medical doctors is that

> Occasional masturbation is a normal behavior of many infants and preschoolers. Up to one third of children in this age group discovers masturbation while exploring their bodies. . . . They find it feels good to touch themselves in this way and continue to do so. Most children do this as a comfort measure much like a pacifier is for infants. During masturbation, a child often appears dazed, flushed, and preoccupied. The frequency of this behavior may range from once per week to several times per day. It occurs more commonly when a child is sleepy, bored, watching T.V., or under stress. . . . Masturbation does not cause physical injury or harm to the body, promiscuity, or sexual deviance. . . . Masturbation is not abnormal or excessive unless it is deliberately done in public places after the age of five or six. Masturbation can cause emotional harm (e.g., guilt or sexual hang-ups) only if adults overreact to it and make it seem dirty or wicked. (Steele, 2008)

An estimated 15 percent of normal boys and girls continue public masturbation during their preschool or early school-age years (ages 2 to 6). For the nursery-school or primary-grade teacher, children who engage in self-stimulation become a problem if they do so obtrusively. Thus, teachers and parents are advised to instruct such children that fondling their genitals should be done only in private.

The habit of masturbating may subside in later childhood, then return and accelerate with the onset of puberty. Whereas during infancy the act is apparently not accompanied by fantasized encounters with a sexual partner, self-stimulation during and after puberty typically involves the youngster envisioning sex acts with one or more companions. For the postpubescent male, masturbating consists of stimulating the penis by pumping it rapidly until the pleasurable sensation of orgasm is reached and semen is ejaculated. For the female, masturbating consists of thrusting a cylindrical object (finger, candle, carrot, banana, or the like) rhythmically in and out of the vagina to stimulate the vagina's sensitive clitoris and thereby achieve orgasm.

Jargon that teenage boys use in referring to masturbation include *wanking, jerking off, jacking off, beating the meat, beating off, whacking off,* and *spanking the monkey*. Surveys among youths who admit that they masturbate suggest that around 55 percent of 13-year-olds (both boys and girls) do it, a figure that rises to more than 80 percent of 15-year-olds. One summary of surveys reported that around 94 percent of teenage males and about 70 percent of teen females admitted that they masturbated (Masturbation, 2008). Among American adults, an estimated 90 percent of men and 65 percent of women practice masturbation (Masturbation, 2005).

Different groups in American society continue to hold conflicting attitudes about masturbation. Some think masturbating is natural and, in moderation, quite healthy. Others believe it's abnormal, sinful, and damaging. The view that masturbating is deviant has been particularly prominent in Christian tradition. For example, the official position of Roman Catholicism is that masturbating is a sin because it wastes semen and thus "spills the seed" that should be used solely to produce a child.

> Both the Magisterium of the Church, in the course of a constant tradition, and the moral sense of the faithful have been in no doubt and have firmly maintained that masturbation is an intrinsically and gravely disordered action. The deliberate use of the sexual faculty, for whatever reason, outside of marriage is essentially contrary to its purpose [of producing children]. For here [in masturbation] sexual pleasure is sought outside of "the sexual relationship which is demanded by the moral order and in which the total meaning of mutual self-giving and human procreation in the context of true love is achieved." (Bloom, 2008)

However, not all Christian theologians espouse such a belief. For example, in his advice to youths, Dr. James Dobson, who founded the evangelical Focus on the Family movement, has written,

> I don't believe a loving God would put a raging fire in an immature kid and then damn him for doing what he can't help doing. . . . It is my opinion that masturbation is not much of an issue with God. It is a normal part of adolescence that involves no one else. It does not cause disease. It does not produce babies, and Jesus did not mention it in the Bible. I'm not telling you to masturbate, and I hope you won't feel the need for it. But if you do, it is my opinion that you should not struggle with guilt over it. Why do I tell you this? Because I deal with so many Christian young people who are torn apart with guilt over masturbation; they want to stop and just can't. I would like to help you avoid that agony. (Dobson, 2008)

The opinion that self-stimulation is a despicable sin has a long history in America. By the beginning of the 20th century, some parents were so bent on preventing their children from masturbating "that they forced their daughters to wear gloves made of a steel-wool-like material (like Brillo pads) at night and put a [stinging] powder on their genitals that made them painful to touch," while other parents put metal chastity belts on their sons at night to make it painful for the youths to have an erection (Masturbation, 2008).

Traditional views of masturbation are replete with myths intended to deter the young from the practice. Some people still contend that masturbating will cause acne, insanity, blindness, various diseases, and hair growth on the masturbator's palm. Some say masturbating can make a teenager homosexual, stunt growth, and—for boys—use up all their semen so they could never have children. Critics of self-stimulation often contend that God punishes masturbators with afflictions, ill fortune on this earth, and an after-death eternity in hell.

Prior to the advent of the Internet, the young usually drew their opinions about masturbation from their peers, older siblings, parents, religious tracts, Sunday school lessons, and sex education at school. However, the sources of fact and fiction about masturbation have expanded enormously with the Internet's World Wide Web. A student at a school computer can enter the term *masturbation* into such a search engine as Google and access more than 60,700,000 websites on the subject. Youngsters who sample those sites receive a profusion of advice about ways to masturbate (including pictures), ostensible dangers of the practice, masturbators' experiences, the opportunity to join others in masturbating, and more. Consequently, teachers can face a problem of students spending school time visiting such sites, thereby neglecting their studies, becoming erotically stimulated, and being tempted to masturbate at school.

For a sexually aroused teenager, masturbation has several advantages. It requires no partner, it can be practiced in private so that no one else knows about it, and it avoids the risk of unwanted pregnancy or infection. However, for youngsters who believe that self-stimulation is sinful or that it produces dire maladies (blindness, insanity, or acne), masturbation can cause distressing anxiety, guilt, and shame.

So it is that during childhood and adolescence, the young are obliged to make decisions about masturbating—whether to practice it, in what manner, how often, when, where, and how to feel about it. Likewise, school personnel are compelled to decide how they will respond if they apprehend—or receive reports about—students masturbating. And teachers who conduct sex-education lessons need to decide what they will say about masturbation.

Voyeurism

Voyeurism is the act of gaining erotic pleasure from viewing other people's naked bodies, genital organs, or sexual acts. The classical prototype of voyeurism is found in the tale of an 11th-century Anglo-Saxon noblewoman, Lady Godiva, who rode naked on horseback through the streets of Coventry in England to win remission of the oppressive tax that her husband had imposed on his tenants. According to legend, the townspeople were forbidden to look at the rider, but a fellow named Tom could not resist; he did look and was struck blind—hence, the label "peeping Tom" that is applied to voyeurs today.

Voyeurism comes in two main varieties—*real life* and *pictorial*. In the typical real-life version, a peeper watches furtively from a hiding place to see someone undress, take a bath, engage in a sexual act, or the like. Sometimes the voyeur takes photos of the unsuspecting subject or else masturbates during the viewing or afterwards. Some state laws make voyeurism a crime—laws that prohibit anyone from photographing or videotaping persons without their consent in their home or in other private places. In order for voyeurism to be considered a personality disorder,

> the fantasies, urges, or behaviors to watch other persons must cause significant distress in the individual or be disruptive to his or her everyday functioning. . . . Once voyeuristic activity is undertaken, it commonly does not stop. Over time, it may become the main form of sexual gratification for the voyeur. Its course tends to be chronic. (Voyeurism, 2008)

In voyeurism's pictorial version, the peeper gets an erotic thrill from looking at photos, drawings, movies, or videotapes of people who are naked, are posed in sexually suggestive garb and positions, or are involved in sex acts. The number of youths who engage in real-life voyeurism is miniscule compared to the number involved in pictorial voyeurism. Furthermore, thanks to the Internet, the amount of pictorial voyeurism practiced today is astonishingly greater than it was in past decades. During the 1940s, an adolescent boy interested in viewing sexually stimulating pictures was pretty well limited to ogling the ladies' underwear pages of the Montgomery Ward catalogue or to looking at the tiny illicit booklets that offered crudely drawn imitations of such comic-strip characters as Moon Mullins or Tillie the Toiler engaged in erotic acts. But during the past two decades, the paucity of readily available pornography has changed radically as the Internet has offered millions of sites portraying people in all manner of sexual behavior. A teenager, seated before a home or school computer, can enter the term *pornography* into the search engine Google and generate over 30 million websites to visit. Some sites offer sexually enticing pictures, whereas others denounce pornography as despicable and provide advice to parents for combating online erotic material. By 2006 there were 4.2 million sites (12 percent of all websites) that furnished pornography, with locations that included more than 420 million pages of pornography. Hence, students have almost unlimited access on the Internet to scenes of sexual positions, parts of the human body, combinations of participants, and equipment that make erotic acts novel adventures. Web pages include images of heterosexual and homosexual intercourse, fellatio, cunnilingus, masturbation, bestiality, sadomasochism, bondage, rape, incest, and more. Never before have youngsters been able to witness such an abundant display of eroticism.

The task of providing Internet pornography has become a major industry that yielded an estimated annual income of $1 billion by 2002, with the total increasing to $2.5 billion in 2005 and $2.84 billion in

2006 (Ropelato, 2006). The industry's money comes chiefly from two sources—subscription fees for access to a site and advertising that appears on sites that provide free access. By 2002, there were more than 100,000 subscription sites in the United States (each included multiple web pages) and about 400,000 for-pay adult sites globally (Thornburg & Lin, 2002).

The free-access websites are ones students visit at no expense. Supposedly, the free web pages offer only lightweight porn, with the raunchier varieties relegated to pay-to-view sites that ostensibly are available only to adults. However, in practice free-view pages can include all sorts of eroticism for youngsters to witness. On those sites, the pages' creators frequently include cautionary advice designed to promote the fiction that the producers of porn are protecting the young from viewing extreme erotic behavior. Here are three ludicrous examples that more likely encourage youngsters to enter the forbidden territory rather than desist:

- Parental Advisory—Explicit Contents Follow.
- Some of the posted links on this website may contain adult content or lead to it. If you are a minor, please leave.
- WARNING! If you are under 18 years of age, or if it is illegal to view adult material in your community, it is your responsibility to leave this site now. We can't be held responsible for your actions. We are not acting in any way to send you this information; you are choosing to receive it! Continuing further means that you understand and accept responsibility for your own actions, thus releasing the creators of this web page and our service provider from all liability.

Although it is difficult to collect trustworthy data about the extent of online voyeurism among the young, available studies suggest that a great many children and adolescents view Internet pornography, with the number of viewers increasing as youths advance in age. From a University of New Hampshire telephone survey of 1,422 American students ages 10 to 17, researchers reported that

- 42 percent of youths age 10–17 had seen Internet porn in the past year.
- Two thirds of youth exposures to Internet porn were unwanted. (However, not all unwanted exposure to porn was unintentional: 21 percent of the time, kids knew they were entering X-rated websites.)
- Boys were exposed to Internet porn far more often than were girls.
- Boys are nine times more likely than girls to seek out Internet porn.
- Teens, especially those age 16–17, are far more likely than younger kids to view online porn, either accidentally or on purpose. For example, more than two thirds of boys 16–17 had been exposed to online porn.

- Youth exposure to Internet porn is fairly common. Unwanted porn found its way to 17 percent of 10- to 11-year-old boys and 16 percent of girls 10 to 11 years old.
- Most youths said they were not upset by the images they saw.
- Some youths—those who report victimization by others when not on the Internet, and those with borderline or significant depression—may be especially vulnerable to the negative effects of Internet pornography. (DeNoon, 2007)

In responding to a question about how harmful Internet pornography is for youngsters, the principal investigator in the University of New Hampshire survey wrote:

> Sexual curiosity among teenage boys is normal, and many might say that visiting X-rated web sites is developmentally appropriate behavior. However, some researchers have expressed concern that exposure to online pornography during adolescence my lead to a variety of negative consequences . . . [including] the undermining of acceptable social values and attitudes about sexual behavior, earlier and more promiscuous sex, sexual deviancy, sexual offending, and sexually compulsive behavior. (DeNoon, 2007)

For a student, pictorial voyeurism as an outlet for the hormonal sex drive has several advantages. It (a) can be pursued at the voyeur's convenience, (b) can be enjoyed either individually or with companions (such as when a group views a sex video), (c) enables a voyeur to gain erotic sensations without risking pregnancy or disease, and (d) entails no expense (unless the student subscribes to a pay-for-view pornography site). However, voyeurism can become compulsive, with youngsters spending so much time viewing pornography that they neglect their responsibilities (school studies, family chores, jobs) and friends. Furthermore, if news about their habit becomes public, youths' reputations may suffer.

Decisions students make in regard to Internet pornography concern whether to search the World Wide Web for erotic pictures, how much time to spend in such activity, and which—if any—porno acts to attempt in their own lives.

School personnel—mainly teachers—are obliged to cope with problems of students (a) viewing pornography on school computers, (b) wasting study time on such activity, (c) storing pornography in computer files, and (d) attempting to pursue erotic acts while on school property or during school-sponsored events (dances, sporting events, excursions).

Oral Sex

The two principal forms of oral sex are *fellatio* and *cunnilingus*. Fellatio involves a girl or boy either licking a boy's penis or taking the penis into her or his mouth. Slang terms for fellatio include *blow job, giving head, sucking off, cock sucking,* and *going down*. Fellatio may be performed to induce orgasm and the ejaculation of semen or it can serve as foreplay prior to vaginal or anal forms of intercourse.

Cunnilingus consists of a boy or girl inserting his or her tongue into a girl's vagina and stimulating the sensitive vulva or clitoris to induce orgasm. Like fellatio, cunnilingus is sometimes called *giving head*.

Oral sex among middle-school and high-school students has been common and is apparently on the rise. A 2002 interview survey of more than 12,500 Americans between ages 15 and 44 revealed that 28 percent of 15-to-17-year-old boys reported giving oral sex to a female, and 40 percent reported receiving oral sex from a female. Among girls aged 15 to 17, 30 percent said they had given oral sex to a male, while 38 percent reported receiving oral sex from a male. Among men aged 18 to 19, two thirds reported having vaginal sex, whereas half reported giving oral sex to a woman, and two thirds said they had received oral sex from a woman. By ages 18–21, the percentage of women who had had vaginal sex was similar to those who had had oral sex (Hitti, 2005).

A host of information about oral sex—pro and con, accurate and inaccurate—is available to students on the Internet. Entering the term *fellatio* into the search engine Google generates more than 6,430,000 sources; while the more limited term *female fellatio* identifies 2,890,000. The word *cunnilingus* finds 10,600,000 sites.

For teenagers, an advantage of oral sex over vaginal intercourse is that the oral variety avoids the risk of pregnancy, which is an important reason that youths choose it. However, some teens believe that they are also protected against sexually transmitted diseases when they practice fellatio and cunnilingus, but they are mistaken. Infections contracted during oral sex can include syphilis, gonorrhea, HIV (human immunodeficiency virus) which causes AIDS (acquired immune deficiency syndrome), HPV (human papillomavirus), genital herpes, and chlamydia. (See chapter 7 for descriptions of those maladies.) Some youths seek to protect themselves from infection by encasing the penis in a condom (perhaps a flavored condom to enhance the taste) before engaging in fellatio.

Earning the reputation of engaging in oral sex has both advantages and disadvantages. Such a reputation may enhance a youth's stature in the opinions of some peers and thereby attract new potential sexual partners. But in the eyes of other schoolmates, an oral-sex reputation is viewed as unsavory, and parents are likely to consider such a reputation quite damaging.

Decisions that students are obliged to make about oral sex include whether to engage in it, and if so, with whom, when, where, how often, under what circumstances, and with what precautions. Frequently, youngsters are very reluctant to try fellatio or cunnilingus but do so to satisfy a partner they adore, or else they yield to social pressure from a group of peers whose friendship they value and who assure them that "Everybody's doing it."

Two responsibilities that school personnel bear are those of (a) monitoring students' activities at school and on school trips so as to minimize opportunities students have to engage in oral sex and (b) making clear in health-education lessons that fellatio and cunnilingus entail substantial risks.

Coitus

Nonslang terms for the act of inserting the male penis into the female vagina include *coitus, sexual intercourse, copulation,* and *fornication*. There are also slang euphemisms for coitus, expressions intended to soften the potentially embarrassing mention of "that very private act"—*having intimate relations, marital embrace, making love, sleeping together, hanky panky,* and *going to bed with*. In addition, there are slang terms regarded as vulgar and foul-mouthed—*bang, drill, frig, fuck, lay, plow, ride, root, screw,* and *shag*.

Over the past two decades, around half of American high-school students reported having had sexual intercourse at least once. From 1991 through 2005, the incidence of coitus declined gradually from 54 percent to 46.8 percent. The trend by gender and grade level in 2005 is shown in table 3.1. Whereas in ninth grade slightly more than one third of students had engaged in coitus, by grade 12 nearly two thirds had done so, with girls' participation only slightly less than that of boys by grade 12 (62.4 percent for girls and 63.8 percent for boys).

The host of physical positions in which vaginal intercourse can be practiced, the risks of disease and pregnancy entailed in coitus, and ways of

Table 3.1. Students Who Had Engaged in Sexual Intercourse—2005

	All Grades	*Grade 9*	*Grade 10*	*Grade 11*	*Grade 12*
All Teens	46.8%	34.3%	42.8%	51.4%	63.1%
Girls	45.7%	29.3%	44.0%	52.1%	62.4%
Boys	47.9%	39.3%	41.5%	50.6%	63.8%

Source: *Surveillance Summaries*, 2006.

protecting oneself against infection are readily available to teens on the Internet. Entering the expression *sexual intercourse* on Google identifies over 4,550,000 websites.

Teenagers' decisions about whether to engage in copulation can be affected by a variety of conditions, including the age at which youths experience the hormonal drive of puberty, the values and eroticism practices of their peers, their parents' child-rearing skills, their rebellion against authority, and how they react to frustration in their lives.

> Factors that are associated with earlier onset of intercourse include a history of sexual abuse, absence of supportive parenting, poverty, poor academic achievement, high risk behaviors, and an earlier than average onset of puberty. On the other hand, factors that encourage a later initiation of sexual intercourse in adolescents include consistent and firm parenting, emphasis on abstinence, goal orientation, high academic achievement, and religiosity. . . . There is no evidence that availability of contraceptives will lead to earlier sexual intercourse, or lack of availability of contraceptives will result in postponement of sexual intercourse. Also, there is no evidence that giving adolescents information about contraception will lead to earlier age of first intercourse, increased sexual activity, or greater numbers of lifetime sexual partners.
>
> Some females initiate intercourse at an early age due to a partner's persuasion, being in love, wish to please a partner, receipt of gifts, or to arouse jealousy in another partner. Studies have shown that some adolescent females have felt retrospectively that they initiated intercourse at an age that was too young. (Sexual intercourse, 2008)

Youths' fear of contracting sexually transmitted infections has apparently been a significant cause of the past decade's decline in the incidence of coitus. In particular, students seem to have been influenced by widely publicized warnings about the danger of contracting HIV and AIDS through intercourse.

An alternative to vaginal coitus is anal sex, which involves the male penis being inserted into the anus of either a male or female. The term *sodomy* in its most limited meaning refers to anal sex. In a 1995 survey, 11 percent of adolescents between ages 15 and 19 admitted having engaged in anal sex (Kaiser Family Foundation, 2005). Whereas anal sex avoids the chance of pregnancy, it still carries the risk of disease unless some such protective device as a condom or dental dam is used.

As in the case of oral sex, schools bear a dual responsibility: (a) to monitor students' activities at school and on school trips so as to minimize opportunities students have to engage in sexual intercourse and (b) to make clear in health-education lessons that vaginal copulation entails significant risks—unwelcome pregnancy, multiple kinds of infection, and an unsavory reputation.

Paraphilias

The word *paraphilias* identifies erotic acts that are unusual, extraordinary, deviant, weird, unconventional, or abhorrent. A common slang term for paraphilia is *kinky sex*. However, the meaning of the term *paraphilia* is problematic, because acts that one person deems unusual, deviant, or disgusting are acts that others consider quite ordinary, attractive, and respectable. Furthermore, some erotic behaviors qualify as paraphilias only when they are compulsive and excessive in amount. Such is the case with viewing photos of naked people or of lightly spanking one's partner during a sexual encounter. It is important that school personnel know about paraphilias because most of those practices begin in late childhood and adolescence, then persist throughout adulthood. In effect, some students that teachers, counselors, and administrators meet daily may be involved in paraphilias.

One system for classifying paraphilias comprises eight main categories (*fetishism, transvestism, voyeurism, exhibitionism, sadomasochism, pedophilia, bestiality, obscene messages*) and five rare types (*coprophilia, urophilia, klismaphilia, frotteurism, necrophilia*; Paraphilia, 2002). To qualify as a true paraphilia, a sexual practice must involve an obsessive preoccupation with an object (women's undergarments, young children, sheep) or a behavior (exhibiting one's penis or vagina, inflicting pain, being tortured) in order to gain sexual gratification.

> The focus of a paraphilia is usually very specific and unchanging. For example, for someone who derives sexual pleasure from exposing his genitals, watching others engaging in sexual activity will not generally provide sexual gratification. Most paraphilias are far more common in men than in women. (Paraphilia, 2002)

Fetishism

Sexual fetishism involves a person fixing attention on an object that is not essentially sexual, then compulsively using the object to gain sexual gratification. The fetish typically accompanies masturbation or erotic acts with a partner as a requirement for sexual gratification.

Things that can serve as fetishes seem almost endless. Among the more common items are masks, body parts (feet, hair, hands), garments (underwear, chastity belts, scarves, shoes, leather goods, orthodontic braces), photographs (in magazines, on the Internet), erotic videos, sculptured figures (dolls, robots, mannequins, statues), inflatables (balloons, plastic dolls, clowns), furry objects (toy animals, gloves), and sharp clutching objects (fingernails, talons, claws). Actions that may function as fetishes include taking enemas, smoking, carrying, lifting, sneezing, and being hypnotized.

Transvestism

Students are engaging in transvestism or *cross-dressing* when they wear garments that typify the opposite gender. So, to qualify as a transvestite, a boy dons feminine clothes and accoutrements while a girl wears masculine garments and accessories. Over recent decades it has become increasingly difficult to accuse girls of transvestism because females in America have almost universally been cladding themselves in garments traditionally considered the province of males—pants (both short and long), shirts, vests, baseball caps, and athletic shoes. No such trend has occurred among boys, except, perhaps, for the recent fad of youths wearing earrings or a necklace (usually an amulet on a gold or silver chain). Other than in settings frequented by homosexuals, males wearing women's garments or accessories are not considered "normal" and socially acceptable.

Students who contemplate dressing in the traditional garb of the opposite gender must decide where, when, and under what circumstances they can safely do so. Likewise, school personnel who observe a student cross-dressing must decide what to do about it. Here are two examples in which schools differed in their responses to incidents of cross-dressing.

An 18-year-old boy at West Side High School in Gary (Indiana) was turned away from attending the senior prom by the school principal because the youth was wearing a pink dress and high-heeled shoes. The student later complained, "I was hurt. [The principal] took something from me I can't get back. I have no formal pictures, no memories, nothing. You only have one prom." When Ken Falk, the director of the Indiana Civil Liberties Union, was later asked about the episode, Falk said that in 1999 he had helped an Indianapolis (Indiana) youth win a lawsuit against a school for stopping the boy from attending a prom in a dress. On that occasion the court had found the school at fault because, as Falk explained,

> All students have First Amendment rights of freedom of expression. Those rights can be overcome for the legitimate [instructional] needs of the school. For example, you can't [stage protest rallies because] that runs the risk of disrupting instruction. But the court found that at a prom, those risks are lessened. It's not a scholastic activity. (Gay boy, 2006)

In contrast, when a second-grade boy in a Douglas County (Colorado) elementary school wanted to attend class dressed as a girl and to be called by a girl's name, school authorities permitted the child to do so. A spokesman for the school district explained, "As a public school system, our calling is to educate all kids no matter where they come from, what their background is, beliefs, values, it doesn't matter." Teachers would refer to the pupil by name instead of using *he* or *she*. The child would not use the regular boys' or girls' bathroom. Instead, two unisex bathrooms in the building would be available. Packets of information about "transgender people" would be distributed to other children's parents who had questions about the arrangement (Garcia, 2008).

Exhibitionism

In its eroticism form, exhibitionism consists of an individual displaying his or her private parts to other persons who have not invited the display and who usually find the act offensive. Boys' private parts are the penis and buttocks. Girls' parts are their breasts, vagina, and buttocks. The act of boys showing off their penis or girls exposing their breasts or vagina is commonly called *flashing*. Exhibiting the buttocks is dubbed *mooning*.

A typical legal prohibition of exhibitionism is the provision in the Wisconsin Child Sexual Assault Law that states: "Whoever, for purposes of sexual arousal or sexual gratification, causes a child to expose genitals or pubic area or exposes genitals or pubic area to a child is guilty of a Class A misdemeanor."

Cases of exhibitionism that involve the schools can concern the behavior of either students or staff members or both. An example involving students and a bus driver is an episode in Crystal River (Florida). When students boarded a school bus outside Crystal River High School, the driver confiscated a bottle of Gatorade from a ninth-grade boy. In response to the driver's act, the boy's 10th-grade girlfriend told the driver she would show him her breasts if he returned the drink to the lad. Other students reported that the driver just laughed and pointed to the bus's security video camera. When the girl pulled up her shirt and bra, other students laughed and some rushed to the front of the bus. The girl later admitted that she had then "flashed another student, and I heard people saying [that the driver] was laughing" and not paying attention to the road. When school officials the next day were investigating the episode, an 18-year-old senior reported that the bus "had gotten so out of hand" that students, not the driver, "seemed to rule the bus." None of these events were recorded by the security camera because the camera was not operating at the time. Six students, including the 10th-grade girl, said the driver did little to stop the ruckus; and he had failed to report the incident to his supervisor. The superintendent of schools recommended that the driver be fired (Ramirez, 2007).

Sadomasochism

Sadists gain erotic excitement from intentionally inflicting pain on someone or from threatening to do so. Masochists are the opposite; they experience erotic pleasure from being subjected to pain or the threat of pain. Sadomasochists are individuals who enjoy both inflicting pain and receiving pain.

> Forms of sadism run the gamut from the fairly common carefully controlled play-acting with a willing partner, in which the mild forms of pain that result from such acts as spanking or biting are not actually experienced as painful (think of having one's back scratched—the same intensity can sometimes feel good and sometimes hurt depending on the circumstances), to the very rare assaultive behaviors that may include torture, rape, or even murder. Some extreme sadists require an unwilling victim to derive pleasure; others become sexually aroused only when they see their victim suffering. (Paraphilia, 2002)

Types of masochism can range from an individual enjoying mild teasing to a person reveling in extreme torture—whipping, near strangulation, beatings, or being trampled.

Sadism and masochism in school usually come under the topics of *bullying* and *sexual harassment*, with bullies regarded as sadists and with their victims—whenever they seem willing to submit to the bullying—deemed masochists.

An example of a sadistic sexual act is an incident in Germantown (Virginia). While riding home on a school bus from Roberto Clemente Middle School, an 11-year-old girl was held down on the bus floor by six older boys. They groped her breasts and groin and lay on top of her. Not until the next day, when she boarded the bus and the boys threatened to "finish what they started," did the girl tell an assistant principal what had happened. School officials transferred two of the attackers to a different school and two others were suspended (Williamson & Aratani, 2005).

Pedophilia

Pedophiles are older teens or adults who prefer getting sexual excitement from fantasizing about, or engaging in sexual activity with, prepubescent children. Most pedophiles are males. Nearly two thirds of pedophiles' victims are girls, typically between ages 8 and 11. Most pedophiles prefer children of the opposite sex.

Although various sorts of people can be pedophiles, the typical pedophile, according to M. J. McGrath (2008),

- Is an adult male, often a hard-working, family man
- Is better educated and more religious than the average person
- Is well liked by parents and children. A pedophile teacher is often one of the most popular teachers in a school and finds ways to be alone with children, as is often the case with athletic coaches, music teachers,

and counselors. He (or she) lavishes attention on other children—ones who are not molested—in order to build a sense of trust by parents and students.
- Seeks out children who need attention or have problems at home
- Collects child pornography and photographs his or her victims
- Gradually seduces children rather than force them into submission

Some of the most publicized cases of pedophilia involve school personnel—teachers, coaches, or administrators—who have enticed students into erotic liaisons. For example,

> After pleading guilty to two counts of felony child seduction, a popular theater-arts teacher at Broad Ripple High School in Indianapolis (Indiana) received a one-year jail sentence for having oral sex with a 16-year-old girl from his theater class. A yearlong relationship between the two had begun with a kiss in a darkened school auditorium.
>
> Things progressed to fondling in his truck and then sexual encounters at his home. In interviews with detectives, the girl said she was confused several times by the relationship, which included daily phone calls, e-mail, and instant messaging with [the teacher]. Despite assurances that he loved her, eventually she broke off their encounters.
>
> In addition to the jail term, the teacher was required to register as a sex offender and to pay $2,100 for the victim's counseling sessions that had resulted from the victim's need to cope with the distress of guilt and shame from the affair. (Corcoran, 2005)

Bestiality

The term *bestiality* is the usual label applied to a person's engaging in sex acts with animals. If such acts—either actual or in fantasy—are frequent or are the sole means of sexual gratification, the label becomes *zoophilia*. Individuals usually choose bestiality out of curiosity, desire for novelty, or a need to release a pent-up sexual urge when a human partner is not available. Bestiality at a school site is likely to occur only in rural high schools that include agricultural programs in which animals are kept on school premises.

Far more common than the rare instances of actual bestiality in schools are controversies over the mention of bestiality in books that students are assigned to read. For example, the 1999 novel *The Perks of Being a Wallflower* by Stephen Chbosky was dropped from a remedial summer-school class at Newton North High School (Massachusetts) when the guardian of one student complained that the book included "extremely, explicitly graphic" descriptions of bestiality, anal sex, and homosexuality. Chbosky's novel is built around a series of letters from a shy teen named Charlie to an unnamed friend, letters in which Charlie describes his struggles to find his identity. When Chbosky learned that the book had been eliminated from the class's reading list, he said he was not surprised by the objections: "That people have a moral, or religious, or ethical stance, I completely respect that, [but] the severity (of the objections) surprises me. The book is not advocating the things people find objectionable. [I think] it's appropriate for high school readers" (School systems, 2001).

Obscene Messages

Some people seek erotic sensations from offering sex-related suggestions over the phone or on Internet websites. Such callers either identify themselves or choose to remain anonymous. Students may be either the callers or only the recipients of calls.

An instance of teenagers being pestered by older adults is the case of a 31-year-old man who repeatedly phoned girls in Shenango Township (Pennsylvania) with sexually odious suggestions and questions about their feet (an apparent fetish). The man was sought not only by Pennsylvania police but also by authorities in Florida and Tennessee for the same offense. Because the caller used a cell phone and constantly moved from one location to another, the police had difficulty finding him (Morris, 2006).

A case of sex predators employing the Internet to entice students into erotic encounters concerned a husband and wife in Las Vegas (Nevada) who used an Internet chat room for enticing a 15-year-old Florida girl to travel to Las Vegas to become the husband's sex partner. After weeks of Internet correspondence between the husband and the 15-year-old, the husband sent the girl a nude photo of himself along with an electronic plane ticket for the trip. His plan was to have the girl run away from home and live with him in Nevada—"to escape without a trace." But what the 39-year-old Las Vegas man and his 33-year-old wife failed to realize was that their chat-room acquaintance was not a 15-year-old student at all. Instead, they had been corresponding with a detective in the St. Lucie County (Florida) Sheriff's Office who was posing as a 15-year-old named Suzy. The detective was a member of the LEACH Task Force that consisted of local, state, and federal law-enforcement officers who investigated child pornography and child exploitation on the Internet. On evidence that the detective compiled, the Nevada couple were arrested and sentenced to prison (the wife for 10 years, the husband for 15) on a charge of soliciting sex from a minor over the Internet (Couple gets prison, 2007).

Rare Paraphilias

Several types of deviant erotic behavior are so unusual that they are very seldom practiced by either students or school personnel. *Apotemno-*

philia is the condition of being sexually attracted by amputations, whereas *coprophilia* consists of gaining erotic stimulation from contact with feces, and *urophilia* involves getting excited over contact with urine. Being sexually thrilled while receiving enemas is *klismaphilia*. *Frotteurism* is erotic arousal from rubbing one's genitals against the body of a fully clothed person in a crowded setting, as in a packed subway train. *Necrophilia* consists of being elated by viewing or sexually manipulating a corpse.

Conclusion

Children and adolescents may engage in diverse erotic acts that range from the most popular (masturbation and pictorial voyeurism) to the rare (frotteurism, coprophilia, and bestiality). Each type of act carries its own advantages and disadvantages for students. Advantages can include the pleasurable release of sex-hormone build-up and the social acceptance of others who practice that same behavior. Disadvantages can include undesired pregnancy, disease, and an unfavorable reputation in the opinions of people who disapprove of the particular act.

To eliminate—or at least to diminish—the disadvantages of sexual acts, students can adopt protective methods. Those methods and their effectiveness, popularity, strengths, and weaknesses are reviewed in the following pages.

METHODS OF PROTECTION

Students who engage in erotic behavior with partners need protection from unplanned pregnancy and sexually transmitted diseases. The following section describes nine prevention measures—*abstinence, early withdrawal, intercourse substitutes, condoms, birth-control pills, diaphragms, fertility awareness, the patch,* and *additional options*.

Abstinence

Not everyone assigns the same meaning to *sexual abstinence*. For some people, abstinence is the avoidance of vaginal intercourse, but such a definition then allows individuals to be considered abstinent if they practice masturbation, oral sex, or anal sex. For others, abstinence requires the rejection of any kind of erotic expression, including masturbation, the pictorial voyeurism that provides sexual satisfaction from viewing pornography, and the hugging and kissing that, during different eras in the past, has been called *spooning, sparking, necking,* and *making out*. However, in the following discussion, *abstinence* is defined as the avoidance of vaginal intercourse, oral sex, anal sex, and open-mouth kissing, but it allows masturbation, pictorial voyeurism, and hugging. Such abstinence, in effect, protects individuals from potential pregnancy and sexually transmitted diseases while still allowing some release of hormonal sexual pressures.

Both the social acceptability of abstinence and reasons for practicing it have a long history. The final decades of the 18th century's Industrial Revolution witnessed an increase in sexual freedom that was followed by the chaste values of the Victorian era in England and America that encouraged abstinence over the last two thirds of the 19th century and throughout the first decade of the 20th century.

> World War I began a return to sexual freedom and indulgence, but more often than not, the appearance of conforming to the earlier moral values of abstinence before marriage was retained. With the conclusion of World War II, the societal importance of abstinence declined swiftly. The advent of the first oral contraceptive pill and widely available antibiotics suppressed many consequences of wide and free sexual behavior, while social mores were also changing. By the 1970s, abandonment of premarital chastity was no longer taboo in the majority of western societies; perhaps even the reverse: that members of both sexes would have experienced a number of sexual partners before marriage. Some cultural groups continued to place a value on the moral purity of an abstainer, but abstinence was caught up in a wider reevaluation of moral values. (Sexual abstinence, 2008)

In the 21st century, abstinence is still a policy strongly endorsed by such groups as evangelical Christians, while the practice of abstinence continues to decline among teenagers. As noted in chapter 2, during the mid-1990s the U.S. Congress passed legislation providing funds to schools that established sex-education programs that taught abstinence as the sole form of acceptable premarital sexual behavior. No programs that included information about other forms of contraception—such as condoms or pills—could receive federal moneys. By 2007, the government was spending about $176 million annually on such programs. However, over the past decade, studies of how well abstinence-only instruction deters youths from practicing coitus, oral sex, or anal sex have cast serious doubt on the wisdom of such a funding policy. The preponderance of evidence from carefully conducted studies has suggested that "Students who participated in sexual abstinence programs were just as likely to have sex a few years later as those who did not" (Abstinence students, 2007).

In summary, everyone agrees that, among all of the protective measures, abstinence is the surest way for students to avoid pregnancy, infection, and a soiled reputation. However, in view of the apparent reality that students in abstinence-only programs often fail to practice what has been preached, increasing numbers of educators favor including other methods of contraception as well in schools' sex education.

Early Withdrawal

The expression *early withdrawal* refers to the practice of the boy, during sexual intercourse, removing his penis from the girl's vagina before he ejaculates semen. The intention of early withdrawal is to prevent any sperm cell in the semen from entering the girl's uterus to merge with a ripe ovum and thereby cause pregnancy.

Withdrawal is one of the least effective ways to prevent pregnancy, and it offers no protection at all against sexually transmitted infections. Even when withdrawal is performed perfectly, it still will result in pregnancy about 16 percent of the time because

> (a) Fluid emitted from the penis prior to ejaculation contains about a half-million sperm, so being inside a partner even prior to ejaculation can risk pregnancy, (b) it's often not easy for a man to sense, predict, and control his ejaculation well enough to pull out in time, and (c) sperm can get into the vagina if they are deposited near the vaginal opening. (Withdrawal, 2008)

In a 1997 survey of high-school students' sexual practices, 13 percent of respondents said they had used withdrawal in their most recent intercourse episode, a decrease from 18 percent in 1991 (Everett et al., 2002).

Intercourse Substitutes

Students can attempt to avoid the disadvantages of coitus by adopting other modes of sexual stimulation, such as masturbation, oral sex, or anal sex. Whereas pregnancy and infection can be avoided by masturbation, students may find such a substitute not entirely satisfying and thus may choose not to limit their sexual expression to masturbation. Although pregnancy can be averted by practicing oral or anal sex, the risk of contracting a disease remains.

Condoms

When people speak of a condom, they are usually referring to a latex sheath (rather like a noninflated rubber balloon a few inches long) that fits over an erect penis to prevent any semen from passing into the vagina during intercourse. The condom, when properly worn, also prevents carriers of infection from passing from the male to the female and vice versa. Among contraceptive devices, condoms are the best ones for protection against both disease and pregnancy. When used properly and consistently, condoms reduce the chance of pregnancy to 3 percent. When they are used inconsistently, the chance of pregnancy rises to 12 percent (Condoms, 2008).

Male condoms come in various types. Some are flavored. Others are lubricated to provide smoother use, with the lubrication frequently being a spermicide—a substance that kills sperms—thereby furnishing additional protection against pregnancy.

Whereas the term *condom* most often refers to a penis-encasing device, the term can also apply to another type used by females. The female variety is a loose-fitting, prelubricated, seven-inch polyurethane pouch that fits into the vagina as a barrier to the passage of sperm. The female condom also protects against certain sexually transmitted diseases, including HIV (human immunodeficiency virus).

Over the past decade and a half, teenagers have been adopting condoms at an increasing rate. Between 1991 and 1997, condom use rose from 46 percent to 57 percent of sexually active teens.

If condoms are so successful as protective devices, why don't all adolescents use them? There are several reasons. Some youths don't know about condoms, as can be the case with teens enrolled in abstinence-only sex-education programs. Or no condom may be at hand when an unexpected sexual encounter is in the offing. Or the cost of a condom can be considered an undue expense. Or a young teenager may be too embarrassed to be seen buying condoms at a drug store. Furthermore, using a condom is frequently considered frustratingly inconvenient, so that during a passionate embrace in the back seat of a car a youth is reluctant to pause and install a condom before engaging in coitus. Finally, some youths say the pleasure of coitus is greater without a condom.

More schools have been including information about condoms in their sex-education programs—information sometimes accompanied by a demonstration of how to install a condom, with the demonstrator using a banana or cucumber to simulate a stiffened penis. More high schools, as well as some middle schools, have also been furnishing condoms at little or no cost, either in dispensers in bathrooms or in the school's health center. By 1995, more than 400 schools in 50 of the nation's school districts offered condom-supply services, with that number markedly increasing over the next decade (Schuster, Bell, Berry & Kanouse, 1998). Critics of such programs have charged that making condoms available to students encourages intercourse. However, studies of high-school students in such places as Seattle (Washington) and Massachusetts have convinced a growing number of researchers that "Making condoms available in high schools does not increase sexual activity among students, but it does raise condom use by students who are already sexually active" (Condoms do not, 2003).

Table 3.2. Percent of Canadian Youths Using Condoms

	15–17	*18–19*	*20–24*
Males	85.2%	74.8%	60.9%
Females	71.2%	60.0%	51.2%

Source: Facts and Statistics: Sexual Health and Canadian Youth Condom Use, 2008.

In typical communities, the move toward furnishing condoms in schools has not gone unchallenged. When Holyoke (Massachusetts) school officials sought to reduce teen pregnancies by making condoms available to students in grades 6 through 12, the region's Roman Catholic bishop condemned the plan, accusing officials of making the school system "an endorser and an enabler of early adolescent sex. I am profoundly disappointed and disturbed [by school officials reducing sex to] meaningless self-gratification" (Abel, 2004).

The belief that teens who adopt condoms early in their sexual life will continue to use condoms in later years was called into question by a 2003 Canadian study that revealed that between ages 15 and 19 the number of boys and girls who used condoms decreased, then declined further in their early 20s (table 3.2). Apparently part of the reason for the trend was girls' increased use of antipregnancy pills as they grew older. The researchers observed, "This is an important finding in that it suggests that older teens may be at higher risk for sexually transmitted infection because of their relative lack of condom use" (Facts and Statistics, 2008).

Birth-Control Pills

The regular use of orally ingested birth-control pills began in the United States nearly half a century ago. The types of pills available today are 98 percent effective in preventing pregnancy when taken consistently each day. However, pills offer no protection against sexually transmitted diseases. Most pill varieties contain synthetic versions of two female hormones—estrogen and progesterone—in proportions that prevent an ovum from moving into a position in the fallopian tube that will permit the ovum to merge with a sperm cell. In addition to regular birth-control pills that are taken prior to sexual intercourse, emergency contraceptive pills ("morning-after" pills) are available to be taken after intercourse so as to interrupt potential pregnancy.

The use of birth-control pills can be accompanied by several minor side effects, such as initial nausea, slight vaginal bleeding, mood changes, breast tenderness, and reduced sex drive. Rare side effects include increased blood pressure, blood clots, and benign liver tumors. On the positive side, the pill may improve the acne that teens often suffer.

King Middle School in Portland (Maine) stirred up a nationwide controversy in October 2007 when the Portland School Committee (school board) authorized the school's health center to make anti-pregnancy pills available to girls ages 11–13. The committee passed the pill regulation on a 7–2 vote in response to 17 pregnancies during the past 4 years and further information about miscarriages and terminated pregnancies not reported to the school nurse. The board's decision was opposed by a considerable number of parents. According to the King plan, a prescription for pills would be given to a student only after she passed a physical exam by a physician or nurse practitioner. The new regulation made King the first middle school in Maine to provide a full range of contraception methods, including birth-control pills and patches. Condoms had been available at the school's health center since 2000 (Maine middle school, 2007).

A spokeswoman for the National Assembly on School-Based Health Care said that the King plan was not apt to be copied by many of the nation's other middle schools, because parents rarely allow middle schools to dispense birth-control supplies. She reported that about one third of the 1,708 school-based health centers nationwide (nearly all of them in high schools) provide contraceptives (Others not likely, 2007).

Diaphragms

A diaphragm is a shallow, dome-shaped latex cup with a flexible rim that fits into a girl's vagina to prevent sperm from swimming into her uterus and merging with an ovum. As added protection against pregnancy, the diaphragm can be coated with spermicide (sperm-killing cream or jelly) before the device is inserted into the vagina. Because diaphragms come in different sizes, a medical expert must select one that properly fits the particular girl. Each time the girl expects to have coitus, she should coat the latex cup with a spermicide before inserting it. The diaphragm should be left in place for 6 to 8 hours after intercourse.

Diaphragms have several advantages. During the course of coitus, neither partner can feel the diaphragm. And if the girl has inserted the diaphragm prior to the sexual encounter, the couple's sex play is not interrupted by the need to install the device in the midst of intercourse. Because the same diaphragm can be used multiple times, its cost as a birth-control method is modest.

However, the use of a diaphragm is not entirely problem-free. The girl may have trouble installing it properly, the device must be used every time the girl has coitus, it may be pushed out of position during copulation, and the girl may be allergic to latex.

> When diaphragms are used perfectly—this means they are used correctly with spermicide every time a couple has intercourse—the chance of becoming pregnant is 6 percent. But, if the diaphragm isn't inserted correctly, is bumped out of place, or is removed too soon, the risk of pregnancy increases. The average risk of becoming pregnant is 20 percent. Because the diaphragm only covers a woman's cervix, it offers only limited protection against sexually transmitted infections. Using a condom with the diaphragm gives the greatest protection. (Diaphragms, 2008)

Fertility Awareness

This technique for avoiding pregnancy is often called the *rhythm method*. Its success depends on a girl understanding the pattern of her monthly menstrual cycle so she can estimate when during the month she will least likely become pregnant from vaginal intercourse. Conception is most likely to occur during the girl's "fertile period," which includes 4 to 5 days before ovulation (when a mature egg descends into the fallopian tube) or the day of ovulation. To identify this period, a girl can chart the pattern of her basal body temperature and cervical mucus by taking her temperature every morning and also noting the amount and consistency of mucus each day.

If the method is to succeed, the girl needs to avoid vaginal intercourse during the fertile period. If correctly used during every monthly cycle, the chance of pregnancy is between 1 percent and 9 percent.

Advantages of the method are that it is inexpensive, enables a girl to understand her menstrual cycle, and may suffice if her religious beliefs do not permit her to use such contraceptive methods as condoms, pills, or diaphragms.

A serious disadvantage is that the rhythm method offers no protection at all from sexually transferred diseases. The method also requires training in its proper application and constant diligence in the daily monitoring of body temperature and cervical mucus.

Patch

A birth-control patch is a thin, 1¾-inch-square beige-colored patch that, like birth-control pills, releases estrogen and progesterone hormones into a girl's bloodstream to prevent pregnancy. The hormones prevent ovulation—the release of an ovum from the ovaries during the girl's monthly menstrual cycle. The patch is put on her skin on the first day of the cycle, then replaced once a week for the next three weeks. The patch can be attached to any one of four areas of the body—abdomen, buttocks, upper arm, or upper torso (except the breasts).

To obtain a supply of patches, a girl must receive a prescription from a medical doctor or nurse practitioner on the basis of a physical examination that includes blood-pressure measurement and pelvic inspection. The cost of using patches is slightly more than one dollar a day.

Potential side effects of patches are similar to those of birth-control pills, including:

- Irregular menstrual bleeding
- Nausea, weight gain, headaches, dizziness, and breast tenderness
- Mood changes
- Blood clots. These are rare in women under age 35 who do not smoke, but there may be a higher risk with the patch than with the pill. (Hirsch, 2007a)

Users of the patch may also suffer problems with (a) skin irritation where the patch is placed, (b) menstrual cramps, or (c) vision changes, including problems using contact lenses.

The effectiveness of the patch in preventing pregnancy is similar to that of the pill. Between 5 percent and 8 percent of consistent users of the patch experience an unintended pregnancy. The patch does not protect a girl from sexually transmitted infections.

Additional Options

Other protective methods include intrauterine devices, dental dams, Fem caps, and Lea's shields.

An *intrauterine device* (IUD) is a small, flexible, T-shaped, plastic contraceptive that is surgically implanted in a girl's uterus. The two main types in the United States are the Paragard-copper-T and Progestasert. In the Paragard version, the copper affects the lining of the uterus by not allowing an egg to implant; the copper also stimulates the production of chemicals that affect the hormones needed to support a pregnancy. A Paragard implant may be left in for as long as 8 years.

> The Progestasert IUD prevents pregnancy by releasing the hormone progestin, which thickens the cervical mucus. This acts as a barrier to prevent sperm from entering the uterus. The Progestasert also affects the lining of the uterus to prevent an egg from being implanted. Because of the hormonal component of the Progestasert, it must be replaced yearly. (Intrauterine device, 2008)

A *dental dam* is not a device for preventing pregnancy but, rather, is intended to reduce the risk of infection during oral or anal sex. Dental dams are thin, square pieces of latex that a person performing oral sex holds against the vulva or anus of the receiving partner, serving as a barrier to bodily fluids that may carry such infections as herpes, genital warts, and HIV (human immunodeficiency virus).

Cervical caps and *shields* are latex devices that fit into the girl's vagina and are held by suction to cover the entrance to the cervix and thereby prevent sperm from entering the uterus and fertilizing an ovum. The three main types are the cervical cap, Fem cap, and Lea's shield. As in the use of a diaphragm, a cap or shield should be treated with a spermicide jelly or cream each time it is used as further protection against pregnancy. In terms of effectiveness in preventing pregnancy, the typical pregnancy rate (the rate of failure to prevent pregnancy) for cervical caps is 16 percent per year, for Fem caps it is 14 percent, and for Lea's shields 15 percent (Cervical cap, 2008). Caps and shields do not prevent sexually passed diseases.

Conclusion

When youngsters contemplate engaging in sexual acts, one of their important considerations is usually their estimate of how likely a given act will place them at risk for unwelcome pregnancy, sexually transmitted infections, and a damaged reputation among people whom they consider important for their welfare. Thus, as a guide to decision making, it is useful for youths to receive information about kinds of erotic acts and the associated risks.

However, students' receipt of the sort of information described in this chapter is obviously not the only determinant of how they decide to behave in sexually enticing situations. A variety of other conditions in their social environments also affect their decisions. Marston and King (2006) have suggested that such conditions follow seven key themes found in all cultures: "Worldwide, not only is sexual behavior strongly shaped by social forces, but those forces are surprisingly similar in different settings, with variations of the extent to which each theme is present rather than of kinds of themes." The seven themes are:

- Young people decide whether to have risky sex based on whether they see their partner as "clean" or "unclean." This determination is largely based on social position and behavior perceived as socially appropriate.
- The nature of young persons' sexual partnership influences not just their condom use but their sexual behavior in general.
- Condoms are stigmatizing and associated with a lack of trust.
- Gender stereotypes determine social expectations and behavior. For example, men are expected to be sexually experienced while women

are expected to be innocent—yet women also are expected to be responsible for pregnancy prevention.
- Society offers both penalties and rewards for sex. For example, an unmarried pregnancy can stigmatize a woman—yet it can also offer escape from her parents' home.
- Reputations and social displays of sexual activity or sexual abstinence are important.
- Social expectations hamper communication about sex.

Therefore, in Marston's and King's opinion, it is not enough simply to offer sex education and distribute condoms to the young. School personnel and parents also need to understand which social forces in the particular culture cause youngsters to deviate from that society's traditional expectations about proper erotic behavior.

> Social expectations, especially ideas about how men and women should behave are a powerful influence on behavior. The influence of sexual partners is also considerable, as are young people's ideas about stigma and risk; and social pressures make it difficult to communicate clearly with partners, which makes safer sex unlikely. (Marston & King, 2006)

INTERPRETATIONS

Chapter 1 introduced six vantage points from which to interpret students' eroticism—(a) decision making (by students and school personnel), (b) heredity and environment, (c) *could-be*, *is*, and *should-be* beliefs, (d) sources of evidence, (e) power and authority, and (f) implications for schools. In these final paragraphs, the six perspectives are used for summarizing erotic acts and protection measures.

Decisions. Choices that students face about erotic acts and methods of protection concern such questions as: Which acts should I try—at what age, where, when, with whom, and with what likely consequences? What protective methods are available and how do they compare in (a) preventing pregnancy and disease, (b) their sources, (c) their costs, (d) their convenience of use, and (e) their effect on the amount of pleasure derived from a particular type of erotic act?

Heredity and environment. Young people's inherited DNA patterns influence their sexual activities by determining the basic (a) genetic timing of the sexual functions of puberty, (b) intensity of the sexual drive at different periods of child and adolescent development, and (c) erotic attractiveness of a student in the eyes of potential sex partners—that is, how "sexy" a student appears to be. Genetic inheritance may also affect a student's gender preference—heterosexual, homosexual, or bisexual (see chapter 8). But it is through environmental encounters that students and school staff members build their beliefs about which erotic acts students could, do, and should engage in at different junctures of childhood and adolescence. Those beliefs are not genetically inherited. Instead, they are learned from whichever sources of evidence students have chosen to trust—parents, religious authorities, teachers, peers, books, television programs, and Internet websites. Some sources have more authority and power than others for influencing the sexual beliefs and erotic acts of both students and school personnel.

Implications for schools. School personnel are obliged to decide which erotic acts or displays of affection should be permitted in schools, how students and their parents should be informed about prohibited acts, and what sanctions should be applied to students and staff members who violate those prohibitions. In addition, schools have increasingly accepted responsibility for teaching youths about the likely consequences of different erotic acts and about methods of protection against unwanted pregnancy, infections, and a soiled reputation.

Chapter 4

Cases: Breaching Schools' Eroticism Rules

Chapter 1 briefly described 10 cases in which students or school personnel were required to make decisions about matters of sex. Chapter 3 added a half dozen more instances. However, those few descriptions fell far short of depicting the diversity of eroticism problems in schools, the conditions affecting such events, and the responses of school or judicial personnel. Thus, in order to expand readers' purview of schools' eroticism cases before we move ahead to the chapters about sexual abuse, pregnancy, and disease, chapter 4 offers 18 additional cases in which students or school personnel were either the perpetrators or the victims. Following the description of the 18 cases, a summary identifies conditions that significantly influenced the nature and outcomes of those episodes.

EXAMPLES OF EROTICISM MISCONDUCT

The following cases are presented under a potpourri of topics: *pornography, exhibitionism, oral sex, coitus, same-sex offences,* and *administrative decisions*. Examples under each topic have been described in considerable detail to illustrate the sorts of conditions that determined the particular nature of each case and its disposition.

Pornography

The two most prevalent sources of sexually objectionable descriptions and photos in schools are (a) books and articles that students are assigned to study and (b) cyberspace, with *cyberspace* defined as *the domain of electronic communication devices and networks* (computers, cell phones, the Internet, and the like).

Offensive Books

As suggested in chapter 2, one of the most contentious school-policy issues in the early 21st century has been what role, if any, books containing blunt descriptions of erotic acts should be permitted to play in American schools. School personnel have been obliged to answer such questions as: Should students read about and discuss masturbation, copulation, oral sex, seduction, rape, and homosexuality? If so, should such behavior be portrayed as deviant and sinful or, in contrast, as part of a normal, acceptable lifestyle?

Case 1. A group of parents representing North Shore Student Advocacy objected to students in Deerfield (Illinois) High School's Advanced English course being assigned to read *Angels in America: A Gay Fantasia on National Themes—Parts I and II.* The group wanted the two books removed, charging that they were "laced with graphic sexual content, pervasive expletives, and mockery of religion" (Winn, 2008).

In support of the complaint, the executive director of North Shore Student Advocacy cited passages from Angels in America that portrayed a pair of male characters planning to painfully "fuck" each other after one of the pair put his hand inside the other's pants, then removed the hand in order to smell and taste the fingers before the two kissed (Winn, 2008).

In response to the parents' challenge, school officials assigned a committee to study the books and offer a recommendation about the volumes' suitability for high-school students. To help clarify the books' status as works of American literature, a representative of the conservative Americans for Truth About Homosexuality reported that the books' content was taken from a drama about AIDS that had won a Pulitzer Prize and two Tony Awards. He said that critics had called the drama

> one of the great American plays of the 20th century. It is defended as a literary work that shows forgiveness, kindness, and compassion. Of course, the first question that comes to my mind is, how many classical works of literature are there that show these virtues without delving into graphic homosexual sodomy? (Winn, 2008)

The school committee recommended that *Angels in America* be removed from the required reading list and placed on an "optional title" list.

Case 2. A group of parents requested that Fond du Lac (Wisconsin) High School stop teaching Maya Angelou's autobiography, *I Know Why the Caged Bird Sings,* after a mother objected to her daughter's being assigned to read the book.

In *Caged Bird Sings*, Angelou tells of her early life as an African American child who is shunted from one home to another and on the way suffers neglect, insult, emotional abuse, rape, and self-doubt. These experiences contributed to her becoming an adult social activist honored by three American presidents—Ford, Carter, and Clinton—for her contributions to racial equality and justice.

Angelou's tale is a blunt recital of distressing life events, cast in the vocabulary of her childhood environment. But some critics have objected to her candor, arguing that it soils the minds of teenage readers. As a consequence, *I Know Why the Caged Bird Sings* was the third most frequently banned book of the 1990–2000 era.

There have been multiple charges against the autobiography—its rampant profanity, childhood sexual encounters, graphic portrayals of masturbation and rape, homosexuals, blatant child abuse, racial hatred, and disrespect for the law.

Typical complaints about *I Know Why the Caged Bird Sings* are illustrated in passages cited on the Internet website of Citizens for Literary Standards in Schools:

> The [book's] crude language includes many references and comparisons to urine, pee, farting, and defecation, as well as general profanity and racial slurs such as Goddammit, shit, bitch, ass, titties, niggers, jigs, spooks, whore, hell, dykes, bulldaggers, pecker, peckerwood, and "give me some trim." Sometimes the words are used as part of the actual conversation of the characters, but often, the words are used as Maya's personal choice of descriptive writing, "the plump brown face had been deflated and patted flat like a cow's ordurous dropping" or "the cotton truck spilled the pickers out and roared out of the yard with a sound like a giant's fart" or "I cried and hollered, passed gas and urine." Or "I decided I wouldn't pee on her if her heart was on fire." (Citizens, 2007)

In reacting to critics, proponents of *I Know Why the Caged Bird Sings* praise such features of the book as its unblinking realism and its portrayal of black women of strong character.

> Though Maya struggles with insecurity and displacement throughout her childhood, she has a remarkable number of strong female role models in her family and community. Momma, Vivian, Grandmother Baxter, and Bertha Flowers have very different personalities and views on life, but they all chart their own paths and manage to maintain their dignity and self-respect. None of them ever capitulates to racist indignities. (I know why, 2007)

At Fond du Lac High School, officials responded to the parents' request by having the daughter of the main complainant substitute a different book for *I Know Why the Caged Bird Sings*. The school principal explained that the book had been taught at Fond du Lac High for more than a decade and would continue to be used because "It is Angelou's own account of growing up. . . . It has a number of attributes and it's historically relevant" (Mathias, 2006).

Offensive Cyberspace Products

As noted earlier, the greatest modern-day source of pornography is the Internet, while the most effective instruments for creating and distributing pornography are desktop computers and such wireless handheld devices as cell phones, digital cameras, and media players. Schools are constantly challenged to find ways to control students' and staff members' access to, and storage of, forbidden erotic matter.

Case 3. The experience of a substitute teacher at Kelly Middle School in Norwich (Connecticut) illustrated the problem of deciding who is to blame for pornography appearing on school computers.

The 40-year-old teacher had seventh-graders in an English class use a classroom computer to search the Internet for information about hairstyles. In the midst of the search, the teacher briefly left the room. Upon her return she found the students clustered around the computer, astonished by the sex acts displayed on the screen. The teacher, in a state of panic, ordered the students to stop looking at the images and ran to the principal's office for help because, as she later testified, she did not know how to turn off the computer. She was subsequently charged with four counts of risk of injury to a minor from pornography the students saw on the computer screen. In a court trial, the jury found her guilty as charged, with their decision based on the prosecutor's claim that she had deliberately selected such websites as *meetlovers.com* and *femalesexual.com*. She then faced a possible sentence of up to 40 years in prison.

However, after the trial, when investigators inspected the classroom computer, they discovered that it had been invaded by computer *malware* (viruses and *spyware* surreptitiously installed by malevolent computer *crackers*) that automatically switched to pornography sites when certain harmless websites were visited. On the basis of this new evidence, school authorities were blamed by computer-security experts for failing to keep the computer's protection programs up-to-date. The judge in the case threw out the jury's decision in the first trial and granted a new trial. A computer-security expert predicted that if the teacher's defense lawyer in the new trial would be "allowed to show the entire results of the forensics examination in front of experienced computer people, including a computer-literate judge and prosecutor, [the teacher] will walk out the court room as a free person" (Kaplan, 2007). A computer-virus researcher said that malware's ability to bring up pornographic images "is not unlikely. This stuff happens pretty commonly. There's a lot of malware that can make this happen, [and] school computers in particular seem to be pretty insecure" (Washkuch, 2007).

Case 4. The difficulty schools face in controlling the images students distribute with their electronic devices was demonstrated at Parkland High School in Allentown (Pennsylvania) when two girls, ages 14 and 17, took sexually explicit photos of themselves and then sent the pictures to at least 40 schoolmates' cell phones. The photo of a third girl copulating with her boyfriend was also included in the transfer. County prosecutors warned that, because the girls were below "the age of consent," anyone who retained the images could face charges of possessing child pornography. In an effort to prevent the photos from circulating, county officials contacted 40 students and their parents, asking the students to come forward and show that the images had been deleted from their cell phones. However, school and county authorities found the case difficult to handle. First, they probably could not prevent the photos from spreading to other people's cell phones and computers. Second, prosecuting the two girls would be awkward, because the pair were both the crime's perpetrators and its victims (Third girl, 2008).

Exhibitionism

The expressions *exhibitionism* and *indecent exposure* refer to people violating standards of morality by intentionally displaying their "private parts" to other people in inappropriate settings. Case 4 above, in which girls distributed nude photos of themselves, exemplifies one form of exhibitionism. Three other forms are illustrated in the following cases.

Case 5. Some sexual incidents qualify as more than one type of erotic behavior. An example is the behavior of a 28-year-old man who served as a computer-laboratory technician and baseball coach at Fox Creek Elementary School in Highlands Park (Colorado). On two dozen occasions he had taken a pair of 10-year-old boys from the baseball team to his home where the three showered together. Although the coach did not touch either boy, he did masturbate in front of them while showering. Apparently he was erotically stimulated as both an exhibitionist performing before the two boys and as a voyeur viewing the naked preteens. When the episodes were eventually revealed to school authorities, the coach was placed on administrative leave and charged by police with unlawful sexual conduct (Nicholson, 2008).

Case 6. The desire of school officials to protect students from sexual exhibitionism is implied in dress codes that identify styles of clothing considered too erotically suggestive. For example, the following regulations are part of the dress code for public schools in Pinellas County (Florida).

- All shirts and blouses must cover midriff, back, sides, and all undergarments (including bra straps) at all times. All shirts, tops, and dresses shall have sleeves and cover the shoulders.
- All trousers, pants, or shorts must totally cover undergarments.
- All clothing, jewelry, or tattoos shall be free of sexually suggestive phrases or images.
- Form-fitting leotard/spandex-type clothing (including sport bras) is not allowed unless proper outer garments cover it.
- See-through or mesh fabric clothing may only be worn over clothing meeting requirements.
- Clothing not properly buttoned, zipped, fastened, or with inappropriate holes or tears shall not be worn.
- Clothing traditionally designed as undergarments or sleepwear shall not be worn as outer garments. (Dress code, 2005)

Case 7. Exhibitionists who are guilty of negatively affecting students' welfare are often not officially connected to schools. For instance, as a busload of fourth graders from Wood View Elementary School in Bolingbrook (Illinois) were traveling to a theater performance, a naked man in a minivan drove beside the bus for several miles, masturbating all the while. The bus driver phoned the 911 emergency operator to alert the police. Officers in a patrol car caught the exhibitionist and jailed him on a felony charge of criminally exploiting children (Police, 2008).

Oral Sex

As explained in chapter 3, oral sex is one of the most common erotic practices among teenagers, with fellatio more frequent than cunnilingus.

Case 8. In the town of Milton (Massachusetts), conflicting opinions were expressed about what kinds of teenage sexual behaviors should be tolerated after five hockey players (between ages 16 and 18) at Milton Academy were expelled for receiving fellatio on several occasions from a 15-year-old sophomore girl.

Clearly, officials of the prestigious private preparatory school deemed oral sex a serious breach of school rules that warranted expulsion. And the five boys' behavior obviously violated a Massachusetts state law that makes it a crime to have sexual relations with anyone under age 16.

But several parents of the academy students appeared to excuse—or at least to rationalize—the hockey players' errant behavior as mainly a symptom of shifting moral standards in American culture. The father of a freshman girl believed that present-day teenagers face a difficult challenge in deciding what sorts of sexual behaviors are proper and what sorts improper. He said, "I think it's difficult for them to realize their own individual responsibility for these acts when they're inundated daily—barraged, if you will—by sexually explicit material from many different angles, particularly items that are broadcast over the Internet" (Slack, 2005). In a letter that academy officials sent to parents to explain the fellatio episodes and why the boys were expelled, the officials implied that they, too, felt that changing moral standards in youth culture were at least partially to blame for such events. Specifically, the letter recommended that parents read up on the "cultural prevalence of hooking up" (Slack, 2005). (In current youth culture, *hooking up* typically refers to people's casual encounters that involve erotic acts that can range from kissing, hugging, and fondling to oral, vaginal, or anal sex.)

Quite a different attitude about the fellatio episodes was expressed by vocal academy students who were appalled that the school and district attorney made such a fuss about the incidents. One senior boy said, "It's no big deal. I think this is something that's typical of high school. We just don't know about it." Another believed that the expulsions were "so stupid. I don't understand why this is happening to them" (Slack, 2005).

Thus, as the Milton affair illustrates, the "sexual revolution"—sparked in the 1960s and continuing today—has produced a generational and conservative/liberal divide that produces conflicts over which standards of acceptable erotic behavior should be applied by schools, parents, and the judiciary.

Case 9. In all instances of forbidden erotic acts, authorities must decide what punishment would be fair and just for the perpetrators of such acts. This matter of justice was the issue at stake in a court decision that sent a 17-year-old honor student and football star to prison for 10 years without the possibility of parole. A jury had convicted him of aggravated child molestation for receiving consensual fellatio from a 15-year-old girl at a 2003 New Year's Eve party that involved alcohol, marijuana, and sex. According to a 1995 Georgia state law, the punishment for "aggravated child molestation" was a mandatory 10 years' imprisonment. The jury's decision drew widespread objections that such a punishment was far too severe. In 2006, the state legislature changed the law to make consensual oral sex between teens only a misdemeanor punishable by a maximum of one year behind bars. In 2007, the youth's case was appealed to the Georgia Supreme Court where the justices, in a 4–3 decision, ruled that he should be freed. In their ruling, the judges noted that the legislature had changed the law that had required a 10-year prison term. The change represented "a seismic shift in the legislature's view of the gravity of oral sex between two willing teenage participants. . . . [The 10-year sentence made] no measurable contribution to acceptable goals of punishment, [and his crime did not rise to the] level of adults who prey on children" (Georgia court, 2007).

Coitus

Vaginal-intercourse incidents frequently involve two or more students (Cases 10 and 11) or else consist of a student and a school staff member (Cases 12 and 13).

Case 10. A 16-year-old developmentally disabled girl at Mifflin High School in Columbus (Ohio) reported that two boys had dragged her into the school auditorium, sexually assaulted her, and forced her to perform oral sex on one boy while the other boy videotaped the act. Even though school authorities are required by law to immediately inform the police of such events, the school principal failed to do so.

In juvenile court, the girl's assailants pled guilty to felonious assault. The victim's family filed a lawsuit against the principal and school district for negligence and failing to take reasonable action to prevent the attack. As a result, the district paid the family $350,000, the principal was dismissed from her job, and three assistant principals were suspended without pay for 10 days, and then reassigned to different jobs (Bush, 2005).

Case 11. Ways that the nature of a community can affect how the sexual misconduct of adolescents is treated were demonstrated in the small, isolated fishing village of Friday Harbor in the San Juan Islands off the coast of the state of Washington. Friday Harbor is a one-square-mile area with a population of 2,150.

Evidence presented in a 2003 juvenile-court trial revealed that in 2000 two 15-year-old boys who attended Friday Harbor High School had challenged each other to defoliate as many virgins as they could manage. Their method would be to invite a girl—a high-school acquaintance—to a private drinking party, ply her with liquor, and engage in vaginal intercourse when she became so intoxicated that she could not resist.

The first victim of the plan was a 13-year-old in 2000. "According to court documents, the girl passed out [from drinking] and, when she came to, the defendant was sexually assaulting her. A friend of the girl saw what was happening and went to the other boy for help. . . . Instead of helping, the second boy tried to sexually assault the victim" (Teen found guilty, 2003). However, the 13-year-old did not report the incident to the authorities because she feared that publicity about the episode would damage her reputation in the close-knit island community. The few school friends who learned of the affair honored the high-school culture's "code of silence" by not revealing the attacks. A second girl, age 15, suffered the same fate in 2001. She, too, failed to report the event to either school or judicial authorities for fear of retaliation by her attackers and of ostracism by her schoolmates. A third girl was given alcohol and assaulted by both defendants in March of 2003. However, this third victim reported the incident to authorities, and the boys were arrested on rape charges.

Although both defendants had turned age 18 by the time of their trials, their cases were assigned to juvenile court because their crimes had been committed when they were still minors. At the end of the first youth's trial, he was sentenced to 30–40 weeks in a juvenile-detention facility for second-degree rape and to 30 days for third-degree rape. He would be on probation until he reached age 21, would have to register as a sex offender for the rest of his life, and could not own or bear firearms. He could not contact the victims or attend the same school as the victims or their siblings, and he was required to write letters of apology to the victims. The second offender was sentenced to 79–120 weeks in a juvenile rehabilitation center and would have to fulfill the same additional conditions as did his fellow rapist.

Each trial featured contrasting attitudes expressed by participants. First were words of contrition by the pair of defendants.

> *First Remorseful Youth.* I cannot take back what has happened or the pain I've caused. My life has not been easy, but I have not made it easier on myself. I want to grow and change and better my life for adulthood and everyone around me. (Ausilio sentenced, 2003)

> *Second Tearful Youth.* This has been a horrific ordeal. There is no winner, everyone here has lost. Time, patience and a lot of love will heal these wounds. I can't erase what happened. If I could, I would. I want to change, I know I can. I am still a boy, scared and confused. I lost my senior year [in high school] and lost respect. [As for having to register as a sex offender], I will either be forgiven, forgotten, or hated, and blamed. I will have to carry this with me to schools, jobs, and relationships. That is the greatest and most fearful punishment I can receive. (Coulter sentenced, 2004)

Next was the judge's response to the suggestion by a defense attorney that the girls were to blame for the sexual encounters by getting drunk.

> *The Judge.* [When girls said,] No, it meant No. The girls acknowledged they did not use good judgment [by drinking alcohol]. They put themselves in a risky position, but that does not mean they are responsible for what happened. (Teen found guilty, 2003)

During the sentencing phase of the second trial, the judge offered the defendant advice.

> *Judge.* You have hurt people. You have not just made mistakes, you committed crimes. It is my firm belief and hope you will stop blaming others, minimizing the effect of your actions and make changes in your life. . . . I have never thought you were all bad. I did think your actions were criminal. I wish the best for you. (Coulter sentenced, 2004)

At the close of the trials, the prosecuting attorney summarized his interpretation of the youths' actions.

> *Prosecutor*. [The girls and boys] all made poor choices. They all engaged in risky behavior [drinking], but [the girls] did it with people they grew up with. People they trusted. [The two boys] exploited that trust and the culture of the school. The boys calculated correctly and got away with it for two years. Only after they humiliated a girl whom everyone loved and respected, did the girls finally say enough is enough is enough. (Teen found guilty, 2003)

The mother of the first defendant spoke in court about her son's recent nine months of sobriety and of the important role he played in their fatherless family as is the oldest of six children.

> *First Mother*. I can honestly tell you [that] right now I am more proud of my son than I have ever been. He is a good son. He feels bad. I love him very much. (Ausilio sentenced, 2003)

In contrast, the mother of the second defendant berated herself.

> *Second Mother*. I have to wonder how my wonderful boy could have caused such damage. I had to look in the mirror. I was a single mother in a community I have always loved. I wanted to believe [that he] wasn't drinking. If I had been more vigilant, these girls and my son could have been spared this ordeal. My home is empty also. He needed me to be a better parent than I was. (Coulter sentenced, 2004)

Finally, the mothers of two of the three victims who had testified in court "broke down as they recounted the changes in their daughters after the rapes. The mothers ended up sending their daughters out of state to live with their fathers and step-mothers" (Coulter sentenced, 2004).

> *One Victim's Mother*. I think of these girls and the time [of suffering] they have already done. They have opened the eyes of the community. It wasn't just the loss of virginity, it was the loss of youth, trust, and home. They should have been in this year's senior class at Friday Harbor High School. (Coulter sentenced, 2004).

Case 12. As in the Friday Harbor affair, the nature of attitudes in a community where many people know each other personally contributed to the suppression of sexual misconduct in the town of Bayonne (New Jersey). However, unlike the "code of silence" among high-school students that led to sexual abuse being kept secret in Friday Harbor, a significant condition that shielded a sex abuser from prosecution in Bayonne was the influential social-class and political status of the abuser's family and friends.

Bayonne is a city of 62,000 on a peninsula that juts into the Atlantic Ocean. Its population consists chiefly of Italian, Irish, and Polish Americans who form a social hierarchy ranging from day-labor families at the bottom to economically well-to-do business and professional families at the top.

In 2001, a 47-year-old woman counselor at Bayonne High School was arrested on a charge of statutory rape of a 15-year-old high-school boy who was living in her home at the invitation of her 15-year-old son. Upon the counselor's arrest, school officials insisted that this single incident was the only blemish on her 24-year record of exemplary service. Officials in 2002

> allowed her to take an early retirement package that fattened her pension, and gave her a farewell party with cake and ice cream. When [she] pleaded guilty in 2005 to sexual assault charges, glowing references from coworkers, supervisors, and friends helped persuade a judge to sentence her only to probation. She was also spared the ordeal of having to register as a sex offender. (Kocieniewski, 2006)

However, a different picture of the offender's past emerged as witnesses came forward to expose a long history of sexual exploitation of teenage boys. In 1980, as an elementary-school special-education teacher, she had astonished observers by fondling a 13-year-old boy at an eighth-grade dance. At the time, several fellow teachers told the school principal that his special-education teacher "has a thing for young boys" (Kocieniewski, 2006). When the principal recommended that the superintendent of schools dismiss the woman, he was amazed to learn that, instead, she had been appointed a guidance counselor at Bayonne High School. The principal said he suspected the appointment was designed to please the woman's father who was one of the community's most prominent business and political figures. Now in the role of counselor, the woman

- Became pregnant in 1984 and told colleagues that the father was a musician in the currently popular musical *Beatlemania*. However, rumors spread that the real father was one of the woman's 16-year-old counselees. When that youth graduated from Bayonne High in 1985, he married her. The marriage produced two more children but ended in divorce in 1996.
- In 2001, the counselor took into her home a high-school athlete to live with her three children. Her relationship with the athlete was

a combination of surrogate mother and secret lover. She "opened a bank account for him, had taken him on vacations to Utah with her children, had set his curfew and bedtime, and had helped arrange an operation on his foot. [The youth said that] several times a week she sneaked him into her bedroom to spend the night" (Kocieniewski, 2006). When the counselor's eldest son objected to the arrangement, the young athlete moved to his aunt's house. From there his relatives filed a statutory-rape lawsuit against the counselor, a suit that was eventually settled for $400,000.

A *New York Times* reporter, trying to account for the incidents of sexual abuse continuing for nearly a quarter of a century without serious consequences to the abuser, concluded,

> Some [Bayonne residents] blame small-town politics; [the woman's] father is a prominent businessman here. Others see a double standard in which people are reluctant to view teenage boys as victims. [The city's mayor] attributes the silence to shock, shame, and misplaced civic pride from people afraid the case would tarnish the reputation of Bayonne schools. "No one bothered to do the math," said [the mayor] who, like many people in town, knew that [the woman] had married a former student, but did not seem to realize that the relationship had started—and that their child had been born—when her husband was still in school. "And the people who suspected didn't want to make it a big issue." (Kocieniewski, 2006)

Case 13. Sometimes an accidental event will lead to the discovery of sexual wrongdoing. A 17-year-old high-school girl's diary that she unwittingly dropped in a school corridor exposed a 41-year-old male teacher's sexual trysts at Green Hills Elementary School in Harlan County (Kentucky). A passerby in the corridor spotted the diary and took it to the principal's office where an administrator who glanced through the log was astonished by entries describing incidents of oral sex and vaginal intercourse between the teacher and the girl who had written the journal. The journal was then given to the police, who, on the basis of the entries, arrested the 41-year-old teacher for third-degree rape and third-degree sodomy of a juvenile.

During the subsequent court trial, the girl testified that the sexual relationship had started with "just talking"—the teacher told her how pretty she was and how he had erotic dreams that involved her. She said such conversations led to her falling in love with him. The two then engaged in oral sex and intercourse after school in the classroom during multiple episodes between December 2004 and April 2005. Finally, the teacher "wanted to call it off, because people were assuming something was going on between them." When the prosecuting attorney asked the girl why she had kept the journal, she said it was because she had no one to talk to; when she tried to discuss the affair with her friends, they didn't believe her (Caldwell, 2007). Her account of the affair was then corroborated by another girl, who testified that she herself had suffered similar treatment by the same teacher. At the end of the trial, the jury found the teacher guilty of both charges and sentenced him to 6 years in prison.

Same-Sex Offenses

Whereas most reports of illicit erotic affairs involve heterosexual encounters, a sizable number are between participants of the same gender.

Case 14. Erotic liaisons between people of the same gender are not necessarily pursued because the initiator of the relationship lacks heterosexual opportunities for satisfying erotic urges. As an illustration, when a 26-year-old married woman at Wharton High School in Tampa (Florida) returned test papers to students in her ninth-grade mathematics class, one 14-year-old girl's paper was accompanied by an envelope containing a note. The note said that the teacher—who was also the girl's basketball coach—found the girl very attractive, and the teacher wondered if the girl felt the same way. When the girl sent a note back saying that she did indeed feel attracted to the teacher, an erotic relationship developed between teacher/coach and student/player. The affair began with the pair kissing in the coach's car after basketball practice or during trips to games. The relationship then advanced to oral sex at the coach's apartment. The affair involved more than 50 occasions over an 18-month period. Although the girl's teammates suspected the nature of the liaisons, none spoke to authorities about their suspicions. Finally, the long-term affair was exposed when the girl told her mother about it and other relatives then told the police, who charged the coach with lewd and lascivious battery—a second-degree felony. When the coach was questioned by detectives, she described her involvement with the teen as "much like a mother/daughter or big sister/little sister" relationship (Another Tampa, 2005).

As soon as school officials learned that police were investigating the coach, they moved her to their Office of Professional Standards where she would have no contact with students. A spokesman for the school district said, "We take these allegations very seriously, and when these things come up, we want to protect the children. That's why we take teachers out of the classroom, even before charges are filed" (Colavecchio-Van Sickler, 2005).

Case 15. The questionable accuracy of young children's testimony can become a critical issue in court cases of sexual abuse, especially when children offer their accounts months or years after the alleged misconduct.

In addition, such cases become additionally difficult when there is also contradictory testimony from adults.

In 2006, a 32-year-old male kindergarten teacher at Key Elementary School in Oak Park (Michigan) was found guilty by a jury for removing two boys—ages 4 and 5—from the school's lunch line one day in October 2005, taking them to an empty special-education room, and forcing them to perform oral sex. The teacher had been convicted on the testimony of the two boys. However, in early 2007 a judge learned that the detective who had originally investigated the incident had failed to visit the special-education room or to interview teachers who worked in that room or near it. Therefore, the judge declared the 2006 conviction a mistrial.

At a new trial convened in March 2008, the witnesses included not only the two boys who purportedly had been molested but also the school principal, a cafeteria worker, and three special-education teachers who had never before been interviewed. At the time of the alleged assaults in 2005, the younger boy at age 4 had been unable to tell investigators how the kindergarten teacher had brought him into the special-education room. But now, at age 7, he offered many new details. He said the teacher had taken him and another boy from the cafeteria, offered them treats, and pulled them by their shirts down a hallway to the special-education room. There, according to the 7-year-old, the teacher assaulted him while the other boy waited outside the door. The teacher then brought the second boy into the room and assaulted him as well. When a defense attorney asked the 7-year-old why, when he was a 4-year-old, he had not told his parents or investigators about the incident, the boy said, "Because I thought they wouldn't believe me" (Brasier, 2008).

The second boy—age 5 in 2005 and now age 8—testified that he had been pulled out of the lunch line and into the hallway by the kindergarten teacher but denied that the other boy was with him. And the 8-year-old's account also differed in several other ways from the 7-year-old's testimony.

When the three special-education workers were questioned, they said the special-education room was always occupied, since special-education children ate lunch there; the kindergarten teacher could not therefore have assaulted the two boys in the room. However, the school principal, on the witness stand, contended that she had ordered the special-education children to eat in different room. And the cafeteria worker testified that she had seen the kindergarten teacher take a boy out of the lunch line.

After hearing all of the witnesses, the jury deliberated for more than a week without reaching a verdict. At one point, the jurors asked the judge to clarify the concepts *presumption of innocence* and *reasonable doubt*.

And notes that the jury sent to the judge suggested that 11 jurors favored acquitting the accused, whereas one juror stoutly held out for convicting him. Finally, as it became apparent that the jury was irreparably deadlocked, the judge declared a mistrial. Jurors estimated that there was "low probability of conviction should he be tried again" (Martindale, 2008).

Although the teacher had weathered two mistrials, he still could be tried again. He remained under bond and was obliged to abide by three conditions set by the judge—he had to report weekly to judicial authorities, he could not reside in his home (which was adjacent to an elementary school), and he could not have any contact with children unless supervised by adults.

Administrative Decisions

Challenges that confront school officials include the need to (a) reassure parents of their children's safety when a sexual abuse incident has occurred, (b) dispose of an abusive staff member in a cost-effective manner that protects the school's reputation, or (c) determine if their school district can be held legally liable to pay punitive damages for sexual abuse by a staff member.

Case 16. Whenever news circulates in a community about a sexual encounter between a school staff member and a student, school officials are prompted to send a letter of explanation to parents of students who attend the school. Such a letter was mailed to parents of students enrolled at Middleton High School in Tampa (Florida) after police arrested a 33-year-old female special-education teacher for engaging in oral and vaginal sex with a 16-year-old ninth-grade boy.

The teacher's sexual assignation with the student was discovered when police stopped an erratically driven Jeep containing six joy-riding youths. After the unlicensed 16-year-old driver told the police that his teacher had lent him the car, the officers summoned the teacher and, while questioning her, discovered that she had been engaged in a series of sexual trysts with the youth at her home.

The school principal, in response to news of the teacher's arrest, sent parents the following letter.

> Dear Parent/Guardian:
>
> I need to inform you about an off-campus incident that had an effect on our school today. One of our teachers was arrested last night and charged with having an inappropriate relationship with one of our students. The teacher, who was new to our school this year, will not be returning the Middleton High School. We anticipate she will be suspended without pay while her case is dealt with within the courts.

> The case has drawn media attention, but we were able to hold class as usual today. Our students and teachers did a great job despite the potential distraction. We have talked with the students in her classes so they understand what's going on.
>
> I want to reassure you that this is an isolated incident. Our teachers know they have a sacred responsibility to our students and they do a tremendous job day in and day out. We don't want an incident like this to reflect badly on our teachers or on our school. This will not distract us from our goals of increasing student achievement and helping students reach their potential. If you have any questions, please contact me.

As for the student who had driven the Jeep so ineptly, the police did not cite him for driving without a license because they believed he was a victim exploited by his teacher (Kalfrin & Poltilove, 2007).

Case 17. Eight girls at Claggett Creek Middle School in Salem (Oregon) in 2004 complained to school authorities that a male teacher had inappropriately touched them—clutching their waists, touching their buttocks, and massaging their shoulders. The school's administrators responded to the complaints by offering the 44-year-old teacher an easy way to escape sexual-abuse charges: If he resigned, they would conceal his alleged conduct from the public. And if future potential employers phoned to the school to ask how the teacher had performed, Claggett Creek officials would attribute his departure to "personal reasons" and make no mention of the agreement under which he had left. When the Oregon Teacher Standards and Practice Commission learned of the agreement, the commissioners revoked the man's license in January 2005. He then secured a teaching job at a charter school in Tucson (Arizona) during the 2006–2007 school year and drew no complaints or reprimands, according to administrators there, but he left after one year for "personal reasons." In 2008, he obtained a teaching post at Cardigan Mountain School, a private, all-boys school in New Hampshire, where the headmaster reported that their newly appointed instructor had not revealed his misconduct in Oregon at the time he was hired, and background checks conducted by the school had revealed nothing. The headmaster reported, "We have been pleased with his performance" (Hsuan, Navas & Graves, 2008).

When editors at *The Oregonian* newspaper learned of the Claggett Creek case, they sought information about similar secret negotiations at other schools and discovered that

> During the past five years, nearly half of Oregon teachers disciplined for sexual misconduct with a child left their school districts with confidential agreements. Most [agreements] promised to keep alleged abuse quiet. Some promised cash settlements, health insurance, and letters of recommendation

> as incentives for a resignation. The practice is so widespread, school officials across the country call it "passing the trash." (Hsuan et al., 2008)

In such a fashion, authorities often rid their school of a sexually abusive teacher, coach, or administrator. For abusers, the advantages of "cutting a deal" are that the deal allows them to seek a job with another school district, it permits them to keep their teaching or administrative license, and it avoids the damaging publicity and costs of a court trial. For school officials, the advantages are that the deal immediately rids the school of the abuser, it avoids trouble with the teachers union, it saves the cost of placing the abuser on paid administrative leave while the case is investigated, it is far less expensive than a court trial, and it prevents damage to the school's reputation that could result from newspaper and television publicity about abuse.

Whereas secret arrangements enable some abusers to retain their teaching licenses, many others lose their credentials. A nationwide study revealed that sexual misconduct allegations led states to revoke, deny, or surrender licenses of 2,570 educators from 2001 through 2005 (School sex predators, 2007).

Case 18. In legal parlance, *vicarious liability* refers to an individual or organization being obliged to pay damages for a crime that the individual or organization did not commit. Such liability was the matter argued before the U.S. Supreme Court in the 1998 case of *Gebser vs. Lago Vista Independent School District* (Leander, Texas). The question was whether the school district was vicariously liable for sexual harassment that a student, Alida Gebser, allegedly suffered at the hands one of her high-school teachers, Frank Waldrup.

The relationship between Alida and Frank Waldrup began when Alida, age 13, was a student in Mrs. Frank Waldrup's eighth-grade class and Mrs. Waldrup invited the girl to join a Great Books discussion group led by her husband at the local high school. The next autumn, when Alida entered high school, she enrolled in Frank Waldrup's class, where he singled her out for flattery and

> made numerous suggestive remarks to her in private and in front of other students. Ms. Gebser believed that this special attention resulted from the mentor/mentee relationship she shared with Mr. Waldrup. In the Spring of 1992, Mr. Waldrup visited Ms. Gebser at her home when her parents were away. He took advantage of the situation by kissing and fondling Ms. Gebser. Ms. Gebser was stunned, confused, and terrified. She was unsure how to react to the situation. Soon after this incident, Mr. Waldrup began a sexual relationship with Ms. Gebser that included numerous acts of sexual intercourse.

> Around this time, the school district had severely cut back the Gifted and Talented Program, in which Ms. Gebser participated. Mr. Waldrup offered to Ms. Gebser, with the school district's consent, one-on-one instruction in advanced course work. Oftentimes, these "classes" were mere fronts for Mr. Waldrup to continue his sexual relationship with Ms. Gebser. Ms. Gebser believed that if she were to report their relationship, then she would lose Mr. Waldrup as her instructor and her only opportunity for an honors education. (Gebser, 2008)

Alida told no one of the affair, which continued for a year and a half until the pair was caught by the police while engaged in sexual activity. Mr. Waldrup was arrested and Lago Vista terminated his employment. Alida then filed a lawsuit against the school district, charging that the district had violated her rights by not protecting her from sexual abuse by a district employee. Her lawyers adduced two arguments to support her claim: (a) Mr. Waldrup, in his intentional misconduct, was serving as an agent of the district, and (b) the district had failed to issue a policy statement defining sexual harassment and the way violations should be reported.

The district court in which the suit was filed rejected Alida's line of reasoning and declared that the school district was not liable. The appeals court to which her lawyers next carried the case agreed with the district-court decision on the grounds that vicarious liability could be assigned only if an employee who was vested with supervisory power by the school board (a) actually knew of the abuse, (b) had the power to end the abuse, and (c) had failed to end the abuse. The judges ruled that those conditions did not apply in the Gebser affair.

When the case was further appealed to the U.S. Supreme Court, the justices, in a 5–4 ruling, supported the appeals-court decision in ruling that

> Damages may not be recovered for teacher-student sexual harassment in an implied private action under Title IX [of the federal Patsy T. Mink Equal Opportunity in Education Act] unless a school district official who at a minimum has authority to institute corrective measures on the district's behalf has actual notice of, and is deliberately indifferent to, the teacher's misconduct. (O'Conner, 1998)

A representative of NOW (National Organization of Women) suggested that when the Supreme Court removed vicarious liability of a school district for its teachers' behavior, the justices

> created a veritable "smoking gun" requirement for harassment suits, forcing the victim to prove that the school district knew of the teacher's actions and consciously ignored them. This places a heavy burden upon the victim, especially when faced with a district [that] may have been sympathetic to the student's concerns, yet refused action upon them. (Gebser, 2008)

CONDITIONS SUMMARY

Each of this chapter's 18 cases featured conditions that influenced the nature and outcomes of that particular case. In order to illustrate the variety of conditions that were involved and their frequency, the following list cites 21 types. The figures in parentheses following each type are the identifying numbers of the cases in which that condition played a significant role.

Influential conditions included:

- The kind of sexual act involved (1, 2, 3, 4, 5, 7, 8, 9, 10, 11, 12, 13, 14, 15, 16, 17, 18)
- Criminal laws (3, 4, 5, 7, 8, 9, 10, 11, 12, 13, 14, 15, 16, 17, 18)
- The kinds of sanctions applied to individuals who were involved in sexual-abuse events (3, 4, 5, 7, 8, 9, 10, 11, 12, 13, 15, 16, 17, 18)
- The ages of students involved in a sexual-encounter incident (5, 7, 8, 9, 10, 11, 12, 13, 14, 15, 16, 17, 18)
- The genders of the individuals engaged in a sexual act (5, 8, 10, 11, 12, 13, 14, 15, 16, 17, 18)
- The settings in which school personnel interacted with students, such as classrooms, counseling rooms, excursion sites, and practice/performance locations (athletic, music, drama) (5, 7, 12, 13, 14, 15, 16, 17, 18)
- The ages of school personnel involved in a sexual-encounter incident (5, 12, 13, 14, 15, 16, 17, 18)
- The discrepancy between teachers and students in the amount of power or authority that accompanied their roles (5, 12, 13, 14, 15, 16, 17, 18)
- School officials attempting to prevent—or at least to minimize—the damage that publicity about a sexual-abuse event might cause their school (8, 11, 12, 14, 16, 17)
- Parents seeking to influence school policies and practices (1, 2, 8, 12)
- School officials attempting to negotiate policies acceptable to competing constituencies (teachers, students, parents, political groups, religious sects, social-class levels, and more) (1, 2, 6, 12)
- Students' intellectual abilities, (10, 13, 15, 18)
- School personnel attempting to provide students with a wide selection of learning resources (1, 2, 18)
- The social-class status of participants in an erotic encounter (8, 12)
- Conflicts between different constituencies (students, school personnel, parents, political groups, religious bodies, social-class levels, age groups) over the seriousness of an erotic encounter (8, 11)
- The size of a community (11, 12).

- How such terms as *unacceptable language* and *coarse language* are defined (1, 2)
- Individuals' levels of expertise in electronic technology (3, 4)
- The clarity of school policy statements (6)
- The responsibility of school personnel to prevent sexual abuse of students (10)
- The involvement of liquor in sexual abuse (11)

Chapter 5

Eroticism Gone Awry 1—Abuse

Several types of eroticism can qualify as sexual abuse. The five types described in this chapter are (a) harassment and bullying, (b) seduction, (c) statutory rape, (d) forcible rape, and (e) date rape.

HARASSMENT AND BULLYING

Sexual harassment consists of unwelcome sexual advances, requests for sexual favors, and other verbal or physical conduct of an erotic nature. Harassment assumes two forms: (a) *quid pro quo* (exchanging *this for that*), where submission to harassment is used as the basis for educational or employment decisions, and (b) *hostile environment*, where harassment creates an offensive learning or working environment (American Bar Association, 2008).

Actions that qualify as harassment include:

- Using words that refer to someone's sexuality as a general put-down, such as calling something *gay* to mean it is undesirable
- Using sexual words to insult a person, such as calling a girl a *slut* or a boy a *pimp*
- Joking about serious and frightening subjects, such as *rape* and *syphilis*
- Gossiping about a schoolmate's or a faculty member's sex life
- Using graffiti to cast sexual slurs on a schoolmate or faculty member, such as spray-painting insulting comments on the wall of a school restroom

- Touching someone in a way that makes the person feel uncomfortable
- Commenting about a schoolmate's appearance, attractiveness, or pubertal development (size of breasts or penis)
- Proposing sexual acts (fellatio, cunnilingus, coitus, mutual masturbation)
- Making sexually explicit gestures

In addition, a group of elementary-school teachers in Minnesota classified the following as instances of sexual harassment:

- "Spiking" (forcibly pulling down pants)
- "Snuggies" or "wedgies" (forcibly pulling up pants)
- Flipping up skirts
- Forcing kisses
- Grabbing or touching another's genitals
- Calling others sexually offensive names
- Asking others for sex or to perform sexual acts
- Threatening rape
- Passing sexually explicit notes
- Making gender-demeaning comments
- Commenting on body parts
- Using sexual profanity
- Exposing genitals
- Participating in organized harassment of girls
- Circulating pornography (Strauss, 1994)

Harassment often takes the form of bullying, when bullying is defined as aggressive behavior by one or more students aimed at causing discomfort or injury to schoolmates. Such behavior can include name calling, making faces, obscene gesturing, malicious ridicule, threats, rumors, physical hitting, kicking, pushing, and choking.

Students as well as school personnel can be the perpetrators or the victims of harassment, as illustrated in the following examples.

A *quid pro quo* episode concerned a high-school girl in the history class of a teacher who has asked the girl to come to his classroom alone after school to discuss her schoolwork.

> When she shows up, he only talks about how pretty she is and has twice put his hand on her knee. He always asks for a hug before she leaves. He is now suggesting that they hold these after-school meetings at a café in town. He tells her that she must continue to attend these extra discussion sessions if she wants to earn a good grade in his class. (Equal Rights Advocates, 2008)

A *hostile-environment* case involved a high-school girl's soccer-team coach telling her sexual jokes, making erotic suggestions, and whistling and winking when she ran by during practice. After the girl told him his actions made her uncomfortable, he said she needed to learn how to accept compliments. Once he showed her a calendar of bikini-clad female athletes and said she was sexy enough to pose for such a magazine. The girl thought of resigning from the team to avoid the constant harassment (Equal Rights Advocates, 2008).

Another girl suffered a hostile environment caused by classmates:

> There were two or three boys touching me . . . and I'd tell them to stop but they wouldn't. This went on for months. Finally I was in one of my classes when all of them backed me into a corner and started touching me all over. . . . After the class I told the principal, and he and the boys had a little talk. After the talk was up, the boys came out laughing because they got no punishment. (Office of Civil Rights, 2008)

A 44-year-old female guidance counselor sent text messages to a 15-year-old boy's cell phone during the school day with such sexually suggestive expressions as "see u soon" and "how about now?" The counselor would then issue a pass for the boy to leave class and meet her in her office. Thus, as illustrated by this case, the advent of such electronic communication media as cell phones, e-mail, and social-network sites (MySpace, Facebook, YouTube) has enhanced harassers' ability to send messages and photos to the objects of their affection (Maxwell, 2007).

Sometimes harassment continues unchecked for years. For example, a first-grade boy in a Minnesota elementary school was repeatedly called sexually insulting names by two classmates who pulled his pants and underwear down to his knees and told him to have sex with his mother, sister, and animals. When the young victim complained to his teachers, they told him to "Go play somewhere else" or "Stay away from them." So the torment grew. By the time the pupil was in third grade, 13 schoolmates were taunting him in the classroom, playground, hallways, bathrooms, and buses. He had tolerated the torture for a year and half before telling his parents, who then demanded that school officials put a stop to the bullying. However, the principal dismissed the incidents as, "Just squabbles between third-grade boys." The boy then took a tape recorder to school and recorded examples of his assailants' obscene taunts. When the principal listened to the tape, he suspended 5 of the 13 schoolmates and called the parents of all 13 for a conference. Yet the harassment continued, even after more than 20 additional complaints from the victim's parents. School officials insinuated that their son needed psychological attention to discover why his classmates treated him so badly. In effect, school personnel appeared to blame the boy for his victimization. Finally, the angry parents filed sexual-harassment charges with the U.S. Department of Education's Office of Civil Rights. At first investigators at the office planned to pursue the case but then changed their mind, "stating that the reported behavior did not constitute sexual harassment because it was a case of other kids simply not liking [the boy]" (Strauss, 1994).

The Incidence of Harassment

A 1993 survey—repeated in 2001—was titled Hostile Hallways. Researchers sampled the responses of students nationwide (grades 8 through 11) about their experiences with sexual harassment. On both occasions, students reported widespread persecution. Whereas the frequency of harassing was essentially the same over the 8-year period, in 2001 more students reported that their schools had established antiharassment procedures than was true in 1993. The results of the 2001 study showed that

- Eight in 10 students (81 percent) experience some form of sexual harassment during their school lives: 6 in 10 (59 percent) often or occasionally and one quarter (27 percent) often. These levels did not change from 1993.
- Girls are more likely than boys to experience sexual harassment ever (83 percent versus 79 percent) or often (30 percent versus 24 percent).
- Three quarters of students (76 percent) experience nonphysical sexual harassment at some point in their school lives, more than half (54 percent) often or occasionally.
- Six in 10 students (58 percent) experience physical harassment at some point in their school lives, one third (32 percent) often or occasionally.
- One third (32 percent) of students are afraid of being sexually harassed. Girls are more than twice as likely as boys to feel this way (44 percent versus 20 percent).
- Students who experience physical harassment are more likely than those who experience nonphysical harassment to feel very or somewhat upset (56 percent versus 26 percent).
- Seven in 10 students (69 percent) in 2001, compared to just 26 percent in 1993, say their schools have a policy to deal with sexual harassment issues and complaints. (American Association of University Women, 2001)

Significant Conditions

Whether or not behavior constitutes harassment can depend on such factors as age, the nature of an offensive act, intent, reciprocity, and custom.

Age was an issue in the case of a 5-year-old kindergarten boy at Lincolnshire Elementary School in Hagerstown (Maryland) who was cited for sexual harassment when he pinched a girl's bottom in the hallway. School officials said that act fit the Maryland State Department of Education's definition of harassment as "unwelcome sexual advances, requests for sexual favors and/or other inappropriate verbal, written or physical conduct of a sexual nature directed toward others." Actually, in such episodes, age is not the significant variable in itself but serves as a surrogate for "knowledge of right and wrong." The 5-year-old's father complained that his son "knows nothing about sex. There's no way to explain what he's been written up for. He knows it as playing around. He doesn't know it as anything sexual at all." But the school principal replied, "Anytime a student touches another student inappropriately, it could be sexual harassment" (Cunningham, 2006).

The question of whether an act has truly been sexual in nature arose when a 6-year-old boy at Joseph H. Downey Elementary School in Brockton (Massachusetts) was suspended from school for 3 days because he had touched the skin on a girl's back when he reached two fingers inside the rear waistband of her pants. The Downey principal said that the child had breached the school's sexual-harassment policy, which prohibited any "uninvited physical contact such as touching, hugging, patting, or pinching." The boy's mother was outraged at the suspension, saying that the child was too young to know anything about sex. The boy said the girl had touched him first and that he had just touched her back. In support of the mother's claim that her family held very strict rules about morality, she said that her son was raised according to the conservative moral tradition of Haitian evangelicalism, so she and her husband did not even let their son watch secular television. Instead, they subscribed to a cable-television channel that broadcast religious cartoons (Ranalli & Mischa, 2006). The parents subsequently filed a lawsuit in federal court, claiming that school authorities had violated the boy's civil rights, because their son was "still obviously a child incapable of forming criminal intent . . . and obviously immature sexually from both a physical and psychological-awareness standpoint" (Mulvihill & Bergantino, 2007).

The matter of intent can be critical in schools' decisions about harassment. If an act was planned to be both sexual and likely offensive to its recipient, then the actor is considered more culpable and deserving of punishment than if the act was not so intended. However, proving intent is difficult—often impossible—as in the cases of the 5- and 6-year-old boys. Intent also becomes important in distinguishing between flirting and harassment. One way to differentiate flirting from harassment is in terms of *mutual intent* and *mutual attraction*. Permissible flirting involves two people exchanging eroticism-toned comments and movements that reflect their feelings of mutual fondness, with neither of them meaning to denigrate the other. In contrast, intent that warrants a charge of harassment involves one person seeking to exploit, abuse, humiliate, or embarrass the other. Hence, nonexploitive flirting would be considered an act of pleasurable reciprocity, whereas harassment would be an act of malice and exploitation.

Another condition affecting judgments of harassment is *custom,* in the sense of behavior regarded as ordinary and acceptable within a given culture. The rapid cultural change in American society over the past several decades has been accompanied by some confusion over what constitutes sexual harassment. Acts that were labeled in the past as *only teasing, kid stuff, just playfulness,* or *boys will be boys* have since become condemned and illegal. So it is that, during the transition from past to present, disagreements are apt to arise over whether or not a particular act has infringed on someone's rights and thus deserves censure.

Sexual Harassment and the Law

The U.S. Supreme Court's ruling in the 1999 case of *Davis vs. Monroe County Board of Education* became a landmark judicial decision about sexual harassment in schools. The case concerned a lawsuit filed on behalf of a fifth-grade girl, LaShonda Davis, who attended a Monroe County (Georgia) elementary school. The petition contended that a fifth-grade boy continually tried to touch LaShonda's breasts and genitals, he rubbed against her in a way she considered sexual, and he said things like, "I want to get in bed with you."

The suit charged that Monroe County school authorities'

> deliberate indifference to [the boy's] persistent sexual advances toward LaShonda created an intimidating, hostile, offensive, and abusive school environment that violated Title IX of the Education Amendments of 1972, which, in relevant part, prohibits a student from being "excluded from participation in, being denied the benefits of, or being subjected to discrimination under any education program or activity receiving Federal financial assistance." (O'Conner, 1999)

When the case was tried in a federal district court, the judge dismissed the suit, reasoning that student-on-student or peer harassment provided no ground for a Title IX private cause for damages. When the plaintiff's attorney appealed that ruling to the Eleventh Circuit Court, the judges there concurred with the dismissal. However, when the U.S. Supreme

Court later reviewed the case, the justices, in a 5–4 decision, reversed the lower courts' verdict.

In penning the Supreme Court's majority decision, Justice Sandra Day O'Conner wrote that convincing evidence suggested

> LaShonda was the victim of repeated acts of harassment by [the boy] over a 5-month period, and allegations support the conclusion that his misconduct was severe, pervasive, and objectively offensive. Moreover, the complaint alleges that multiple victims of G. F.'s misconduct sought an audience with the school principal and that the harassment had a concrete, negative effect on LaShonda's ability to receive an education. The complaint also suggests that petitioner may be able to show both actual knowledge and deliberate indifference on the part of the [County School] Board, which made no effort either to investigate or to put an end to the harassment. (O'Conner, 1999)

The decision in *Davis vs. Monroe County Board of Education* made clear that school districts can be held financially liable for ignoring complaints of student-on-student harassment or for failing to protect students from sexual abuse. For example, a Kansas school district paid $45,000 to a pair of high-school girls to settle a claim that school authorities were deliberately indifferent to a boy's continually assailing the girls with rude, violent, and sexually suggestive comments. On several occasions he had exposed himself and tried to make them touch him. At one point the girls had received a protective order from the police. However, according to the girls, school officials ignored their attempts to report such abuse on a daily basis. District representatives said they settled the claim so as to avoid litigation costs, but they did not admit liability. The representatives claimed the girls' relationship with the boy was actually friendly, thereby suggesting that some of the alleged harassment was consensual. However, as a result of the lawsuit, officials changed their sexual-harassment policies and appointed a staff member to cope with Title IX discrimination complaints (Kansas school district, 2008).

Schools' Responses to Sexual Harassment

As a result of the Supreme Court's decision in *Davis vs. Monroe,* school districts became increasingly diligent about establishing antiharassment procedures and in distributing information about those procedures to students, their parents, and school personnel. Such information is typically published in schools' student handbooks. A typical policy statement is one included in the booklet distributed to students at Mount Miguel High School handbook in the Grossmount Union High School District (Spring Valley, California).

> Students may not engage in conduct constituting sexual harassment such as, but not limited to, unwelcome sexual advances, requests for sexual favors, or other verbal or physical conduct of a sexual nature, including harassment for sexual orientation, severe enough to have a negative impact upon another student's academic performance or to create an intimidating, hostile, or offensive educational environment.
>
> Students should report any sexual harassment to their school principal, vice principal, counselor, or teacher. Students who violate this policy shall be disciplined appropriately, including suspension or possible expulsion. Employees who violate this policy shall be disciplined, pursuant to Board Policy 4119.11.
>
> Complaints must be initiated no later than six (6) months from the date when the alleged discrimination occurred or when the individual first obtained knowledge of the facts of the alleged discrimination. Investigation of alleged discrimination complaints shall be conducted in a manner that protects confidentiality of individuals and the facts. The District prohibits retaliatory behavior against any complainant or any participant in the complaint process. The initiation of a complaint of sexual harassment will not reflect negatively on the student who initiates the complaint nor will it affect the student's academic standing, rights, or privileges.
>
> Sometimes harassment complaints can be settled at the school and sometimes at the District office. If the complaint is not settled after mediation and/or investigation, you have the right to discuss your concerns with the Superintendent. If it is not resolved there, you may go to the Governing Board, Child Protective Services, and/or law enforcement agencies including the U.S. Office of Civil Rights, which may also investigate complaints of sexual harassment. The U.S. Office of Civil Rights may be contacted directly to file complaints. (Sexual harassment policy, 2005)

In addition to publicizing antiharassment procedures, schools can adopt other means of coping with offences. Girls can be taught assertiveness skills as ways to confront harassers, and boys can be schooled in socially acceptable ways to communicate with girls. A faculty meeting or workshop can be dedicated to training school personnel in techniques of coping with the sexual harassment of students.

SEDUCTION

Sexual seduction has been defined various ways. During the latter half of the 19th century, seduction in legal parlance was "the offence of a man who abuses the simplicity and confidence of a woman to obtain by false pretenses what she ought not to grant" (Litigating morality, 1997). In a similar vein, early-20th-century criminal law defined seduction as "persuading or inducing a woman of previous chaste character to depart from the path of virtue by any species of arts, persuasions, or wiles which are calculated to have and do have that effect, and which result in her ultimately submitting to the sexual embrace of the accused" (Underhill, 1910, p. 663). A definition from common law has called seduction "conduct on the part of a man, without the use of force, in wrongfully inducing a woman to surrender to his sexual desires" (Ferrara, 2007). However, none of these definitions adequately encompasses the sort of abuse that can result from erotic liaisons in which present-day students and school personnel become involved.

Thus, for present purposes, seduction will be redefined as "an individual (male or female) enticing another person (male or female) to perform a sexual act which that person performs only with great reluctance." Hence, such a definition distinguishes between (a) a couple engaging in a sexual act with mutual enthusiasm, so that the episode is not an instance of seduction, and (b) one of the pair consenting to the act but with marked misgivings, thereby qualifying the event as seduction and sexual abuse. Unlike the above-mentioned legal definitions of seduction, this revised version recognizes that abuse can be suffered in any kind of erotic activity (unwelcome kissing, fondling, masturbation, coitus, fellatio, cunnilingus, or sodomy) and that both males and females can be seducers and victims.

Girls in particular can face a difficult decision about whether they should capitulate to seduction attempts. If a girl readily succumbs, she may strengthen her relationship with the boy, may attract many other suitors, and may gain the reputation of being popular. However, such a reputation may include being labeled *roundheels, ho, easy lay,* or *slut butt.* And boys interested in establishing a serious long-term relationship with such a girl could be frightened away, suspecting that she was prone to infidelity.

STATUTORY RAPE

The expression *statutory rape* refers to the sex crime of an older person engaging in an erotic encounter with a child or adolescent who is *under the age of consent,* meaning the age at which an individual is believed to be competent to agree to a sex act. Prior to that age, youngsters are considered ill prepared to judge the likely consequences of their sexual behavior. Therefore, the question of whether young participants in sexual encounters with older people have willingly engaged in erotic acts is irrelevant, because juveniles are deemed incompetent to make that decision. Thus, whether willing or forced, the young are considered victims of statutory rape.

The realm of statutory rape is quite muddled, because age of consent, types of sex acts, and appropriate punishments can differ markedly from one jurisdiction to another. Even the generic term *statutory rape* is not universally used. Other expressions that refer to underage sex include *sexual assault, rape of a child, corruption of a minor, carnal knowledge a juvenile, sexual intercourse with a child, sexual assault of person under the age of consent, first degree rape of a minor, criminal sexual penetration, sexual battery to penetrate a child, sexual offense with a person under age 14, criminal sexual abuse, unlawful sexual intercourse,* and *aggravated child molestation.*

Age-of-consent laws are not descriptions of what eroticism development *could be* or *is,* but rather what legislators and the courts believe eroticism development *should be.* The phrase *age of consent* has been defined differently in different U.S. states, with most states setting it at 16 years old. In other states the age at which consent can be given varies from 14 to 18.

The age difference between the two participants in an erotic act is often a significant issue in determining the penalty for violating an age-of-consent law. Jurisdictions can vary widely in the penalties they assess, with the range extending from an 18-month jail term in New Mexico to a possible death sentence in Oklahoma. In general, the greater the difference in age between the two participants, the greater the blame assigned to the older person and the more severe the punishment. For example, in Georgia the penalty for statutory rape is 10 to 20 years in prison if the offender is age 21 or older, but it is only one year in prison if the victim is age 14 or 15 and the offender is no more than 3 years older. In some states, juveniles of similar age who engage in intercourse are given a light sentence or no jail time at all.

Louisiana law uses age in distinguishing between a felony and a misdemeanor

> Felony carnal knowledge of a juvenile is sexual intercourse with consent between (1) someone age 19 or older and someone between age 12 and 17 or (2) someone age 17 or older and someone between age 12 and 15. The penalty is up to 10 years in prison, with or without hard labor. Misdemeanor carnal knowledge of a juvenile is sexual intercourse with consent between someone age 17 to 19 and someone age 15 to 17 when the difference in their ages is greater than two years. The penalty is up to six months in prison.
>
> In Arkansas, statutory rape consists of engaging in sexual intercourse with someone under age 14 who is at least three years younger than the perpetrator, with the act leading to a prison sentence of 10 to 40 years. However, the crime is called *fourth-degree sexual assault* if someone age 20 or older engages in sexual intercourse with someone under age 16, and the violation is punishable by up to one year in prison. (Norman-Eddy, Reinhart & Martino, 2003)

The eight states that have separate ages of consent for males and females are Montana, Idaho, Iowa, Massachusetts, South Carolina, Utah, and Wyoming. In Wyoming women at age 16 and men at age 18 may legally consent to sex with an adult. In South Carolina, the age of consent for females is 14 and for males is 16. West Virginia provides separate ages of consent for heterosexual and homosexual acts, whereas virtually every other state has one age of consent for both types or ignores age for homosexual acts altogether.

Sometimes age-of-consent laws are written in a manner that renders them difficult to apply. Such was the case when Utah's law—which deems children under age 14 too young to give consent—was used for the arrest of a pregnant 13-year-old girl and her 12-year-old boyfriend. Each of the young teens was charged with *sexual abuse of a child*, so that each was both a perpetrator and victim of the same offense. The girl's attorney wondered, "How can they be old enough to commit an offense if they're not old enough to consent to it?" (Age-of-consent, 2006).

In school settings, statutory rape usually involves a staff member and one or more students. Staff members whose jobs place them in close, informal relationships with students are ones most likely to become involved in sexual liaisons. For instance, a 29-year-old male security guard at an intermediate school in Harlem (New York City) was arrested for statutory rape after engaging in sex more than 20 times with a 12-year-old sixth-grade girl, usually inside the guard's van (Onishi, 1994). A former Wake Forest University football star who was now a 23-year-old teacher/coach at a Chattanooga (Tennessee) private school was charged with seven counts of "statutory rape by an authority figure" (Former private, 2008). A 25-year-old first-year woman teacher who served as Gallatin (Tennessee) High School's softball and volleyball coach was arrested for having sex with a 17-year-old boy in her home on six occasions. Although the liaisons were consensual (the youth voluntarily drove to the coach's home each time), the fact that the coach was an authority figure and was 8 years older than the boy caused her behavior to be judged a misdemeanor (Heatherc, 2007).

Frequently, a sexual escapade between a faculty member and a student is brief. But sometimes the affair can extend over a period of months or years. An instance of a brief liaison is a case involving three sex incidents over a 4-month period. A 37-year-old male social-studies teacher at Columbia High School in East Greenbush (New York) engaged in consensual oral sex with a 16-year-old boy in the social-studies classroom. The teacher was arrested for a felony third-degree criminal sex act and a misdemeanor of endangering the welfare of a child. In addition to teaching, the accused also coached baseball and wrestling (Gardiner, 2007).

A more extensive series of sexual encounters was pursued by a 50-year-old drama coach, who had taught at Jefferson Middle School (Oak Ridge, Tennessee) for 20 years. Between June and September, 2006, he had engaged in sex "almost every day" with a 15-year-old girl who had been his student. A judge sentenced him to a pair of 4-year prison terms on two counts of aggravated statutory rape (Fowler, 2007).

A very long-term sexual relationship—extending from the time a girl was age 14 until she reached 21—involved a 51-year-old male gymnastics coach who initiated the affair when the girl was a Massachusetts middle-school student. Before long, news of the coach's apparent misconduct reached officials of a national gymnastics association that placed his name on a list of banned instructors. When the girl became pregnant at age 17, the coach drove her to an abortion center to have her pregnancy terminated. Their affair then continued until 3 years later when the illicit relationship was exposed publicly and the coach was charged with statutory rape (Ertelt, 2007).

FORCIBLE RAPE

The most frequently quoted definition of *forcible rape* is from the federal government's Universal Crime Reporting (UCR) program, which identifies forcible rape as the carnal knowledge of a person against that person's will, or when a victim is mentally or physically incapable of giving consent. Attempts to commit rape also fall within that definition. In the past, only females could be considered victims of rape, but recently some states have enacted gender-neutral rape statutes that prohibit forced sexual penetration of either sex by any sort of object. Under some definitions, *instruments of forcible compulsion* include substances—alcohol or drugs—administered without a victim's knowledge so as to render the victim physically or mentally incapable of making an informed consent to sexual intercourse.

A typical instance of in-school forcible rape is one from Leesville Road High School in Raleigh (North Carolina), where a 17-year-old boy lured a 14-year-old girl into the boys' locker room after school and attacked her. However, rape in schools has been rare in North Carolina, with only 29 cases reported over the 1993–2003 decade (Lamb, 2003).

Teenagers who rape fellow students can be charged with multiple crimes that can lead to successive jail sentences. For example, three boys—ages 15, 16, and 18—were arrested for dragging a girl into a restroom at Mount Hebron High School in Ellicott City (Maryland) where one boy raped the girl while another held her down and the third served as a lookout to warn the others if anyone was coming. All three offenders were charged with first- and second-degree rape, first- and second-degree sexual offense, conspiracy to commit rape, and conspiracy to commit a sexual offense (Three high school, 2004).

The question of whether a sexual encounter qualifies as forcible rape rather than consensual sex can be a difficult issue for judges to determine. Some help in deciding such cases was provided in 2003 when the California Supreme Court considered the question of whether a girl can withdraw her consent to coitus in the midst of sexual intercourse and thereby change a sex act from seduction to forcible rape. The case concerned a 17-year-old girl who initially agreed to have sex with a 17-year-old schoolmate at a party. However,

> after intercourse had begun, she resisted and told the boy that she had to go home. He repeatedly asked her to "give me some time," but she kept saying, "No, I have to go home." He did not stop until several minutes later. At the subsequent trial, the court found the boy guilty of rape and sentenced him to time at a youth ranch. (Guido, 2003)

As in California, at least five other states' supreme courts have ruled that a youth who fails to stop when consent is removed during coitus can be charged with forcible rape. However, applying the rule fairly can be difficult. For instance, precisely how long after consent is withdrawn may a youth continue with intercourse before he is guilty of rape? And if the girl and boy disagree in a court trial about exactly what occurred, which one should be believed and why?

Sometimes cases of rape are so dramatic that they provide the impetus for legislators to create laws intended to prevent—or at least to reduce—future occurrences. By way of illustration, in 1995 at McCluer North High School in Florissant (Missouri) a freshman girl, while walking from her fifth-period class to her sixth-period class, was forced into a restroom by a 15-year-old male schoolmate who pummeled her severely, raped her, and drowned her by flushing a toilet while holding her head in the water. A classmate later found the girl lying dead on the restroom floor, jammed between the toilet and a wall. Evidence presented at the 15-year-old offender's trial revealed that, on the day before the rape and murder, he had been transferred to McCluer North High from another school. However, McCluer teachers and administrators were not told that the boy had been suspended from his former school for "behavioral problems." Later that year, the Missouri state legislature was prompted by the McCluer rape-and-murder case to pass a Safe Schools Act that required schools to send along a student's discipline record when the student was transferred to a different school. Observers proposed that if the Safe Schools Act had been in effect before the 15-year-old boy enrolled at McCluer North High, the staff at McCluer would have had prior warning of the youth's penchant for violence (Anderson, 1999).

A similar law aimed at warning school personnel of sex offenders was passed by the Washington state legislature in 2006. The statute required sheriffs' offices to notify a school principal when a juvenile sex offender or convicted kidnapper sought to enroll in the principal's school. The law forbade schools from giving parents information about other people's children; only school employees would be notified of a sex offender's joining the school's student population. In the following fashion, a spokeswoman for the state Department of Public Instruction explained the rationale behind the *staff-members-only* provision in the legislation:

> We tried to make it perfectly clear to principals that there are confidentiality laws. It's up to law enforcement [rather than the schools] to inform the public. We're not there to inform parents or other kids, and we're especially not there to create hysteria and negativity, or chaos and the fear factor. (Gutierrez, 2006)

DATE RAPE

One form of abuse that can be a combination of seduction and forcible rape involves a victim's being lulled into complacency by an intoxicant. This is known as *date rape* or *acquaintance rape*. The seduction usually occurs when a couple going out on a date ends up with one member of the pair—almost always the male—forcing unwanted sexual intercourse on the other member. Or *acquaintance rape* can happen at a party where more than one male takes advantage of a female partygoer, often preparing the attack by first weakening the intended victim's ability to resist by plying her with liquor or drugs.

A government survey reported that 96 percent of date rapes are male-on-female, 2 percent male-on-male, 1 percent female-on-male, and 1 percent female-on-female (Larsen, 2005). And a study of 81,247 ninth- and twelfth-grade boys and girls in Minnesota public schools showed that nearly 1 in 10 girls and 1 in 20 boys reported experiencing violence or being raped on a date (Ackard & Neumark-Sztainer, 2001). Another study revealed that one in five Massachusetts teenage girls, from ages 14 to 18, had been physically or sexually abused on a date (Gehrke-White, 2001).

In short, date rape or acquaintance rape is widespread and typically involves alcohol and drugs as perpetrators seek to relax their intended victims' inhibitions by serving them conscience-numbing substances. Younger chronological age, age at first date, and age at first sexual activity have all been shown to increase vulnerability to sexual assault in adolescent girls. Furthermore, youths who have suffered past sexual abuse or sexual victimization appear to be prime candidates for date or acquaintance rape. Adolescents with a history of sexual abuse are five times more likely to report date or acquaintance rape than nonabused peers (Rickert & Weinmann, 2000).

> A 15-year-old girl accepted an orange-juice-and-vodka drink given to her by one of the four young males who had organized a small party at a Grosse Ile (Michigan) apartment. Shortly after finishing the drink, the girl lost consciousness, and the young men placed her on the bathroom floor. Another girl also passed out and was placed on the floor next to her friend. When the two girls had failed to recover by 4:00 a.m., the young men—ages 18–26—took the pair to a hospital, where the first girl died. Vomit had entered her lungs and had stopped her breathing. It was then discovered that one of the men had spiked the girls' drinks with the drug GHB (gamma hydroxybutyrate)—an odorless, colorless liquid often referred to as a "party drug." In response to police questioning, one of the youths admitted that "We thought if we put a little into the drinks, maybe they'll liven up a bit." When the four were indicted and tried in court, the jury found three (two age 18, one age 19) guilty of involuntary manslaughter and poisoning charges. The 26-year-old was found guilty of being an accessory to manslaughter after the fact, poisoning, and possession of GHB. (A deadly trip, 2000; Cohen, 2000)

GHB is one of several substances known as date-rape drugs that are used at an increasing pace to "loosen up" girls who would otherwise be unwilling to engage in sex acts. Drug-use experts usually prefer the expression "drug-facilitated sexual assault" to the term "date-rape drugging." Effects that can result from ingesting GHB include: relaxation, drowsiness, blurred vision, dizziness, nausea, vomiting, sweating, dreamlike feeling, unconsciousness, breathing difficulties, slow heart rate, inability to recall what happened during the drugged state, tremors, seizures, and coma (Date rape drugs, 2005).

Another popular date-rape substance is Rohypnol (flunitrazepam), known on the streets as *roofies, ruffies, roche, R-2, rib,* and *rope*. Rohypnol acts as a very potent tranquilizer, similar to Valium (diazepam) but far stronger. It produces amnesia, muscle relaxation, and a slowing of psychomotor responses. Sedation appears 20 to 30 minutes after administration and lasts for several hours (Staten, 1996).

A third date-rape substance is ketamine (ketamine hydrochloride), a white powder that can cause such reactions as hallucinations, loss of sense of time and identity, distorted vision and hearing, slurred speech, feeling out of control, breathing problems, distorted memory, dreamlike sensations, vomiting, convulsions, loss of coordination, numbness, and violent behavior (Date rape drugs, 2005).

As noted earlier, acquaintance rape does not always involve an encounter between a male and a female:

> A 24-year-old male teacher at Middleboro (Massachusetts) High School was arrested on a dual charge of rape of a child with force and indecent assault and battery. The victim of the attack was a 15-year-old male student. Earlier suspicions that the teacher was engaged in illicit sexual activity were aroused by his habit of chatting with students over the Internet and having them visit him at his apartment. According to the police, the teacher had taken the boy to a hockey game, and after the game he drove to an empty parking lot where he raped the 15-year-old. A police officer said the boy "tried to get out the door, but it was locked, [and then] he tried to fight the teacher, but he could not get him off." (Former Middleboro teacher, 2004)

Constructive steps that schools can take to discourage date rape include:

- Enrolling middle-school and high-school students in social-orientation sessions early in the school year to inform them of the dangers of date rape and of how to avoid being either a victim or perpetrator. Such sessions can profitably include definitions of *consent* and *statutory rape,* of legal penalties for date rape, of the contribution of alcohol and drugs to such violence, and examples of specific cases.
- Providing counseling for girls who have a history of victimization and for boys who are at high risk for sexual aggression.

INTERPRETATIONS

As illustrated in chapter 3, six vantage points that can serve for summarizing the essence of a chapter are those of (a) decision making (by students and school personnel), (b) heredity and environment, (c) *could-be, is,* and *should-be* beliefs, (d) sources of evidence, (e) power and authority, and (f) implications for schools. In these final paragraphs, the six perspectives are used for recapping key points of sexual abuse as it relates to schools.

Decisions. As children approach and pass through puberty, they are obliged to decide what constitutes abusive erotic behavior and under what circumstance—if any—they would engage in such behavior—where, why, when, with whom, and with what potential consequences. Children and teenagers are also often confronted with problems of deciding if, how, and to whom they should report instances of their being abused by others—harassed, bullied, seduced, or raped.

Heredity and environment. Two ways that students' genetic inheritance can affect whether they sexually abuse others are by how their genetic structure establishes (a) the basic strength of their erotic drive at different times during their development and (b) the intellectual ability they need to understand how their abusive acts likely influence their victims' welfare and their own future. Then youths' social environments (peers, parents, teachers, magazines, newspapers, the police, popular music, television, the Internet) define for them what constitutes sexual abuse, the circumstances under which they might abuse others with impunity, and the consequences they might suffer for abusing particular persons under particular conditions. Social environments can also suggest how to respond to abuse the young may suffer.

Could-be, is, and should-be. Youths can receive different advice about *should-be* behavior and abuse from different sources in their environment. Which advice the young trust depends on the frequency with which they encounter the different sources and on which sources they regard as the most authoritative and powerful for affecting their fate.

Implications for schools. Schools are expected to cope with sexual abuse by (a) explaining what constitutes abuse in school and illustrating abuse with examples of forbidden acts, (b) specifying the punishments meted out by the school for different kinds of abuse, (c) establishing procedures for processing reports of infractions, and (d) providing students, parents, and school staff the definitions, illustrative examples, and steps for processing allegations of abuse.

Chapter 6

Eroticism Gone Awry 2—Pregnancy

In this chapter, the expressions *unplanned pregnancy* and *unwelcome pregnancy* refer to teenage girls unintentionally becoming expectant mothers.

ADOLESCENT UNPLANNED PREGNANCY

The following discussion of unintended pregnancy is presented under four headings—(a) frequency and trends, (b) causes, (c) consequences, and (d) responses.

The Frequency and Trends of Unplanned Teen Pregnancy

In 1991, among American girls ages 15 through 19, there were 61.8 births per 1,000 female teenagers. The annual number of births then declined steadily until there were only 40.5 births per 1,000 in 2005, with the decrease attributed to a more consistent use of contraceptives and a higher proportion of adolescents delaying vaginal intercourse until they were older. Almost all—82 percent—of teen pregnancies are unplanned, about one in five of all unintended pregnancies annually. The great majority of the teen pregnancies happen to unwed girls. Throughout the 1991–2005 period, an annual average of 750,000 girls became pregnant—a rate higher than in most other developed countries: two times higher than in England, Wales, and Canada, and eight times higher than in the Netherlands or Japan (Guttmacher Institute, 2006).

The likelihood that teen pregnancy rates would continue to decline was cast in doubt when figures for 2006 were announced by the Centers for Disease Control. According to the CDC report, from 2005 to 2006 the birth rate among younger teens, ages 10–14, declined by 5 percent from 0.7 to 0.6 per 1,000. However, among girls aged 15 through 19, births rose 3 percent (from 40.5 live births per 1,000 in 2005 to 41.9 per 1,000 in 2006). Among girls aged 15–17, the increase was 3 percent and among those aged 18–19 it was 4 percent. The rate for the 18–19 age group (73 births per 1,000) was three times higher than the rate for the 15–17 group (22 per 1,000). So, the older the teen, the more likely she would have an unplanned pregnancy (Ventura, 2007).

Although the trend in unintended motherhood over the past decade and a half was encouraging, the fact remains that unplanned teenage pregnancy is a grave societal and personal problem, one that the nation's schools are compelled to take seriously.

Causes

A number of conditions in adolescents' lives are related to higher rates of pregnancy. Those conditions include poverty, strained family life, single-parent homes, low levels of education, gang-infested neighborhoods, and cultural traditions that make teen pregnancy common. However, those conditions are not the direct causes of high teen pregnancy rates. Instead, they are proxy variables—easily recognized circumstances that tend to be correlated with teen pregnancy. The real causes are the opportunities and beliefs of people who live in circumstances of poverty, stressed families, low levels of education, and cultural traditions.

First, consider opportunities. Low levels of education lead to peoples' employment chances being limited to poor-paying jobs. Often, parents with poor-paying jobs must work long hours, leaving little opportunity to supervise their children after school and at night. This is a particularly serious problem in single-parent families, which most often are single-mother families; unsupervised teenagers are apt to engage in erotic activities that may lead to pregnancy. Furthermore, low levels of education can contribute to parents being ill equipped to offer their children accurate guidance in sexual behavior, such as how best to avoid pregnancy and infection. Poor-paying jobs can also lead to crowded housing conditions that contribute to friction within a family; teens from stressed families are more likely to engage in unsafe sex than are ones from amicable family settings. A study by Dougherty and Kurosaka (1996) led the authors to conclude that girls reared in fatherless homes are more than twice as likely to become teen mothers than are girls whose fathers are present.

> Teens who have been raised by both parents (biological or adoptive) from birth, have lower probabilities of having sex than teens who grew up in any

> other family situation. At age 16, 22 percent of girls from intact families and 44 percent of other girls have had sex at least once. Similarly, teens from intact, two-parent families are less likely to give birth in their teens than are girls from other family backgrounds. (National Campaign, 2006b)

It is also the case that dysfunctional families can offer men opportunities to impregnate adolescent girls. Over 60 percent percent of teenage mothers had been seduced or raped by a man over age 20 who was living in their home (Pryor, 2006).

Next, consider beliefs held by segments of American society that encourage or tolerate teen pregnancy, a result of cultural traditions passed from one generation to the next. Birthrates in the nation's principal ethnic groups seem to reflect such beliefs.

> The Mexican-American teen birthrate is 93 births per every 1,000 girls, compared with 27 births for every 1,000 white girls, 17 births for every 1,000 Asian girls, and 65 births for every 1,000 black girls. To put these numbers into international perspective, Japan's teen birthrate is 3.9, Italy's is 6.9, and France's is 10. (MacDonald, 2006)

Some analysts account for the high incidence of teen births in Latino communities by proposing such causes as "psychological effects and family separation because of immigration, limited access to health care, language and economic barriers, and the process of acculturation and assimilation" (Laureano, 2003). However, observers of Mexican traditions have also claimed that another important contributor to high birthrates among adolescent girls has been a tradition in Mexican culture of emphasizing submissiveness for teenage girls and virility and *machismo* for boys. The trait of machismo is widely seen as featuring sexual promiscuity and the aggressive exploitation of females. However, some defenders of machismo have contended that it can also include a sense of responsibility for the family, trustworthiness, respect, and courtesy (Laureano, 2003).

In present-day African American culture, an *absent-father syndrome* has been cited as contributing to a high incidence of pregnancy and unwed motherhood among black teens. Nearly 70 percent of all black children are born to single mothers, more than twice the national average and almost triple the rate of whites. At least 48 percent of all black children live without their fathers, which is double the rate of any other American ethnic group (Tucker, 2006). Controversy continues over the likely causes of the absence of fathers in so many black families. Some critics blame a widespread attitude of self-indulgent irresponsibility among black males—an attitude that requires nothing from men for child care. However, other observers blame high unemployment rates and poor-paying jobs among blacks (twice the rates among whites), so that black men hesitate to take on the burden of supporting a family. In addition, a high incidence of imprisonment (half of the nation's prison and jail inmates are blacks) means that many black males are unable to be with the women whose children they fathered.

A further influence that has increased the ranks of unwed mothers has been the attitude about sexual freedom and formal marriage among virtually all ethnic groups since the "cultural revolution" of the 1960s. Today there is a far higher rate of couples cohabiting without the benefit—or burden—of marriage than was true before the mid-20th century.

Not only does teenage motherhood yield immediate damaging consequences for pregnant girls, but it also results in low-level education, poverty, and family stress for young mothers, even those who did not come from poverty backgrounds. The daughters of teen mothers will more likely become pregnant during their own adolescence than will daughters from traditional intact families. In effect, teenage pregnancy tends to perpetuate itself from one generation to the next.

> Almost one-half of all teenage mothers and over three-quarters of unmarried teen mothers began receiving welfare within five years of the birth of their first child. The growth in single-parent families remains the single most important reason for increased poverty among children. . . . Out-of-wedlock childbearing (as opposed to divorce) is currently the driving force behind the growth in the number of single parents, and half of first out-of-wedlock births are to teens. (National Campaign, 2006a)

In summary, multiple factors have coalesced to produce America's current high levels of teen pregnancy and unwed mothers.

Consequences

Teenage pregnancy yields consequences for a variety of individuals and social institutions, including pregnant girls, the males who impregnated them, the teenagers' children, teenagers' parents, the schools, and taxpayers.

Pregnant Girls

In a report titled *When Children Have Children*, the American Academy of Child and Adolescent Psychiatry listed a variety of consequences experienced by teen mothers:

> Some may not want their babies.
> Some may want them for idealized and unrealistic ways.

Others may view the creation of a child as an achievement and not recognize the serious responsibilities.
Some may keep a child to please another family member.
Some may want a baby to have someone to love but not recognize the amount of care the baby needs.
Some become overwhelmed by guilt, anxiety, and fears about the future.
Depression is common among pregnant teens.
Many do not anticipate that their adorable baby can also be demanding and sometimes irritating. (American Academy, 2004)

Teen mothers who discover that taking care of an infant can be very difficult often express distress at their plight. As one typical adolescent mother complained,

> What troubles me is when another girl finds out that I have a daughter and she says "That is so neat." A car is neat, an outfit is neat, a baby is not. They take a lot of time and work. When you become a mom, you become responsible (physically, emotionally, and financially) for a child for the rest of your life. There are no weekends or summer vacations; the child will always be there. And no matter how good your relationship was before you became pregnant, the father will most likely have gone on his merry way. If I had been better informed, I would have never had sex in the first place, let alone a child. (National Campaign, 2007)

The experience of teenage pregnancy can also prompt young mothers to offer advice to girls who may contemplate having vaginal intercourse without adopting ways to protect themselves from pregnancy. Consider, for example, this segment of a letter sent to an adolescent girl by a young woman who had borne a child while she was still in high school.

> At age sixteen, I became pregnant. Before my pregnancy, I was a cheerleader and involved with many school clubs. I had many friends and was enjoying my teenage years. I now ask myself, "What happened to me? Where did I go wrong?" Why was I now standing in line at the welfare office waiting for food stamps? Maybe because I was involved with a guy who was three years older than myself. My parents had forbid me to stay in the abusive relationship. My answer to stay with this guy was to become pregnant. I will never forget the tears that my mother shed when my stepfather told her the news. That night, I left my home, my teenage years, and never went back. . . . [A while later,] I finally reached the lowest point in my life. There I was lying in a bed at a shelter for battered women. In the past, I would always leave the relationship [with the baby's father], but always return. That same night, I prayed for the strength and courage to get myself back on my feet. That was also the night that I left him and never went back. Even though my life seems to be going well now, there are emotional scars that I will carry with me each and every day of my life. There is not a day that goes by that I do

> not think about my past mistakes. This letter is not in any way intended to prove how teen mothers can succeed, but rather to prove how one mistake can change the rest of your life! Enjoy your teen years! I never went to my prom; I never got to cheer at homecoming; I never went on my senior cruise; I never went off to college. These things I will never have the opportunity to do again, but you will. Please, think twice before you change the rest of your life! (National Campaign, 2007)

Consequences for girls can include health dangers. Pregnant teens who fail to receive proper medical care can risk fetal death, high blood pressure, anemia, labor and delivery complications (such as premature labor and stillbirth), and a low birth-weight infant. The earlier in the pregnancy that the expectant mother comes under the care of a physician, the better her chances to avoid sickness and to produce a healthy infant (Homeier, 2005).

Becoming a mother during adolescence also reduces girls' chances to further their education. Only one third of teen mothers receive a high-school diploma, and only 1.5 percent have a college degree by the time they reach age 30.

Some critics of unwed teenage girls' bearing children have charged that such behavior is an outcome of irrational decision making in which girls fail to analyze the consequences of their act. Such a charge has been leveled particularly against black teens, because nearly 70 percent of recent births among African Americans have been to single mothers. However, other observers have argued that, for many poor black girls, teen pregnancy makes good sense.

Why is unwed teen pregnancy a rational choice?

> (1) For teens raised in poor areas, with lousy food and lousy medical care, their health will probably peak at around ages 17–19. That makes the teenage years a much better time to give birth than later years. Among poor black girls and women, the infant mortality rate is twice as high among those who wait until their 20s to give birth as it is for those who give birth in their teens.
>
> (2) For those who will be relying on an extended family of older female relatives to help with childcare and support, it makes sense to give birth when mothers, aunts, and older cousins are younger and more able to offer assistance. Furthermore, grandmothers may feel more obligated to offer extensive aid to their 16-year-old pregnant daughter than to their 26-year-old pregnant daughter.
>
> (3) For middle-class whites, the opportunity costs (aka "what you give up") of early childbirth are enormous; college and early career-building are made much harder by a baby or two in tow. Furthermore, the odds of eventually getting married and having a healthy child in wedlock are very good for middle-class teens who wait until they're women to marry and have

> children. For poor teens of color, in contrast, the opportunity costs of early childbirth are much lower. Poor teens can see that their odds of affording a good college followed by a high-paying, high-status career are low. And for poor black girls, the odds of finding someone suitable to marry during peak childbearing years—or even during their 20s—are much lower. So overall, poor girls of color have much less reason to delay childbearing. (Ampersand, 2005)

Males Who Impregnate Teenage Girls

Two thirds of the babies born to teenage mothers are fathered by adult men, while the remaining one third of fathers are adolescent boys who usually are older than the girls (Teen father services, 2008). Males charged with fathering an infant can respond in different ways: (a) deny the parentage, (b) avoid taking any responsibility for the infant or the young mother, (c) offer to marry the girl, or (d) avoid marrying the girl but take some fatherly responsibility for the infant.

Denying parentage. Particularly in cases that involve girls who are suspected of having had recent sexual relations with more than one male, the male whom the girl identifies as responsible for her pregnancy may contest her charge. Either the girl or the male can then seek to expose the truth by means of DNA (deoxyribonucleic acid) analysis or blood-type matching conducted by laboratory technicians. Matching the father's blood type with the infant's and mother's types is the cheaper and simpler method, but it only tells if the male *might* be the father. If the blood types fail to match, the male could not possibly be the father. But if the blood types do match, it means that this male *might* be the father, and a DNA test is needed to settle the matter for sure. Each individual has a distinctive DNA pattern in his or her body cells. Thus, an infant's DNA pattern will reveal an unmistakable combination of the mother's and father's patterns, thereby identifying who the two parents were. By 2006, the cost of blood tests and DNA tests ranged from $450 to $2,500, so which tests—if any—a pregnant girl or an accused male would choose depends partially on their financial resources (A guy's perspective, 2006; Hardcastle, 2008).

Avoid any responsibility. Men or boys who have impregnated teenage girls may attempt to wash their hands of the whole affair, assuming no responsibility for the care of the child, even though they are legally liable for the child's support. Such fathers are often referred to as *deadbeat dads.* In some cases, they may send money to help finance their child's upbringing, but they have little or no contact with the child. The children of such fathers are at increased risk of becoming personally distressed, socially delinquent, and academically unsuccessful.

Assume responsibility. Whether they wed the girl or cohabit without marrying, fathers who assume their parental role are, on the average, positive forces in children's lives. When teenage or adult fathers participate in parenting programs, their children show (a) positive development of their gender roles, (b) more constructive social adjustment, (c) improved cognitive development, and (d) greater school success (A resource guide, 2008).

Teenagers' Children

Difficulties suffered by infants of teenage mothers include premature birth and low birth weight accompanied by physical disabilities, including brain damage. Such problems are more likely to occur when young mothers fail to receive professional prenatal care early in the pregnancy as a result of delaying pregnancy testing, denying the pregnancy, or fearing to tell others about it. The chance that an infant will be born with physical disorders is greater if the mother uses tobacco, alcohol, or drugs during pregnancy. After infants are born, their development may be impaired by their young mother's neglect, irritability, impatience, or lack of knowledge about how best to care for a child (Weiss, 2008).

Teenagers' Parents

When it becomes apparent that a girl is pregnant, or when she gives birth, her parents are typically distressed. They often imagine that their acquaintances will consider them ineffective parents, and they foresee a bleak future for their daughter. Because pregnant girls usually continue to live at home, their parents find their newborn grandchild a costly, time-consuming burden that they are obliged to bear.

The unplanned birth of a child who has been fathered by a teenage boy can also yield consequences for the boy's parents if they admit to their son's fatherhood and accept responsibility—at least partial—for the financial and emotional support of the child.

Schools

Teen pregnancies can yield financial, curriculum, staff, and student-services consequences for schools.

Public schools typically receive support funds from the state based on the number of students who daily attend class. Thus, when girls either drop out of school or are absent because of their pregnancy, the school loses the funds represented by the missed days.

In recent years, an increasing number of pregnant students have continued to attend high school rather than dropping out. Therefore, schools have felt obliged to add new material to the curriculum—information about ways to prevent unplanned pregnancy, about prenatal care for expectant mothers, and about wise child-rearing practices.

As more pregnant girls attend classes, school officials need to introduce policies governing the treatment of such students. In addition, staff members (teachers, coaches, secretaries, counselors) need training in how to cope with the conditions of pregnant girls (limitations on physical activity, likely mood changes, prescribed medications, noxious substances to avoid, potential miscarriage).

Taxpayers

Because nearly 80 percent of unwed teen mothers end up on welfare, taxpayers must foot the costs of supporting the majority of teen mothers and their offspring (National Campaign, 2006b).

Responses

The kinds of people whose reactions to teen pregnancy are significant include the pregnant girls themselves, their parents, their peers, and school personnel.

Pregnant Girls

Girls react in various ways to news that they are pregnant. Most are apparently shocked, distressed, and despondent as they speculate about their future and the need to decide what to do about the prospective birth. However, other expectant teen mothers are pleased.

> Studies of pregnant teenagers have shown that they may be motivated by hopes of achieving adult status, prestige or autonomy through pregnancy, by a desire to demonstrate love or commitment to a partner, and/or by the wish to replace a real or threatened loss of a significant person. [Girls from lower socioeconomic families are apt to see] having a child as the best way to find love and support and make a commitment to the future. (Adler & Tschann, 1993)

Teen girls' three choices for resolving their pregnant condition are (a) to have an abortion, (b) to bear and raise the infant, or (c) to bear the baby, then put the baby out for adoption.

The abortion option. Abortion involves the unborn fetus being removed from the pregnant teen's womb before the fetus could survive birth. Nearly one third of teenage pregnancies end in abortion (Guttmacher Institute, 2006). Abortions either occur spontaneously or are induced surgically or by medication.

Spontaneous abortion—referred to as *miscarriage*—is the loss of a pregnancy without outside intervention; it occurs in up to 20 percent of confirmed pregnancies, usually within the first 12 weeks of pregnancy. The causes of miscarriage are not entirely clear, but some may be due—at least in part—to a poor match of the genetic components (sperm and egg) at the time of conception, to the pregnant teen's heavy use of harmful substances (alcohol, tobacco, drugs), or to serious infections during pregnancy. Once a miscarriage has started, little can be done to stop it (Miscarriage, 2006).

Induced abortion involves someone—usually a physician—removing the fetus from the pregnant teen's womb by surgery or by administering a medication in pill form—such a medication as mifepristone or methotrexate taken together with a third pill, misoprostol. The pills successfully empty a girl's uterus of the embryo in about 96 percent of the cases (What is medical, 2008).

Three common surgical procedures are (a) *suction curettage* (vacuum aspiration technique) that involves expanding the cervix with special instruments, inserting a tube connected to a strong vacuum motor, and extracting the embryo by suction (99 percent effective); (b) *dilation and curettage* that consists of dilating the cervix and inserting a sharp-loop instrument into the uterus to scrape the uterus walls, then removing the lining and embryo by suction; and (c) *dilation and evacuation* that involves widening the cervix with material made from seaweed (*laminaria*), then removing the fetus with forceps (First trimester, 2008).

Which abortion method—medical or surgical—will be most suitable depends on several conditions, including how long the girl has been pregnant, the girl's preference, her health status, and whether the fetus would likely be born with serious defects.

As a guide to which abortion technique will be preferable, the 9-month period between conception and birth is divided into three 3-month periods called *trimesters*. The safest time for a girl to have an abortion is during the first trimester when the abortion will usually be performed medicinally. Surgery is rarely used during the first two months of pregnancy because the embryo or fetus is so small. Near the end of the first trimester (after 9 weeks), surgery becomes the safer option because medications do not work well after that time. About 90 percent of abortions occur during the first trimester, whereas 9 percent are performed during the second trimester (months 4 through 6).

During the third trimester (months 7 through 9), the fetus is considered to be *viable*, that is, likely to be an alive infant if born during that period. In virtually all of the nation's states, third-trimester abortion is illegal unless an infant's birth would threaten the mother's life or the infant would be born with extreme deformities.

In our discussion so far, we have been focusing on abortions performed by well-trained medical personnel working under sanitary conditions with proper equipment. But some abortions are performed by incompetents under frightful conditions. Such is the case when a teenager tries to terminate her own pregnancy by inserting a knife or wire coat hanger into her uterus to scrape out the embryo or fetus, with her clumsy attempt breaking the uterus wall and setting off an infection. Or a *quack abortionist* conducts a clandestine business of ending the pregnancy of teenage girls as a profit-making venture in the bacteria-infested back room of a sleazy hotel. Or an untrained, unregistered midwife operates in the bathroom of her home to rid girls of the fetus they carry. Abortions conducted by such people under such conditions can easily result in serious physical and emotional damage to adolescent girls.

In recent years, teen abortions have been legal in all states except South Dakota. Twenty of the other 49 states and District of Columbia require the permission of one or both parents or an adult relative for adolescents under age 18 to have an abortion. However, nearly of those states allow for *judicial bypass*, which means that a judge can set aside the permission requirement if a girl appears sufficiently mature to make a responsible abortion decision on her own. The remaining 30 states do not require the permission of a girl's parents, but 13 of them stipulate that parents must be told before the abortion takes place unless a judge removes that requirement through judicial bypass. (Teen abortion laws, 2008)

Many of the teens who have had an abortion are apparently pleased with their decisions, for it has allowed them to continue with their lives unencumbered with rearing a child during their adolescent years. But other girls regret their decision as they later envision what they imagine would have been a happy state of motherhood.

> When I was 16, I had an abortion. It has been only five months since then. I was messing around with someone much older than me, always thinking that it was not going to happen to me. However, it did; and it felt like a ton of bricks hitting you in the face. To look down at your pregnancy test saying positive, saying you have a baby on the way. I looked for the easy way . . . abortion. It was the only way to keep it from my parents and not let my friends know about it. So the guy and I went for the abortion. At first I was happy. I no longer had worries or responsibilities, but that changed.
>
> Now I look around my school, and I see girls younger than me carrying a child. Why couldn't I do it? Their life is no different than mine. I could have raised a child. To think that I could have been a mom . . . have a little girl in my arms . . . to know that I brought her into this world. But, no, I did the opposite. . . . I took her out because I chose the easy way out. (Brianne, 2008)

The adoption choice. If a pregnant teen wishes to deliver the baby yet be freed of responsibility for raising the child, she can do so by placing the newborn out for adoption. She does this by signing consent papers that permit the infant to be adopted by adults who will become the child's parents. If the male who fathered the infant is known and admits to being the father, he also must sign the consent forms. Adoption may be arranged through an agency or, in some states, arranged independently between the birth mother and the adoptive parents, so long as the prospective parents and their home setting are approved by a court and by the state agency that oversees adoptions.

There are three varieties of adoption—open, closed, and semi-open. In open adoption, the teen mother and the people who accept the baby (adoptive parents) may meet and share names and addresses. In a closed adoption, the birth mother and the adoptive parents do not meet or know each others' names. In a semi-open adoption, the adoption agency provides the birth mother information about the baby from the adoptive parents and vice versa, but there is no direct contact between the birth mother and the infant (Pregnancy choices, 2005).

A teenager's putting her infant up for adoption is not without potential problems. After the adoption has been finalized, the birth mother may change her mind and wish to have the child back—a change of mind that may be immediate or may occur only months or years later. Or, in a closed adoption, the birth mother or father may seek the names and locations of the adoptive family in an attempt to establish a relationship with the child. Furthermore, the adoptive parents may wish to return an adopted child who turns out to have a physical or psychological disorder that they find very time consuming and expensive. And rather frequently, adopted children, as they grow older, try to discover who their birth parents were and attempt to contact them.

Teenagers' Parents

Parents respond in various ways to their daughter's pregnancy. Many, upon learning of the pregnancy, angrily berate the girl, telling her what a disgrace she has been to the family and predicting that she will suffer a disastrous future. They may order her to get an abortion. Some order her out of the house. Others demand that she marry the fellow who fathered the child. However, after weathering the initial shock of the unwelcome pregnancy, parents often cherish the newborn and assume a constructive role in the child's development.

Parents' reactions are often conditioned by the cultural traditions of the subgroup of society with which they are associated. Thus, the typical response of wealthy suburban parents can differ from the response of parents living in an inner-city ghetto whose residents are chiefly immigrant families that frequently include unmarried pregnant teens. Likewise, the religious affiliation of a family can affect the parents' response to unplanned pregnancy, with some parents more harshly condemning their daughter's condition than do others. Religious convictions are particularly influential in decisions about whether or not the girl should have an abortion. Abortion is more readily approved in families that subscribe to a woman's right-to-choose philosophy than in families dedicated to a child's right-to-life position.

Teenagers' Peers

Becoming pregnant can be expected to alter a girl's relationships with her schoolmates as her new status forces her to forgo former activities and social connections. Events in which she had participated earlier are no longer open to her—cheerleading, acrobatic dancing, softball, basketball, high jumping. Boys who had taken her to parties, hip-hop concerts, and dances are no longer interested. Former friends who now feel that the unplanned pregnancy has tainted the girl's reputation begin to avoid her.

After she bears her child, the girl's alienation from former friends increases as she must give so much attention to her newborn, and her fate as a mother provides an object lesson for her peers.

> My friend just became a mom. She has no time for anything else. She comes to school looking so tired and run down. She leaves at lunch to go feed her baby. Sure, babies are cute but they are so much work. I know that now, and I am more careful about using protection when I have sex. (National campaign, 2007)

Schools

Ways that schools have responded to teen pregnancy have included (a) expanding sex-education programs, (b) establishing special schools, and (c) offering daycare services linked to classes on child-rearing skills.

Expanded sex education. As mentioned earlier, the federal government since 1996 has offered schools funds for conducting sex education that exclusively teaches abstinence from sexual acts, thereby leaving students uninformed about other methods of avoiding pregnancy and sexually transmitted diseases. However, an increasing body of research evidence has shown that abstinence-only programs fail to deter youths from oral and vaginal sex before marriage. Consequently, a growing number of schools have forgone the federal dollars and introduced programs that furnish students with information about other means of protecting themselves from unwanted consequences of sexual behavior. (Chapter 9 describes such programs in considerable detail.)

Establishing special schools. Before 1960, school systems typically responded to teenage pregnancy by expelling young expectant mothers or putting them on medical suspension and, if the girls wished to return to school after they had an abortion or gave birth, they were often required to enroll in a different school than the one they had been attending. In New York City—which has had as many as 7,000 pregnant adolescents annually—hundreds of pregnant girls were transferred to social-service shelters where the board of education provided schooling. Then, as the number of teen pregnancies increased during the 1960s' sexual revolution among youths, cities began establishing special schools for pregnant students—four schools in New York City, five in Los Angeles, several in Chicago, and one in each of such smaller cities as Denver and Milwaukee.

From the outset, pregnancy schools were controversial and, as the years advanced, the controversy grew. Advocates of congregating pregnant girls in the special schools said that staff members were specialists in ways of teaching expectant mothers and meeting their physical and emotional needs. In addition, the students were with schoolmates whose life conditions were much the same as their own, so they could understand and support each other. Furthermore, the pregnant girls were not subject to the gibes and social rejection of unsympathetic students in regular high schools. Proponents bolstered this favorable view of special schools with such statistics as those from Milwaukee's Lady Pitts School where, in 2003, "56 out of the 60 students who were eligible to graduate received their diplomas—a rate that far exceeds that at most Milwaukee high schools—[and] only 10 percent of Lady Pitts students get pregnant a second time, less than half the national average" (Pardini, 2003). In 2001, the continuing need for such schools was suggested by a survey that revealed there apparently were more than 20,000 mothers in New York City under age 21 who had yet to finish high school, but there were only 500 spaces in the four special schools for pregnant and parenting teens (Fertig, 2004).

However, critics argued that most pregnancy schools had appalling records of attendance and academic progress. In one New York school in 2004, around 40 to 50 students were eligible to take the statewide exams for graduation, but only one passed the global-studies test and just two passed the English exam (Fertig, 2004). By 2006, the city's pregnancy schools had a daily attendance rate of 47 percent, well below the city average. The typical pregnant student earned only 4 or 5 credits each year, less than half the 11 units available. Upon leaving the pregnancy school, fewer than 50 percent of the students made a satisfactory transition back to a regular high school (Bosman, 2007).

The special schools were also criticized for segregating pregnant girls, separating them from their nonpregnant peers rather than providing facilities to accommodate them within regular middle schools and high schools. In addition, some critics complained that providing special school facilities gave the impression that the school system approved of unwed pregnancy and motherhood. Schools then attempted to combat that impression by curbing practices that glamorize teen pregnancy. As the principal of Milwaukee's Lady Pitts facility explained,

> The school walks a fine line between being supportive of pregnant teens and celebrating the fact that they are giving birth. Although volunteers provide each newborn with a basic layette, the staff avoids activities that might be viewed by teen parents as celebrating, or even condoning, pregnancy. That means there are no baby showers for pregnant teens, public address announcements at school when someone delivers a baby, or visits to hospital maternity wards. . . . Members of a local sorority who last year held a baby shower at the school [were asked, instead, to] sponsor a career day this year. We don't want to reinforce the notion that these girls are special because they are pregnant. (Pardini, 2003)

The enthusiasm for pregnancy schools, generated by increasing rates of teen motherhood from the late 1960s through the 1980s, began to dwindle as rates regularly dropped from 1991 through 2005. In Los Angeles during 2006, declining enrollments led officials to shut down one school and reduce the personnel of another from 19 to 16. In New York City, all four pregnancy schools were eliminated in 2007 as pregnant teens and unwed mothers would henceforth receive assistance in regular schools that maintained parenting classes and daycare facilities for the infants and toddlers of student mothers (Bosman, 2007).

Daycare centers. The numbers of daycare facilities in high schools has increased over the past three decades, so that today there are hundreds of such facilities across the nation. The typical four-part intent of centers is to (a) enable teen parents to continue their high-school education, (b) provide health care and a safe environment and guidance for children, (c) train parents in sound child-rearing practices, and (d) offer parents health care and job-preparation training.

In the typical childcare center, teenage mothers and fathers are not only obligated to enroll in parenting classes, but they are also required to spend time in the childcare facility, observing their child's interactions with others, and practicing constructive child-raising methods—changing diapers, resolving disputes over toys, preparing healthful meals, and talking with children in a fashion suited to children's levels of understanding.

School-based centers vary in the number of children they can accommodate. For example, in Yakima (Washington) the facility at Davis High School supports 11 at a time, whereas the center at Stanton Alternative School can serve 28 (12 infants and 16 toddlers). In both schools, teen mothers and fathers are required to enroll in a parenting class, which one 16-year-old ninth-grade mother said is "really a big plus. It teaches you what to do." Parents are also obliged to abide by three rules—check their child into the daycare before school, eat lunch with their child in the daycare center, and wait until after school to pick up their child so they will not be parading their offspring around campus in a way that could promote teen pregnancy (Joyce, 2008).

The ages of children accepted in childcare centers can differ from one program to another. The facility at Red Lake High School, adjacent to the Red Lake Indian Reservation in northern Minnesota, accepts children between the ages of 6 months and 2½ years (*Teen Parents*, 2008). The childcare program at Options High School in Bellingham (Washington) includes infants aged 1 month to 18 months (Karcher, 2008).

Course offerings for pregnant girls and teen parents typically combine regular high-school classes with classes designed to fill young parents' special needs. The following is a list of available courses at Bellingham's Options High School:

Child Health, Safety, and Nutrition
Global Science
Child Development Theory
Human Science Survey
Basics in Child Care
Applied Math
Project-based Learning
Speech
Parenting
Biology 1 and 2
Surviving on Your Own
Environmental Science Survey
Health
English 1–7
Fine Arts
U.S. History 1 and 2
Physical Education
Self-Directed Study
World History 1 and 2
Math Skills Contact
Washington/World Geography
Nova Net Computer Classes
Independent Reading
Citizenship (Karcher, 2008)

Providing daycare for children of teens can be the source of controversy. Members of the public in some communities charge that daycare is not only expensive, but it also coddles adolescents who have misbehaved by bearing children and it encourages other teens to follow suit. However, daycare personnel, such as those in charge of the center at Rock Island High School (Iowa), say such facilities can discourage some students from engaging in unprotected sex. For instance, after the center's director heard that a girl had been telling her friends that she wanted a baby, the director invited the girl to spend time at the daycare facility, an experience that caused the girl to change her mind about wanting a baby of her own (Luna, 2007).

How successful, then, are high-school programs that include daycare centers? Although the dropout rate of teen parents is usually high, proponents of in-school childcare facilities claim that

- Teenage parents whose children attend [a daycare] facility are more likely to complete their education and less likely to become dependent on welfare.
- Schools benefit through lower dropout rates, improved parent education programs, vocational training for students, and increased performance from faculty who enroll their children in the facility.
- Communities profit from having a lower number of welfare participants and a more efficient use of public funds.
- The children involved benefit from a high-quality preschool education. (Muir, 2004)

Researchers who studied an urban high school's childcare center that catered to low-income teen parents concluded that "participating students showed improvement in overall grade point average. All students graduated or were promoted to the next grade. No participants experienced repeat pregnancies. Most children were current on immunizations and healthcare" (Williams & Sadler, 2001).

Summary

Beginning in the 1960s, rates of teenage pregnancy increased, thereby stimulating school officials to introduce sex-education classes, pregnancy schools, and programs that included daycare centers for teen parents. However, from 1991 through 2005, pregnancy rates regularly decreased, reducing the need for special pregnancy schools. During the same period, critics charged that segregating pregnant girls and young mothers in special schools was unjust, and the special schools began to close. By 2008 the most popular way to accommodate the needs of teens who were pregnant or were parents was to furnish special services and parenting classes within regular high schools, services that often included childcare facilities. In addition, more schools were rejecting the federal-government-financed abstinence-only sex-education program in favor of a broader variety of sex education that included information about ways to avoid pregnancy other than by abstinence.

INTERPRETATIONS

As in chapters 3 and 5, vantage points that can serve for summarizing the essence of pregnancy issues in chapter 6 are those of (a) decision making by students and school personnel, (b) heredity and environment, (c) *could-be, is,* and *should-be* beliefs, (d) sources of evidence, (e) power and authority, and (f) implications for schools.

Decisions. Postpuberal students must decide whether they will engage in vaginal intercourse and, if so, whether they will practice methods that prevent pregnancy. If girls do become pregnant, they need to decide whether to continue going to school, what their relationships will be with their peers, and what to do about the expected birth (abort, bear and raise the infant, put the baby up for adoption). They also need to decide what prenatal care they will seek and from whom they will seek it. If a girl does plan to raise her child, she must decide whether to continue in school, how to care for the infant, and what relationship she wants the child to have with the father. Males who father adolescent girls' babies face decisions about whether they will admit to being the father, whether they will marry the mother, and what emotional and material support they will provide for mother and child. School personnel (board members, administrators, teachers, counselors) are obligated to (a) decide how they will treat students who are pregnant and ones who become parents and (b) offer rationales in support of such treatment.

Heredity and environment. Students' genetic inheritance affects matters of pregnancy by establishing a time range within which a girl produces mature ova and a boy produces mature sperm that could result in pregnancy. Genetic inheritance also influences the intensity of a young person's sex drive at successive stages of development. Then environmental factors affect where within an inherited time range and drive-intensity range the individual's development actually occurs. Such environmental factors include diet, exercise, illness, family composition, family culture, religious convictions, portrayals on television and the Internet of youths' sex lives, and peers' beliefs about teen pregnancy.

Could-be, is, and should-be. Girls' erotic behavior is often influenced by their knowledge about the conditions under which they could become pregnant. Boys' erotic activities may be affected by their beliefs about the conditions under which they could impregnate a girl. Both girls' and boys' sex behavior is also influenced by their beliefs about whether they should engage in vaginal intercourse and whether they should bear children.

Sources of evidence. Students vary in the sources of information about pregnancy and teen parenthood that they access and trust. Especially in their prepuberal years, children's beliefs about sexual behavior and pregnancy are strongly affected by their parents' opinions and the model that their parents' own sexual behavior offers. Parental influence usually continues into adolescence but is often modified or replaced by the opinions of peers and by displays in the mass media—television, movies, videos, magazines, and the Internet.

Authority and power. Certain institutions within a society enjoy official authority that puts them in a stronger position than others for affecting students' beliefs and behavior relating to pregnancy. The church is one such institution. The society's justice system (laws, the police, the courts, juvenile detention centers, prisons) is a second authoritative institution. The school is a third. The school's power and control are illustrated in the instruction it provides in sex-education classes. As noted earlier in this chapter, critics of federal-government-funded abstinence-only sex education have charged that at least some cases of unplanned pregnancy among students who participated in such classes would not have occurred if the students had been taught ways to avoid pregnancy other than abstinence. Schools' authoritative power to affect students' beliefs and actions is also reflected in rules schools establish about eroticism and in the sanctions applied to students and staff members who fail to abide by the rules.

Implications for schools. School authorities are wise to issue public policies (a) about how pregnant students, young mothers, and young fathers will be treated by the school and (b) about those students' rights, opportunities, and responsibilities. As part of the implementation of the policies, in-service-education sessions can be conducted for school personnel, focusing on the kinds of problems that can arise with pregnant girls, with the boys responsible for the pregnancies, with parents of those girls and boys, with other students who may harass their pregnant schoolmates, and with young mothers and fathers who continue attending school.

Chapter 7

Eroticism Gone Awry 3—Infection

The expressions *sexually transmitted diseases, sexually acquired infections,* and *venereal diseases* are alternative labels for illnesses contracted during erotic encounters. Every year 3 million American teens—about 1 in 4 sexually active youths—acquire one or more of those infections. Therefore, sexually transmitted diseases (STDs) are of serious concern to school personnel because STDs so tragically debilitate students and threaten the health of schoolmates who engage in sexual liaisons with their infected peers.

Among two dozen types of infection that qualify as STDs, not even one is the result of heredity. None are caused by a person's genetic structure that was formed when the father's sperm merged with the mother's ovum at the time of conception. So, because all STDs—by definition—are acquired from sexual contact with a person who has the disease, all STDs are preventable. It is true that some infants already suffer from an STD at the time they are born. However, those infants did not inherit the disorder genetically. Instead, they acquired the infection from the intrauterine environment provided by their mother while she was infected by the STD during her pregnancy or while the baby was being born.

The purpose of this chapter is to identify the most common types of sexually acquired infections, their frequency among teens, their characteristics, how they are acquired, and how they can be treated.

COMMON STDS AMONG TEENS

From among the diverse disorders that qualify as sexual infections, the ones most frequently incurred by American children and adolescents are described in this chapter—*chlamydia, gonorrhea, pelvic inflammatory disease, syphilis, HIV/AIDS, genital herpes, genital warts, hepatitis B, pubic lice,* and *trichomoniasis.*

Chlamydia

Chlamydia (pronounced *kluh-mid-ee-uh*) is caused by the bacteria *Chlamydia trachomatis,* which are passed from an infected person to a partner during vaginal intercourse and possibly during oral or anal sex. Contrary to a popular myth, chlamydia cannot be caught from a towel, doorknob, or toilet seat. Because there often are no obvious symptoms, students may be suffering from chlamydia without realizing it.

> If someone touches bodily fluids that contain the bacteria and then touches his or her eye, a chlamydial eye infection is possible. Chlamydia also can be passed from a mother to her baby while the baby is being delivered. This can cause pneumonia and conjunctivitis, which can become very serious for the baby if it's not treated. (Van Vranken, 2006a)

The incidence of chlamydia in the United States reached a record high in 2007—over 1 million cases. The disease is more frequent among teens aged 15–19 than in any other age group (One million, 2007). During 2003, the known extent of chlamydia had risen by 12 percent in the state of Washington, with nearly three quarters of the infected people between the ages of 15 and 24. Health officials responded by recommending that sexually active women under age 25 be tested for the disease at least once a year (Centers for Disease Control, 2004).

Although chlamydia is found in all ethnic groups, the highest frequency is among black women, whose infection rates are double those of Hispanics and more than seven times higher than that of whites.

Ignorance about chlamydia is widespread. One survey reported that when participants were asked to name the sexually transmitted diseases they had heard about, only 34 percent percent of women and 22 percent of men included chlamydia.

Chlamydia infection can be diagnosed by either a urine test or a swab test that involves a health worker swabbing the vagina or penis for bacteria secretions. But the task of identifying and curing the malady is difficult because many people (three quarters of infected females) display no symptoms. Thus, infected persons can unwittingly suffer harm and pass the infection on to their sexual partners. Symptoms that can appear in girls include swelling and soreness of the urethra (where urine comes out) and the cervix. Other signs are a yellowish discharge from the vagina, bleeding after intercourse, spot bleeding in between menstrual cycles, and pelvic pain. The younger a girl is, the more vulnerable her cervix is to infection. Chlamydia may also lead to pelvic inflammatory disease (PID), which damages the uterus, ovaries, and fallopian tubes and thereby can cause infertility or tubal pregnancies in later years. Symptoms in boys can include a yellowish discharge from the penis while urinating, painful swelling of the testes, and inflammation of the epididymis (a tube for transporting sperm from a testicle during intercourse). The disease can be treated with antibiotics, which usually will entirely cure the infection within a period of 7 to 10 days.

Physicians warn teenagers that

> Anyone with whom you've had sex will also need to be tested and treated for chlamydia because that person may be infected but not have any symptoms. This includes any sexual partners in the last 2 months or your last sexual partner if it has been more than 2 months since your last sexual experience. It is very important that someone with a chlamydia infection abstain from having sex until they and their partner have been treated. . . . You can become infected with chlamydia again even after you have been treated because having chlamydia does not make you immune to it. (Van Vranken, 2006a)

Gonorrhea

Gonorrhea (pronounced *gah-nuh-ree-uh* and known popularly as *the clap*) is caused by *Neisseria gonorrhoeae* bacteria passed from one person to another through vaginal, oral, or anal sex, even when the infected partner displays no symptoms. Gonorrhea can be contracted by a newborn during the birth process, which is a principal reason that physicians add silver nitrate or an antibiotic to the eyes of the infant to prevent ocular infection. Like chlamydia, gonorrhea cannot be caught by contact with a towel, a doorknob, or a toilet seat.

An estimated 1 million cases of gonorrhea occur annually in the United States, with the highest rate of infection in girls between ages 15 and 19 and in men between ages 20 and 24. The greatest incidence of the disease is among males and in inner-city populations. Traditionally, gonorrhea had been treated successfully by such antibiotics as penicillin and tetracycline, so rates of infection declined over the years. But in recent decades, rates have begun to rise due to newer strains of the bacteria that are resistant to traditional remedies. For example, in Hawaii a 70 percent increase in cases was reported in 2003. Thus, newly developed antibiotics effective against resistant strains of the disease are now administered—such medications as ceftriaxone, cefixime, ciprofloxacin, or oflaxacin (Gonorrhea, 2005).

Boys infected with gonorrhea are more likely to show symptoms of the disease than are girls. The most common signs in boys are a burning feeling when urinating and a yellow-white ooze from the penis that typically appears between 2 and 7 days after contracting the disease. However, some who are infected exhibit no signs.

Around half of infected girls show no symptoms of the disease. Others experience a burning sensation when urinating, extrude yellow-green pus from the vagina, and bleed between menstrual periods. The disease may also cause fever and pain during sexual intercourse. In around 15 percent of infected girls, the bacteria damage the uterus and fallopian tubes, resulting in pelvic inflammatory disease (PID).

> Gonorrhea can be very dangerous if it is left untreated, even in someone who has mild or no symptoms. In girls, the infection can move into the uterus, fallopian tubes, and ovaries . . . and can lead to scarring and infertility (the inability to have a baby). Gonorrhea infection during pregnancy can cause problems for the newborn baby, including meningitis (an inflammation of the membranes around the brain and spinal cord) and an eye infection that can result in blindness if it is not treated. (Van Vranken, 2006b)

Other parts of the body that occasionally are damaged by gonorrhea include the throat, eyes, heart, brain, skin, and joints.

Although antibiotics can cure a present infection, they do not make a person immune, so the disease can be acquired again through erotic engagements with infected partners. Abstaining from vaginal, oral, and anal sexual encounters is the only sure way to avoid the disease. However, using a new latex condom during each sexual contact will usually prevent infection.

Pelvic Inflammatory Disease

A girl can suffer PID infection when bacteria infest her uterus (womb), fallopian tubes, ovaries, and adjacent organs. Among various bacteria that may cause PID, the most common are the microorganisms that produce chlamydia and gonorrhea. The disease can develop anytime between a few days and several months after a girl has had sexual intercourse with an infected partner.

The presence of PID may be suggested by pain in the lower abdomen, pain during sexual intercourse or while urinating, a smelly fluid discharge from the vagina, irregular menstrual periods, and body temperature above 99.6 degrees. However, some girls show none of these symptoms, so the PID they suffer continues without their realizing that their pelvic organs are likely being damaged.

Teenage girls who are sexually active are more apt to contract PID than are women over age 25, and the incidence of PID is increased for girls who have multiple sex partners or previously had a sexually transmitted infection. Girls who use a douche (a device that squirts liquid into the vagina to rinse out sperm or bacteria) may unwittingly drive chlamydia or gonorrhea germs into the uterus or fallopian tubes.

Girls who suspect that they may have contracted chlamydia or gonorrhea should be examined for that disease and for PID by a doctor or by personnel at a Planned Parenthood center and, if infected, be treated with antibiotics.

Syphilis

Syphilis (pronounced *siff-uh-liss*) is caused by the bacterium *Treponema pallidum*, whose spirochetes are acquired by contact with a sexual partner's open sore during vaginal, anal, or oral intercourse. An expectant mother who has syphilis while pregnant can infect the unborn child in her womb. Like chlamydia and gonorrhea, syphilis cannot be caught from a towel, doorknob, or toilet seat.

Untreated syphilis can advance through primary, secondary, and tertiary stages. At the primary stage, one or more small, firm, round, and painless red sores called *chancres* (pronounced shang-kers) may erupt on the part of the body that had touched the infected sex partner's sores—vagina, penis, rectum, or mouth. In addition, glands may swell. Sometimes no sores appear, so the infected person does not recognize that something could be wrong. At this primary stage, the disease is highly infectious. Within 3 to 6 weeks the sores will heal, but that does not mean the infection has been cured. Instead, the syphilis moves into a secondary phase during which the infected person usually breaks out in an obvious or faint rash (typically on palms and soles of the feet) that is often accompanied by fever and aching muscles. Sometimes sores appear on the lips, within the mouth, on the vagina, and on the anus. The disease continues to be highly infectious during the secondary stage. As in the primary stage, the symptoms of the secondary phase usually disappear within a week or two as the ailment passes into a latent condition that can lull the infected individual into believing the problem is over. The latent, hidden condition can last for months or years.

When syphilis enters its tertiary stage, the spirochetes spread throughout the body, affecting the brain, heart, spinal cord, and bones so that a sufferer can gradually go blind, have difficulty walking, and eventually die.

Medical personnel can diagnose syphilis in several ways: (a) inspect a patient for such symptoms as chancres in the genital area, (b) take a sample of fluid from a suspicious ulcer and examine it under a microscope to detect syphilis bacteria, and (c) search for particular antibodies in the patient's blood—antibodies not aimed specifically at syphilis bacteria but ones often found in people who have the disease.

Syphilis is successfully treated with penicillin. One dose of the antibiotic is usually sufficient during the first year of the infection but a longer course of penicillin is needed in later stages of the disease. However, curing the disease does not immunize a person, so individuals who carelessly engage in sex can be infected again.

Trends in the incidence of syphilis in the United States over the past six decades have featured a dramatic reduction from 1942 (230 reported cases of primary and secondary stage syphilis per 100,000 people) to a low of 10 cases per 100,000 in 1976, then an increase to 20 per 100,000 in 1991, and a drop to 2 cases per 100,000 by year 2000. Reported cases rose slightly in 2004 to nearly 5 per 100,000 for men and 1 per 100,000 for women (Centers for Disease Control, 2005). About 9,800 cases of primary- and secondary-stage syphilis were reported in 2006, compared to about 8,700 in 2005 (up from 2.9 to 3.3 per 100,000; One million, 2007). A significant amount of the recent increase of syphilis has been among men who have engaged in sexual relations with other men. Health authorities in Hawaii reported that 90 percent of primary and secondary cases in 2003 involved men who had sex with men; 60 percent of the men with syphilis were co-infected with HIV / AIDS (STD / AIDS, 2003).

Although some teenagers contract syphilis, the greatest incidence of the disease by 2006 was among women ages 20 to 24 and among men ages 35 to 39 years (Centers for Disease Control, 2008c).

HIV/AIDS

The job of white cells (*leukocytes*) in the human bloodstream is to defend the body against infectious diseases and foreign materials. People whose white cells are weakened are vulnerable to a variety of diseases that can lead to serious illness and death. One type of white cell ($CD4^+$)—crucial to the normal function of the human immune system—can become the victim of attack by a submicroscopic infectious agent called the *human immunodeficiency virus* (HIV). When the $CD4^+$ cells are damaged in a person who had contracted HIV, that person is likely to develop AIDS (*acquired immunodeficiency syndrome*). With their weakened immune systems, such people often suffer infections of the lungs, brain, eyes, and other organs, accompanied by diarrhea and weight loss. The eventual, inevitable result of AIDS is an earlier than otherwise expected death.

The origin of HIV in humans is a matter of debate. However, a widely accepted theory proposes that the virus existed within the monkey population of West Africa and was transmuted into a form acquired by humans when a hunter made a meal of monkey flesh. This transfer of the virus from monkeys to humans occurred perhaps in the 1930s or 1940s. The spread of HIV to the United States began chiefly in the

1980s, probably brought to the country by infected immigrants. Because of the virus's prominence among men who had sexual relations with other men, the disorder in the 1980s was first called *gay related immune deficiency*, a label changed to *acquired immunodeficiency syndrome* after it became apparent that the virus could also be contracted through heterosexual relationships, blood transfusions, infected hypodermic needles, or an infected person's blood or other bodily fluid (semen, vaginal fluid, pre-ejaculate) coming in contact with the blood, broken skin, or mucous membranes of an uninfected person. And a pregnant woman—including teenagers—can pass HIV to her baby during pregnancy, delivery, and breastfeeding.

In the United States, cases of HIV and AIDS rose rapidly in the 1980s, then declined in the 1990s and into the 21st century as a result of information campaigns and by medications that often keep HIV under control before it causes AIDS. By 2009 there was no cure for HIV or AIDS. There were only methods of retarding the advance of HIV.

The chance of acquiring HIV is increased by other sexually transmitted diseases. A person with genital sores caused by syphilis (chancres) or herpes has an estimated two to five times greater risk of HIV infection because HIV can enter the body more readily through a break in the skin during unprotected sexual encounters.

In the United States, the total number of identified cases of AIDS over the quarter century 1981–2006 was 982,498. During that time there were 545,805 recorded deaths from AIDS. In 54 percent of new cases in 2006, the disease had been transmitted by men having sex with men. Another 33 percent resulted from high-risk male/female erotic contact (multiple partners, unprotected sex), 13 percent from drug injection with HIV-infected needles, and 1 percent by other means. In the 5-year period 2001–2006, the number of people newly diagnosed with AIDS decreased from 38,132 to 36,828. In 2006, the highest incidence of the disease occurred within two age decades—35–44 years (32 percent) and 25–34 years (26 percent). One percent of AIDS sufferers were under age 13, and 15 percent were within the age range 13 to 24 (Centers for Disease Control, 2008b).

The task of discovering who has an HIV infection is often difficult because easily observed symptoms may not appear for years, and the amount of time for symptoms to emerge can differ from one person to another.

HIV typically advances through several stages. The initial acute-stage symptoms are much like those of influenza and can include:

- Abdominal cramps, nausea, or vomiting
- Diarrhea
- Enlarged lymph nodes in the neck, armpits, and groin

- Fever
- Headache
- Muscle aches and joint pain
- Skin rash
- Sore throat
- Weight loss (Essig, 2007)

The acute symptoms often disappear after a few weeks and the HIV infection moves to a chronic phase as the virus continues to reproduce itself in the victim's tissues to weaken the immune system. Chronic symptoms, which may not appear for years, can include:

- Mental confusion, difficulty concentrating
- Personality changes
- Diarrhea or other bowel changes
- Unexplained weight loss
- Dry cough
- Fatigue
- Fever
- Loss of appetite
- Mouth sores
- Night sweats
- Swollen lymph nodes in the neck, armpits, and groin
- Pain when swallowing
- Repeated outbreaks of herpes simplex
- Shortness of breath
- Tingling, numbness, and weakness in the limbs
- Yeast infection of the mouth (thrush; Essig, 2007)

If the HIV goes untreated, it morphs into a final stage, that of AIDS, usually within 12 to 13 years after the initial infection. "A small number of people who are infected with HIV are rapid progressors. They develop AIDS within about 3 years if they do not receive treatment" (Essig, 2007). However, medical treatment for HIV may delay or prevent AIDS.

Because hundreds of teenagers become victims of HIV/AIDS each year, protecting students is a serious concern for America's schools whose health-education programs bear responsibility for informing students about

- Ways that HIV is transmitted (vaginal, oral, or anal sex; mucus or blood of an infected person; contact with sores of an infected person; an infected hypodermic needle that has been used to inject drugs)
- Who is likely to infect them with the virus (adult men with multiple male sexual partners; girls and women who have multiple sexual partners; people who engage in unprotected intercourse; HIV-infected persons who display no symptoms)

- How to protect themselves from contracting HIV (abstain from sex; use a condom if they engage in intercourse; avoid injecting drugs; avoid contact with other people's sores; accept blood transfusions only from legitimate, trustworthy sources)

Genital Herpes

Reddish, blister-like sores in girls' and boys' genital regions can be caused by two forms of the herpes (pronounced *hur-peez*) virus—*herpes simplex virus-1* (HSV1) and *herpes simplex virus-2* (HSV2). Although both forms can produce genital lesions, HSV2 is by far the dominant source. HSV1 is more frequently responsible for cold sores or fever blisters around the mouth.

Genital herpes are most often contracted through vaginal, oral, or anal sex, with one or more of the disease's blisters usually appearing on the genitals or anus within 2 weeks after the virus has been transmitted. An uninfected person whose skin touches an infected person's lesions can contract the virus.

When the blisters break, they leave tender sores that typically heal within 2 to 4 weeks. The first outbreak may be accompanied by fever, fatigue, headaches, swollen lymph nodes, and itching, pain, or swelling in the genital area. Another episode of lesions often occurs weeks or months after the first, with each subsequent occasion less severe, less frequent, and of shorter duration that the previous ones. It is also the case that some people who are infected with herpes fail to exhibit any telltale blisters. Thus, they are not aware that they will be infecting future sex partners.

Genital herpes are very common in the United States. An estimated 20 percent of Americans over the age of 12 are infected, a frequency five times greater than 40 years ago. Recent studies suggest that teenage girls have a 46 percent chance of contracting the disease during their first sexual encounter (Meeker, 2002).

As yet, there is no cure for the malady, so the herpes virus remains in infected people's bodies indefinitely to cause further eruptions of painful blisters at any time. Although herpes cannot be cured, the chances of getting infected during intercourse can be reduced if an uninfected person avoids vaginal, oral, or anal intercourse until an infected partner's lesions have disappeared. Even then it is prudent for boys to use a condom in vaginal or anal sex and for both boys and girls to use dental dams in oral sex (Eisenberg, 2006).

Genital herpes are not merely periodic painful nuisances but can lead to more serious problems. They are related to over 99 percent of cervical cancer, can make people more susceptible to HIV infection, and render HIV-infected individuals more infectious (Centers for Disease Control, 2008a; Meeker, 2002).

Genital Warts

Warts can appear on any part of a person's body as white, beige, or brown bumps or growths on the skin that can be flat or raised, single or multiple, small or large. The cause of warts is the *human papillomavirus* (HPV), which comes in more than 100 varieties, most of them harmless. Among the varieties that cause warts are several types that produce growths on the hands, others that cause warts on the feet (*plantar warts*), and still others that cause warts in the genital area. Although about 30 types can cause warts in the genital region, two types (numbers 6 and 11) are responsible for 90 percent of the growths.

Genital warts (*venereal warts*) are highly contagious, usually transmitted from one person to another during vaginal, oral, or anal sex when an uninfected person's skin touches the warts of an infected partner. About two thirds of the people who have sexual contact with someone who has genital warts will also develop warts. The larger the number of sexual partners a person has, the greater the chance of catching the virus. An estimated 50 percent of sexually active American teens and young adults have genital warts (National Institute, 2008). Occasionally the papillomavirus is passed from an infected mother to her baby during childbirth.

Among girls, genital warts can erupt on the vagina, cervix, vulva, and rectum, whereas among boys, the growths are found on the penis, scrotum, and rectum. Although warts typically appear 3 or 4 months after a person is first infected, they sometimes fail to erupt until many months later, and in some cases they are so small that they go unnoticed.

In several ways, genital warts are similar to genital herpes. Both are caused by viruses, their symptoms can disappear spontaneously as time passes, and the lesions can return at a later time because the viruses remain in the body. If warts increase or become embarrassing or bothersome, they can be treated in any of several ways by health-care providers. Small warts can be (a) frozen off (cryosurgery), usually with liquid nitrogen, (b) burned off with electricity (electrocautery), or (c) removed by laser. Large warts may need to be cut off with a scalpel. Medications that can be applied to genital warts include (d) imiquimod cream, (e) a 20 percent podophyllin antimitotic solution, (f) a 0.5 percent podofilox solution, (g) 5 percent 5-fluorouracil cream, (h) trichloroacetic acid (TCA; National Institute, 2008).

> Treatment of genital warts should be guided by the preference of the patient, the available resources, and the experience of the health-care provider. No definitive evidence suggests that any of the available treatments are superior to any other and no single treatment is ideal for all patients or all warts. The majority of patients require a course of therapy rather than a single treat-

ment. . . . The majority of genital warts respond within 3 months of therapy. (Centers for Disease Control, 2006)

Hepatitis B

In the main, there are no vaccines to prevent people from contracting sexually transmitted diseases. However, hepatitis B (HBV) is an exception. In 1982 a vaccine became available in the United States to protect people from the hepatitis-B virus. Since 1991 the vaccine has been routinely administered to children, thereby reducing the incidence of the disease by 80 percent, chiefly among persons born after 1991. The immunization process consists of three injections over a 6-month period (National Center, 2008).

The hepatitis-B virus does its damage by attacking the liver, thereby causing lifelong liver infection, scarring (cirrhosis), cancer, liver malfunction, and death. The virus is transmitted from one person to another through an infected person's body fluids—blood, semen, vaginal secretions, and saliva. The hepatitis-B virus be contracted not only by erotic liaisons (vaginal, oral, anal) but also by infected blood remnants clinging to a contaminated drug-injecting needle or a tainted razor, toothbrush, or tattooing needle. In addition, the virus may be transmitted by contact with blood or open sores of an infected person or by an infected mother passing it to her newborn during the birth process. Using a condom during sexual encounters may reduce the chance of catching hepatitis B but will not provide sure protection. The virus is not spread through food or water, sharing eating utensils, breastfeeding, hugging, kissing, hand holding, coughing, or sneezing (National Center, 2008).

Approximately two thirds of youths who are newly infected with hepatitis B will show flulike symptoms—fatigue, aching joints, nausea, vomiting, appetite loss, and abdominal pain. In addition, victims often show signs of jaundice (yellowing of the skin and whites of the eyes), and their urine may have a brownish cast.

The one third of newly infected persons who display no symptoms are more often children and teenagers than adults. Since they fail to realize that they are infected, they can inadvertently pass the virus on to future sex partners.

Hepatitis B can be either acute or chronic.

> In acute hepatitis the inflammation develops quickly, and lasts only a short period of time. The patient usually recovers completely, but it can take up to several months. Occasionally, a person fails to recover fully, and the hepatitis becomes chronic. In other words, it continues at a smoldering pace. Chronic hepatitis can develop over a number of years without the patient ever having acute hepatitis or even feeling sick. (Jackson, 2006)

By the early years of the 21st century, the number of Americans with chronic hepatitis B was estimated at between 1 and 1.4 million. About 90–95 percent of people who are infected are able to fight off the virus so their infection never becomes chronic. Only about 5 to 10 percent of adults infected with HBV go on to develop chronic infection. The number of reported cases of acute HBV in 2006 in the United States was 4,758 or 1.6 per 100,000 population, the lowest incidence ever recorded. "Because many HBV infections are either asymptomatic or never reported, the actual number of new infections is estimated to be approximately tenfold higher. In 2006, an estimated 46,000 persons were newly infected with HBV" (National Center, 2008).

Once the disease becomes chronic, it cannot be cured. The virus is carried throughout the infected person's lifetime. However, such antiviral medications as Interferon, Telbivudine, Entecavir, Lamivudine, or Adefovir dipivoxil can be administered to help ameliorate the effects and progression of the disorder.

Pubic Lice

Pubic lice are tiny, six-legged insects the size of a pinhead that cling to a person's pubic hairs, feeding themselves by biting the person and sucking blood from the wound. Because their two front feet resemble claws, the lice have been called "crabs" and the disorder they cause has been dubbed "the crab."

The typical way teenagers catch lice is by having sexual intercourse with an infested partner, an act that permits the insects to crawl from one person's pubic hairs to the other's. Lice can also be spread from infested clothing, towels, and bedding. But lice cannot be contracted from pets, since animals neither get lice nor transmit them.

Sometimes teens are unaware that they have lice, but far more often they are alerted to the infestation by severe itching, especially at night. When a suffering person scratches the itching area, the lice can spread to adjacent regions, and harmful bacteria may enter the bite wounds.

> If the infestation consists of many adult lice, symptoms may be noticeable immediately. But if the infestation initially involves a few lice that then lay eggs, a person may not experience any symptoms for 2 to 4 weeks until the eggs hatch. (Hirsch, 2007b)

Pubic lice can be eliminated by applying a lotion or shampoo containing 1 percent permethrin or pyrethrin (available without prescription at a pharmacy) or by using such a prescription medication as Malathion lotion (Division of Parasitic Diseases, 2008).

Trichomoniasis

Trichomoniasis (pronounced *trick-oh-mo-neye-ah-sis* and often called "trich") is a disease caused by the *trichomonas vaginalis* parasite transmitted between a girl and boy during penis-to-vulva intercourse or passed from one girl to another girl in vulva-to-vulva contact. Occasionally the parasite can also be caught from a damp towel, clothing, or toilet seat, which is why teenagers should avoid sharing towels and swim suits.

An estimated 8 million cases of trichomoniasis occur annually in the United States, making it the nation's most common nonviral sexually transmitted infection. However, the disease has not received widespread public attention because the symptoms are usually mild and the infection is readily cured.

Among girls, typical symptoms of trichomoniasis appear between 1 week and 4 weeks after exposure to the parasite. Signs of the disease can include (a) a yellow, green, or gray vaginal discharge (often foamy) with a strong odor, (b) discomfort during sex and when urinating, (c) irritation and itching in the genital area, and (d) lower abdominal pain and swelling in rare cases (Trichomoniasis, 2005). The disease is far less common among boys, whose symptoms feature a yellowish, cloudy discharge from the penis (urethra), perhaps accompanied by itching or pain while urinating. However, many trichomoniasis carriers display no symptoms, so they are unaware that they can infect additional sex partners.

Because the symptoms of trichomoniasis are mild, teenagers are prone to think the infection leads to no serious consequences. However, trichomoniasis is a major cause of inflammation of the vagina (*vaginitis*), it can increase people's chances of getting AIDS, and pregnant teens with trichomoniasis are apt to bear infants with below-normal birth weight.

The only sure way to avoid trichomoniasis is to abstain from sex. But youths who continue to engage in vaginal intercourse can reduce their chance of catching trichomoniasis by using a latex male condom or female polyurethane condom. Teens who practice anal sex should use a male condom. Those who engage in oral sex should use a dental dam.

Trichomoniasis can usually be cured with the prescription drug metronidazole (Flagyl) or tinidazole. Curing the infection does not prevent a person from contracting the disease again during a future sexual encounter.

INTERPRETATIONS

The six vantage points used for summarizing the essence of this chapter are those of (a) decision making (by students and school personnel), (b) heredity and environment, (c) *could-be, is,* and *should-be* beliefs, (d) sources of evidence, (e) power and authority, and (f) implications for schools.

Decisions. The kinds of decisions students face about sexually transmitted infections can be expressed as a series of questions. Should I abstain from any form of sexual contact so as to avoid any chance of catching a disease? If I do engage in sex, what kinds of diseases might I catch? What can I do to minimize the chance of getting one of those infections? How would I know if I've caught a disease? What kinds of symptoms do different infections cause? Should I periodically be examined by a doctor or nurse to discover if I have an infection?

Decisions that school administrators (superintendents, curriculum planners, principals, board members) are obliged to make can also be cast as questions. Should sexually acquired diseases be discussed at all in our schools? If so, should such discussions be a part of the regular curriculum or, instead, a matter addressed only when a problem arises about students contracting infections? If the study of sexual diseases is part of the curriculum, at what grade levels should such study be placed, and why that grade level? Who should be authorized to teach about sexual diseases, and why that person? How should school personnel respond if students, parents, or members of the community object to the mention in school of sexually acquired maladies?

Teachers and counselors also face questions about how they should deal with sexual diseases. What should I say if students ask me about sexually transmitted infections? Should I initiate discussions of sexual diseases with students? If so, under what circumstances?

Heredity and environment. Even though sexual diseases are acquired from students' environments rather than being inherited, heredity can play a role in determining how readily teenagers contract infections and how seriously venereal diseases affect youths. For example, females' and males' genetically determined anatomical structures influence the infections they incur or pass on. By way of illustration, more girls than boys suffer from trichomoniasis because the female sexual/urinary system provides a more receptive environment than a male system. For a similar reason,

> Women are more susceptible than men to infection from HIV in any given heterosexual encounter, due to the greater area of mucous membrane exposed during sex in women than in men; the greater quantity of fluids transferred from men to women; the higher viral content in male sexual fluids; and the micro-tears that can occur in vaginal (or rectal) tissue from sexual penetration. (World Health Organization, 2008)

A host of studies reveal marked ethnic differences in the incidence of venereal diseases. For example, table 7.1 shows the results of a summary

Table 7.1. Sexually Transmitted Infections in Ethnic Groups—2006 (Number of cases per 100,000 population)

	All	*Males*	*Females*
Chlamydia			
African Americans	1,275.0	741.2	1,760.9
American Indians/Alaskans	797.3	317.3	1,262.3
Asians/Pacific Islanders	132.1	59.2	201.2
Hispanics	477.0	211.0	761.3
Whites	153.0	66.0	237.0
Gonorrhea			
African Americans	658.4	702.7	618.1
American Indians/Alaskans	138.3	99.9	175.6
Asians/Pacific Islanders	21.1	19.6	22.6
Hispanics	77.4	70.1	85.3
Whites	36.5	28.3	44.4
Syphilis			
African Americans	1.3	18.3	4.9
American Indians/Alaskans	3.3	4.7	1.9
Asians/Pacific Islanders	1.3	2.5	0.1
Hispanics	3.6	6.3	0.8
Whites	1.9	3.5	0.3

Source: Centers for Disease Control and Prevention. (2007, November 13). *STD Surveillance 2006—Racial and Ethnic Minorities,* www.cdc.gov/std/stats/ minorities.htm

of surveys in the Untied States for chlamydia, gonorrhea, and syphilis in 2006.

However, I have found no evidence that suggests the remarkable differences in table 7.1 are caused by genetic inheritance. On the contrary, differences in rates of sexually acquired diseases across ethnic groups appear to be the result of environmental influences, primarily socioeconomic (poverty vs. riches) and cultural (family and life traditions, conceptions of acceptable gender roles). And because social and environmental influences can be intentionally altered from one generation to the next, there is hope that high rates of infection among ethnic minorities can be reduced with the passing of time. Conceivably, schools can play a role in effecting such change.

Could-be, is, should-be. Adolescents profit from learning the *could-be, is,* and *should-be* of sexually acquired infections. Knowledge of *is* consists of information about how youths can catch the diseases, the frequency of each type of disease among teens, ways to prevent infections, and modes of treatment. Knowledge of *could-be* derives from teenagers estimating how their erotic needs, social environments (family members' attitudes, peers' erotic activities and beliefs, and portrayals of teen sex on television and in the movies), and risk of infection could influence their own well-being. Youths' convictions about *should-be* are founded on such considerations as what their family members regard as appropriate sexual behavior, their religious convictions, the attitudes of peers they respect, and what they regard as their "right" to express their erotic yearnings.

These three aspects of *could-be, is,* and *should-be* are not only concerns often addressed in parents' talks with their teenage offspring but are issues that can profitably serve as the foci of discussions in schools' sex-education programs.

Sources of evidence. In teen society, misinformation abounds about sexually transmitted infections. Many adolescents know nothing about venereal diseases. Furthermore, a host of ill-founded myths circulate among the young about the symptoms, risks, and treatments of sexual disorders. And even when youths depend on their parents for guidance, the parents may be too embarrassed to talk about sexual matters or may be so poorly informed that the accounts they offer are inaccurate, thereby doing more harm than good.

Thus, what children and adolescents need are trustworthy, easily accessed sources of evidence about sexual diseases. One such source is the Internet's World Wide Web. However, the web's nearly limitless cafeteria of facts and opinions about eroticism is not monitored for accuracy or bias. Some websites are more reliable than others, so that students must decide for themselves which sites to trust, which to doubt, and which to reject. This means that students can profit from guidance in judging the accuracy of sources by (a) comparing different accounts for consistency, (b) estimating the likely motives and professional training of the people who are offering information and advice, (c) learning the reputation of the organization that sponsors a particular website, and (d) discovering how and where the data were gathered to support the conclusions and advice that the site offers. This same guidance also helps students judge the accuracy of other sources of evidence—parents, schoolmates, teachers, books, magazines, television, and movies.

Power and authority. As proposed in chapter 1, *authority* is the official decision-making power assigned to an individual or institution. An authority is empowered not only to decide how people should behave but also to apply sanctions—punishments and rewards—to encourage compliance. As an important factor in young people's lives, authorities can influence what the young learn about sexually acquired infections. A 15-year-old boy who is a dedicated member of a fundamentalist Protestant church is likely to respond differently to his minister's warning against oral sex than will another 15-year-old who declares himself an agnostic. The daughter of Hispanic immigrants who thinks her parents are old-fashioned and out of touch with modern life in America can regard her high-school health-education teacher as a more convincing authority than her parents in matters of sexual behavior. An 18-year-old member of an inner-city street gang is apt to follow the sex-activity model provided by the gang leaders in preference to the advice of a YMCA counselor. In effect, children and teenagers can differ in the types of authorities whose word they respect in matters of sex.

Implications for schools. Schools face responsibilities and opportunities in relation to sexually transmitted infections. In the present context, *responsibilities* are defined as obligations that schools cannot avoid; *opportunities* are defined as potential—not obligatory—services that schools might provide to enhance students' welfare.

Schools' unavoidable responsibility is that of establishing a policy governing the treatment of students who have contracted sexually acquired infections. In some schools such a policy assumes the form of an unstated general attitude of disapproval that can lead to different ways of treating students on different occasions. In other schools, the policy is written and available to students and parents, describing what kinds of diseases are involved and what treatments are to be applied under various conditions (a student's age, academic status, girl or boy, how the infection was caught, past record of sexual activity).

Schools have the opportunity to offer sex education that includes information about sexually transmitted diseases—types of infections, their symptoms, their consequences, how they are contracted, how to avoid such infections, and how they can be treated. This opportunity can become an obligation whenever influential members of the public insist that information about sexual diseases becomes a required part of the curriculum. However, how that obligation is implemented can become highly contentious, as explained in chapter 9, "Sex-Education Programs."

Chapter 8

Gender Traits and Role Preferences

In every culture, adults teach children and youths the culture's dominant beliefs about what distinguishes males from females. Those beliefs consist of convictions about differences between the genders in physical structure, abilities, personality traits, proper appearance, and proper behavior. The purpose of such instruction is to equip the young to recognize their culture's distinction between the masculine role and the feminine role and then to adopt the role that matches their own gender—boys are typically expected to prefer the culture's stereotypical masculine traits and girls are to prefer the feminine traits.

Since prehistoric times, the most obvious gender differences that people have recognized have been physical, especially in the distinction between females' and males' sex organs. In addition, males have been credited with greater muscular strength, height, and weight. Many millennia ago, such differences led to females and males assuming different childbearing and child-rearing roles—women and girls became homebodies caring for infants and young children, while men and boys went hunting and fishing. As the centuries advanced, peoples' beliefs about gender differences expanded to include abilities, personality traits, proper appearance, and proper social roles. As a result, well into the 20th century, most Americans held a variety of convictions ("truths") about gender differences, such as the beliefs in table 8.1.

In the early 21st century, schools have been acutely affected by two social movements that concern gender differences—the *feminist movement* and the *gay-rights movement*. Feminist activists argue that traditional attributes assigned to females have been founded on prejudice rather than fact and thus have deprived females of occupational, educational, and

Table 8.1. Traditional American Beliefs about Gender Differences

Females	*Males*
Abilities and Personality Traits	
Physical Abilities	
Weaker, smaller muscles	Stronger, larger muscles
Slower runners	Faster runners
Better finger dexterity	Worse finger dexterity
Less stamina	More stamina
Intellectual Abilities	
Better readers, more verbally adept	Worse readers, less verbally adept
Worse at logical analysis	Better at logical analysis
Worse in math and science	Better in math and science
Better at art	Worse at art
Emotional	
Emotions more frequent, more intense	Emotions less frequent, less intense
More compassionate and empathetic	Less compassionate and empathetic
Decisions based on feelings	Decisions based on logic
Display happiness, sadness, fear	Display anger, stubbornness
Vulnerable, weep easily	Brave, rarely weep
Proper Appearance	
Clothing	
Skirt, blouse, dress, high heels	Pants, shirt, suit, necktie, low heels
Accoutrements	
Necklace, earrings, fancy finger rings, lipstick, cheek rouge, face powder, longer hair	Moustache, beard, shorter hair, plain finger ring
Proper Social Roles	
Dominant vs. Submissive Behavior	
Followers	Leaders
Helpmates for males	Decision makers, activists
Implement males' decisions	Guide and supervise females
Appropriate Occupations	
Housewife, schoolteacher, nurse, salesclerk, stenographer, secretary	Businessman, factory worker, medical doctor, professor, scientist, farmer, politician

Sources: Kallen, 1998; Kelly & Hutson-Comeaux, 1999; Rivers & Barnett, 2007; Study finds, 2008.

social-position opportunities to which they are entitled. Gay-rights activists charge that unwarranted prejudice has long been held against individuals who choose to adopt a lifestyle different from the one traditionally assigned to people by the nature of their sexual equipment. In other words, gay-rights activists have urged the general populace to consider a homosexual or a bisexual life pattern as acceptable as a heterosexual pattern. The purpose of chapter 8 is to inspect these two movements and to identify ways they have influenced schools.

A FEMINIST POSITION

Historically, a political issue in America that reflected public opinion about females' competence was the question of whether women should vote in elections. When the U.S. Constitution was being formulated in 1787, the matter of who would be qualified to vote was left up to the states. By 1807, all states had denied women the right to vote. Yet a significant feminist movement to gain the vote was not mounted until the Anti-Suffrage Society was formed in 1871, with Susan B. Anthony as the leading activist. Over the following years, the women's movement gained strength until the 19th Amendment to the Constitution in 1919 accorded women voting rights. Since that time—and especially over the most recent quarter century—increasing numbers of Americans have engaged in heated debate and vigorous social action over three issues:

1. How accurate—when judged by objective measures—are the portrayals of male and female abilities and personality traits in table 8.1?
2. To what extent are the beliefs about abilities, personality traits, and social roles in table 8.1 rooted in genetic (hereditary) determinants rather than social (environmental) determinants?
3. What do the answers to questions 1 and 2 imply about the opportunities that schools should provide for girls and boys and for the men and women who operate schools?

The Accuracy of Gender Stereotypes

Whereas traditional beliefs about girls' physical skills have changed markedly over recent decades, opinions about their intellectual abilities continue to be vehemently debated.

Physical Abilities

Changes in popular beliefs about females' physical skills and stamina over the 20th century can be illustrated with the sports of basketball and marathon racing.

Basketball. The women's version of basketball was created in 1892 by Senda Berenson, a physical-education instructor at the all-girls Smith

College (Northampton, Massachusetts)—just 1 year after Dr. James Naismith invented the game of basketball at the International YMCA Training School in nearby Springfield. Although Berenson had far more faith in females' athletic potential than did most of the general public, she still believed that girls' physical limitations and their need to exhibit proper feminine behavior required different rules than the ones Naismith had designed for males. Therefore, rather than permitting girls to roam anywhere on the basketball court, Berenson divided the court into three zones, with two players from each team assigned to each zone. The players were forbidden to leave their zone or dribble down the court. Instead, they were confined to tossing the ball to teammates in the other two zones. The zone rule, along with other restrictions on vigorous exertion (in dribbling, the ball could be bounced only three times) were intended to protect players' health and to suit current standards of feminine decorum.

Berenson reasoned that the lines separating the three zones prevented the players from "running all over the gymnasium, thus doing away with unnecessary running, and also giving the heart moments of rest [because] it has been found that a number of girls who play without division lines have developed hypertrophy of the heart." She cautioned that "It is a well known fact that women abandon themselves more readily to an impulse than men, [so without her restrictive rules] the great desire to win and the excitement of the game would make our women do sadly unwomanly things" (Berenson in Pölling-Vocke, 2003). In order to maintain ladylike respectability, girls who played basketball wore confining undergarments (including corsets) and long dresses.

As women's basketball entered the 20th century, the guidelines that Berenson had introduced continued to distinguish the game from the rougher, physically demanding male version. Not until 1938 were the three zones of the female game reduced to two zones, and in 1971 the zones were eliminated entirely so that girls' basketball became nearly identical to the physically demanding male version. Over the years, girl's long dresses gave way to more manageable gym bloomers and middies, then eventually to the present-day's shorts and tank tops.

Thus, a century after the game of female basketball had been introduced, the traditional belief that girls could not develop the physical stamina and agility of boys had been dispelled.

Marathon racing. The evolution of women's marathon racing paralleled that of women's basketball. Females were not allowed to participate in the marathon when it was introduced in the 1896 Olympics in Greece, because the endurance demands of such an event were considered far beyond females' physical capacity. However, one woman known as Melpomene, who was refused permission to enter that first marathon, ran alongside the course when the race began and soon joined the male runners. She finished the race an hour and half after the male winner, thereby suggesting that long-distance running was not beyond women's ability, particularly in view of the fact that only 8 of the 15 male starters finished the race (Women and the marathon, 2008).

In 1926, when the official length of marathons was standardized at 42.195 kilometers or 26 miles and 385 yards, a British woman ran the course in 3 hours, 40 minutes, and 22 seconds (3:40:22). Yet women were still prevented from entering such official marathons as the New York and Boston versions. When women's track and field events were added to the Olympics in 1928, the longest race was 800 meters. But when three women collapsed in that event, Olympic officials ruled that no race longer than 200 meters would be permitted in the future. Not until the 1960 Olympic Games was the 800-meter event restored.

During the 1960s, as the women's liberation movement gained momentum, recreational long-distance running spread rapidly, ultimately forcing directors of the New York (1971) and Boston (1972) marathons to officially include women. From that time on, women's opportunities throughout the world to run long distances grew at a rapid rate. In 1980, at the third Avon International Marathon for women in London, the first five finishers broke the 2-hour 40-minute (2:40) time barrier, thereby convincing the International Olympic Committee to add three long-distance events for women in the 1984 Olympics—the marathon and the 5,000- and 10,000-meter races.

The rapidly growing popularity of women's marathon racing was accompanied by improved running times. Grete Waitz of Norway won the women's division of the New York City Marathon in 1979 in a time of 2:27:33—the first woman to run the distance in under 2:30:9. In 2003, Britain's Paula Radcliffe set a world record at 2:15:25.

According to Stephen Seiler,

> Some years ago, when the marathon was first becoming a competitive event for women, the rapid improvement in female times led some to predict that female performances would soon equal those of men in the marathon. This has not happened, and it won't. The world record for women [by the mid-1990s was] 2:21, compared to 2:06:50 for men, a difference in speed of about 10 percent. This same 10 percent gap is present across the distance running performance spectrum The reason for the performance gap is not that women don't train as hard as men. There are some important physiological differences between the sexes that can't be overlooked or overcome. (Seiler, 1996)

In Seiler's analysis, two physiological conditions that help account for the long-distance performance differences between males and females are (a) males' greater maximal oxygen consumption because males on the average are larger (and thus have larger hearts) and (b) females' greater proportion of body fat. But it is important to recognize that Seiler has focused on the *average* performance of the two genders. Hence, he suggests that "the best women can still beat 99 percent+ of the men. . . . [So] if you ask me 'When will women (on the average) run as fast as men,' I will answer 'Just as soon as they have the same [maximal oxygen consumption] as men'" (Seiler, 1996).

By the first decade of the 21st century, the marathon was still not a usual high-school running event. The longest races in which girls and boys participated were cross-country competitions and two-mile track events. There is no established length for cross-country races, but two miles is a typical distance for middle-school athletes and between 2.5 and 3 miles is common for high-school students. In parallel with the history of the marathon for women, the widespread acceptance of cross-country and two-mile track events for girls reflects a marked change from the past in attitudes about girl's physical stamina.

Other strenuous sports. Because of changed attitudes about female strength and stamina, girls today compete in a wide variety of demanding sports from which they had been excluded in earlier decades when they were viewed as too delicate for such events as soccer, volleyball, field hockey, ice hockey, lacrosse, shot put, discus throw, javelin throw, pole vault, long jump, and high jump. In effect, traditional stereotypical beliefs about females being too frail for physically taxing athletics are now outmoded.

Intellectual Abilities

The main types of empirical evidence offered in debates over gender differences in intellectual aptitude have been intelligence test scores and the incidence of cognitive disabilities.

Intelligence test scores. Since the early years of the 20th century, psychologists have created oral and written tests intended to assess people's intellectual aptitudes. Test items have been designed to measure such abilities as speed and accuracy in reading, in writing fluently, in perceiving meanings, calculating quantities, estimating spatial relationships, reasoning logically, recognizing analogies, and more. When scores on such skills have been combined to form a single overall score, that score has been interpreted as an indicator of *general intelligence,* signified by the letter *g*. Measures of *g* typically are expressed as an *intelligence quotient* or IQ—a number ostensibly reflecting a person's overall mental aptitude or "smartness." Youths with an IQ between 90 and 110 are considered to have average general intelligence. Those above 140 or 150 are considered to be mentally very gifted. Those scoring below 70 are regarded as mentally disadvantaged.

How, then, have males and females fared in comparisons of their test scores for both general intelligence and the more specific aptitudes? Answering this question is confounded by several conditions. First, one intelligence test will contain different types of items than another, so there is a question about whether the two tests have measured the same abilities. Second, the debate over gender differences has not been free from possible gender bias, because test analyses offered by women have more often produced interpretations showing females' general intelligence equal to—or better than—that of males, while interpretations offered by men have more frequently portrayed males as the more gifted gender. Thus, the following discussion should be viewed in light of these two caveats.

First, consider general intelligence. In the early decades of the 20th century, such pioneers of intelligence testing as Lewis Terman and Cyril Burt found no differences between males and females in general intelligence among the test takers they studied. This traditional belief continued throughout much of the century. In 2004, Anna Cianciolo and Robert Sternberg (2004) reviewed the history of general-aptitude studies and concluded that "The general consensus among psychologists is that there do not exist meaningful, systematic differences in overall intelligence among males and females, as indicated by IQ scores" (p. 111). In effect, boys and girls—on the average—were considered to be equal in overall aptitude.

However, other researchers have disagreed. In a 2003 study, Paul Irwing and Richard Lynn analyzed the results of an IQ test given to 80,000 members of the general public and to 20,000 students. The test consisted of a series of matrices (Raven's Matrices) rather than verbal items. On the average, males scored five points higher than females, with far more males in the upper IQ brackets—3 men for each woman with an IQ above 130 and 5.5 men for each woman with an IQ above 145. Irwing suggested, "These different proportions of men and women with high IQ scores may go some way to explaining the greater numbers of men achieving distinctions of various kinds, such as chess grandmasters, Fields medalists for mathematics, Nobel prizewinners and the like." The publication of the Irwing-Lynn report was promptly attacked in the journal *Nature* as being badly flawed and wrong-headed (McKie, 2005). However, the Irwing-Lynn findings were later supported by Douglas Jackson's and Phillipe Rushton's (2006) study of scores earned by 100,000 17-and-18-year-olds on the Scholastic Assessment Test; boys averaged 3.63 IQ points higher than girls.

Hence, there is no definitive answer to the question of gender differences in general intelligence. The issue remains unsettled. However, such is not the case for specific skills that contribute to overall cognitive ability. Some specific skills do reveal gender discrepancies. The most convincing answers about specific cognitive differences in recent years have been provided by *meta-analysis*, a procedure that enables scholars to simultaneously inspect more than just one set of intelligence test scores. In effect, meta-analysis involves combining the results of multiple empirical results to produce an overall conclusion. For example, Hyde and Linn (1988) examined 165 studies that reported data on gender differences in verbal ability. In a similar fashion, Hedges and Nowell (1995) examined mental test scores from six studies of large national probability samples that focused on mathematics, science, reading comprehension, perceptual speed, and associative memory.

> The differences found confirm the generally accepted pattern of gender differences. Males score higher on tests of mathematics, science, and the composite, while females score higher on tests of reading, perceptual speed, and writing. Mean differences in vocabulary do not consistently favor either gender. (Nowell & Hedges, 1998)

Therefore, studies in recent decades have confirmed the traditional stereotypical beliefs about boys being more adept than girls at math and science, whereas girls are better at such literacy skills as reading and writing. However, the average gender differences have generally been quite small. And it is important to recognize that the distributions of boys' and girls' scores in each skill greatly overlap, demonstrating that some girls are better than most boys in science and math and some boys are more adept than most girls at reading and writing. Thus, simply knowing that a particular student is a girl rather than a boy is of no real help in estimating whether that student will be good or poor in math, science, reading, or writing.

In addition to the great overlap in the female and male distributions of test scores, a second feature—extremely high scores—is significant. Hedges and Nowell's results suggested that average sex differences have been generally small and stable over past decades, but the math and science scores of males consistently showed greater variability than those of females. In other words, males' scores stretched across a broader range than did females' scores, so there were more males than females at both the highest levels and lowest levels. In contrast, in tests of reading comprehension, perceptual speed, and associative memory, females typically outnumbered males among the highest scoring individuals.

Therefore, boys—on the average—have continued to hold a modest advantage over girls in performance on tests requiring math and science skills, whereas girls—on the average—hold a modest advantage over boys in such literacy skills as reading and writing. Those advantages are particularly marked among the highest scoring individuals.

Cognitive disabilities. Further evidence of gender differences is found in the proportions of girls and boys who suffer specific types of verbal-skill disorders. Recent meta-analyses have shown no more than slight average female superiority in overall verbal aptitude, a superiority that led Hyde and McKinley (1997) to conclude "there were not (or were no longer) any [significant] gender differences in verbal ability." However, noteworthy differences have appeared in particular types of verbal skills, such as reading comprehension and speech fluency. For example, "mild developmental dyslexia is five times more likely to occur in boys than in girls, and severe developmental dyslexia is ten times more likely to occur in boys than in girls; in addition, there are three to four times as many male stutterers as there are female stutterers" (Hyde & McKinley, 1997).

Summary. The puzzle over whether girls and boys—on the average—differ in general intelligence remains unresolved. The issue is confounded by such variables as (a) a lack of comparability among intelligence tests, (b) unclear or conflicting definitions of intelligence, (c) researchers' possible gender biases, and (d) differences among the groups of people who take the tests.

However, there is greater agreement about gender differences in specific cognitive abilities. Girls are generally better at reading comprehension, speaking, and writing. Boys are generally better at math, science, and spatial relations. But a question remains about whether such differences are inherent, unchangeable characteristics of males and females or, instead, are a result of the conditions under which boys and girls grow up. In other words, to what extent are the differences revealed by tests the consequence of heredity rather than environment?

Heredity and Environment

The question of how hereditary and social influences interact to produce gender differences in abilities has been of particular interest to feminists, especially in relation to traditional beliefs about females' aptitude for mathematics and science. If the observed superiority of males in math and science is seated in genetic endowment rather than in how females are treated in daily life, then girls are forever destined to trail behind boys in these subjects at school, and women are forever fated to be underrepresented in occupations that require mathematical and scientific skills.

A concern about heredity-environment interactions is also voiced by people interested in reducing the greater number of males than females who suffer from problems of reading and speech. If such disorders are due principally to genetic rather than environmental influences, then the chances of reducing the frequency of dyslexia and stammering are far dimmer than if those disabilities are heavily affected by how boys are treated.

There is no generally accepted solution to heredity versus environment puzzles over gender. Instead, there is an abundance of theorists who marshal data and rationales in support of their proposals. The following examples illustrate three conflicting theoretical explanations of cognitive differences between girls and boys.

Genetic Factors

As explained in chapter 2, the sexual attributes of a newly conceived human are determined at the moment of conception when a male sperm fertilizes a female ovum. If a male X sex chromosome pairs up with one of the female's X chromosomes, the resulting XX combination determines that a female child will result. But if a sperm carrying a Y sex chromosome fertilizes the ovum, the resulting offspring will be an XY male. In effect, the Y chromosome carries genes that account for gender differences.

One such difference is physical size. On the average, males are larger than females. In addition, males have larger brains. Richard Lynn (1999) noted that an adult male cognitive advantage of 4 IQ points over females can be obtained by averaging test scores on verbal comprehension, reasoning, and spatial abilities to arrive at an overall IQ. He then proposed that (a) the male IQ advantage can be predicted from the larger average male brain size (by about 10 percent) and (b) the male advantage in both brain size and intelligence is less in children and young adolescents because girls mature more rapidly than boys in general and in brain size in particular. If Lynn's theory is correct, then females, by the time they reach adulthood, will—on the average—always lag behind males' general intelligence (combined verbal, reasoning, and spatial aptitudes) because the gender difference is the result of genetically determined brain size.

Recent studies have supported the notion that girls use different parts of their brains than do boys in performing certain mental tasks. Researchers investigating how people process language and visuospatial information discovered that "male and female participants performed equally on tasks, both in terms of accuracy and timing; they just used different parts of their brains to get the tasks done" (Study confirms, 2006). One potential reason for some of the gender differences is that brain functions are affected by the hormone estrogen, found primarily in females (Study of language, 2006). So a different patterning of genes between females and males may account for numbers of the observed gender distinctions in cognitive functioning. Such may be the case with such disabilities as dyslexia and stammering that might be grounded in an unfortunate combination of genes in males that is less common in females.

Heredity-Environment Interaction

Such evolutionary psychologists as David Buss (1995) have theorized that the male/female division of labor in prehistoric times could help account for why today's physical, cognitive, and emotional gender differences exist. In the primitive ancient world, women's genetically determined child-bearing role required that they not overtax themselves physically and that they be on hand to care for infants and young children. Thus, they were obliged stay close to home and to depend on males for such highly strenuous activities as hunting and fishing. "Male involvement in hunting activities, such as navigating over long distances and bringing down animals, resulted in the development of superior spatial skills, whereas female involvement in foraging activities and childrearing did not promote such skills" (Cianciolo & Sternberg, 2004).

> This [spatial] ability is essential for successful hunting, in which the trajectory and velocity of a spear must anticipate correctly the trajectory of an animal as each moves with different speeds through space and time. Other sorts of skills involved in hunting also show large magnitudes of sex differences, such as throwing velocity, throwing distance, and throwing accuracy. Skilled hunters, as good providers, are known to be sexually attractive to women in current and traditional tribal societies. (Buss, 1995)

Competition among females for suitable mates led women to prefer physically strong, agile, clever men who would be good providers. Competition among males for mates led men to prefer healthy, clever women who would bear healthy, clever children. The offspring who inherited the genetic composition of such parents would be better equipped to survive in changing environments, so they would multiply in greater numbers than would those in their society who were less well endowed with survival skills. The favored offsprings' desirable genes would then be passed on to the next generation, thus contributing to a greater concentration of certain traits (physical size, strength, spatial perception) in males and other traits (finger and hand dexterity, verbal skills) in females as the millennia advanced. Thus, according to evolutionary theory, the principle of "survival of the fittest" could account for most, if not all, present-day physical, cognitive, and emotional differences between genders.

By this same line of logic we might speculate that conditions of life in modern industrialized societies might, over a long period of time, change future patterns of differences between males and females. Because physical strength and agility are no longer required for a male to be a "good provider," other traits (logical reasoning, verbal persuasiveness) might gradually become more prominent characteristics among males, whereas different traits could become more prominent among females (physical strength and stamina, math and science aptitudes) as females gain greater access to opportunities in athletics and occupations.

Social Factors

In contrast to genetic and evolutionary theories of gender differences are sociological theories that account for observed gender traits by how children and adolescents are treated during their formative years. Such theories propose that family members, teachers, religious counselors, and the general public who subscribe to such beliefs as those in table 8.1 become the designers of children's activities and self-perceptions. The debate about such social causes of gender differences has focused chiefly on youths' performance on math and science tests and on the numbers of males and females in math and science classes and occupations.

> From the time that children are very young, parents encourage them to engage in sex-typed activities, which may lead to the development of different intellectual strengths in boys and girls. For example, young boys are encouraged to play with Lego building kits or erector sets and young girls to play with dolls and dollhouses. Similarly, adolescent boys are more strongly encouraged than girls to engage in more science or mathematical-related activities. (Cianciolo & Sternberg, 2004)

Proponents of sociological theories bolster their arguments with evidence that the gap between boys and girls in math and science test scores has been closing as a result of more girls receiving encouragement and opportunities to engage in math and science activities (Nowell & Hedges, 1998). Devin Pope's analysis of test results from the National Assessment of Educational Progress led him to

> attribute the variation in the math gender gap to differences in the educational, social, and cultural environment. This variation is large enough that we conclude that virtually the entire gender gap in math test scores can be explained by environmental differences. We further show that test score differences between boys and girls across geographic regions are correlated with perceptions about math and gender and an existing gender inequality index. (Pope, 2007)

The shrinking gap between boys' and girls' test scores has been accompanied by news of girls' performance in such events as the 2007 Siemens science competition.

> Girls won top honors for the first time in the Siemens Competition in Math, Science and Technology, one of the nation's most coveted student science awards. . . . Janelle Schlossberger and Amanda Marinoff, both 17 and se-

niors at John F. Kennedy High School on Long Island, split the first prize—a $100,000 scholarship—in the team category for creating a molecule that helps block the reproduction of drug-resistant tuberculosis bacteria. Isha Himani Jain, 16, a senior at Freedom High School in Bethlehem, Pa., placed first in the individual category for her studies of bone growth in zebra fish, whose tail fins grow in spurts, similar to the way children's bones do. She will get a $100,000 scholarship. . . . Eleven of the 20 finalists were girls. It was the first year that girls outnumbered boys in the final round. (Millner-Fairbanks, 2007)

If, indeed, the observed gender differences in math and science are caused by the society's traditional child-rearing attitudes that have diminished girls' opportunities, then how long will it take before improved attitudes eliminate the gender gap? Nowell and Hedges (1998) suggested that

> the rate of change is extremely slow and certainly not practically significant. For instance, the trend for mathematics mean differences estimated from [a variety of] surveys predicts closure of the (small) gap in achievement in approximately 40 years and the science trend as estimated from the NAEP [National Assessment of Educational Progress] tests predicts equal average achievement in 30 years. . . . Surely these projected changes cannot be considered substantial progress towards the goal of equality.

Summary

The controversies over gender differences in cognitive skills have not been settled. Debates continue, particularly over such questions as: Do females and males—on the average—differ in general intelligence or specific cognitive abilities? If boys and girls do differ, how large are the differences? To what extent are differences the result of genetic rather than social causes?

More research and more unbiased analyses are needed if persuasive answers are to result.

Implications for Schools

Over the past half-century, social movements and social-science research have effected marked changes in the ways schools address gender differences. The "social-cultural revolution" of the 1960s was a particularly powerful influence on broadening opportunities for girls, as feminist activists pressed schools to offer girls richer opportunities for learning and participation than had been traditionally available.

A significant piece of federal legislation—partly a result of the newly energized women's movement—was the 1972 Title IX amendment of the

Civil Rights Act of 1964, which stipulated that "No person in the United States shall, on the basis of sex, be excluded from participation in, be denied the benefits of, or be subjected to discrimination under any education program or activity receiving Federal financial assistance" (Sadker, 2008). Although Title IX encompassed all aspects of schools' activities (academic, social, and athletic), the legislation's most dramatic effect was on high-school and college sports, which traditionally had drastically favored boys over girls in funding and in the variety of programs. The federal government sought to ensure compliance with Title IX by requiring schools and colleges to meet any one of three criteria: (a) provide athletic opportunities that are substantially proportionate to the student enrollment, (b) demonstrate a continual expansion of athletic opportunities for the underrepresented gender, or (c) fully accommodate the interest and ability of the underrepresented gender. Over the three decades following Title IX's enactment, there was an 800 percent increase in girls playing high-school sports and a 460 percent increase in women playing college sports (Fair game, 2003).

Title IX also emboldened advocates of gender equality to urge greater opportunities for girls to progress in academic fields in which girls had been underrepresented and less successful than boys. The most obvious fields were those of math, science, and such allied technologies as woodworking, mechanical drawing, auto mechanics, computer programming, and architectural design. The campaign to engage more girls in such pursuits not only demanded more openings for girls in classes but also required that girls (a) envision themselves as competent in math and science, (b) regard math and science as appropriate female pursuits, (c) expect to be welcomed and respected by classmates in those classes, and (d) have ways to redress ill treatment.

Developing a Sense of Competence

One nationwide study of math achievement revealed that girls and boys differed little in math ability, effort, or interest until their adolescent years. Then, as girls' awareness of traditional gender stereotypes increased, girls made less effort to study mathematics, thereby limiting their future math education and, eventually, their career choices. The authors of the study suggested that

> gender differences in mathematics performance result from the accumulated effects of sex-role stereotyping by families, schools, and society. Although American society pays lip service to being committed to equal opportunity, public attitudes perpetuate stereotypes that "girls really can't do math" and that "math is unfeminine." As long as such stereotypes exist, females will

> continue to drop out prematurely from mathematics education. (Manning, 1998)

Therefore, one way that teachers, counselors, and school administrators can combat such a tendency is by not spreading the notion that girls are unable to master math and science as well as boys. Furthermore, research has suggested that when boys take math tests, they are more willing than girls to guess the answers to questions whose answers they are not entirely sure about. Therefore, educators not only can profitably emphasize girls' mathematics competence but can also urge girls to take risks when solving math problems. Educators can also advise test constructors to consider how directions about guessing might influence female test takers, because "when instruction and assessment reflect female perspectives, females are just as capable at mathematical analysis as males are" (Manning, 1998).

Another way schools can bolster girls' confidence in their math aptitude is by encouraging adept math students to urge their friends to take math classes. The efficacy of this approach was demonstrated in a study of 6,547 high-school students, showing that by the early years of the 21st century,

> contrary to popular opinion but in line with recent government findings, girls have caught up with boys in terms of the math courses they take in high school. One reason is the kinds of friends and peers they have in high school. All teens—girls as well as boys—with close friends and other peers who made good grades took more higher-level math than other teens. But the connection between these relationships and the math classes was stronger for girls than for boys. (Friends' school achievement, 2008)

Gender Appropriateness

In the past, traditional opinions about what types of occupations were appropriate for women and for men resulted in females being denied access to—or at least being discouraged from entering—vocations considered the exclusive province of males. Such opinions extended to school subjects that were associated with male occupations, such as mathematics, science, electronics, political science, business management, and manual arts (woodworking, metalworking, auto mechanics, architecture, mechanical drawing). However, social change in recent years has opened opportunities for women to enter nearly all of the former "male occupations" and for girls to study subjects leading to those callings.

Today, school personnel increasingly seek to convince girls that they can realistically prepare for vocations formerly regarded as "nonfeminine." In this effort, teachers and career counselors are aided by resources on the Internet's World Wide Web. Entering such terms as *women professions, workplace gender equity*, or *gender jobs* into an Internet search engine (Google, Ask, FreeFind, Yahoo! Search, MSN Search) generates a host of valuable websites. The following two examples illustrate kinds of information useful for expanding students' understanding of vocational opportunities for girls.

Discovering what it takes to succeed. The organization WomensWork created the Role-Model Project for Girls to illustrate the conviction that "girls can grow up to be almost anything." The group's website (www.womenswork.org/girls/index.html) is organized as two levels of information. The first level offers a list of vocational domains and specific occupations within each field. The vocational domains are a mixture of occupational fields and types of workers:

> Arts, building design, computer science, crafts, educators, entrepreneurs, finance, entertainment, historians, journalists, writers, library and information services, management, manufacturing, mass media, medical services, naturalists, politics, government, safety, occupational health, sales, marketing, sciences, sports, technicians, telecommunications, transportation, trades. (Role-model, 1996)

The following examples illustrate specific vocations under four of the domains.

Arts—musician, performer, sculptor, photographer
Building Design—interior designer, electrician, heating/cooling engineer, architect, construction worker, heavy machine operator
Communications (including the Internet)—multimedia developer, public relations, web designer
Computer Sciences—software designer, programmer, tech support, technical writer, systems administrator (Role-model, 1996)

The second level of the website offers dozens of testimonials from women that include their job title, the path they followed to enter their vocation, and comments about their work. Here are two sample testimonials, one from a photographer (the arts domain) and the other from a digital designer (the computer-science domain).

> RESPONDENT: Ann
> JOB TITLE: Horse-show photographer
> PATH TO THE VOCATION: My 7-year-old son wanted to show horses. There was no photographer at the shows, so I went to a "horse-show photography" school—a week—and learned how to do it. I've been doing it now for over 15 years.

COMMENTS: If you love horses, this is the perfect career! I work weekends to take the pictures, then do the order taking and paperwork during the week. It could be a part-time job, but I make it full-time and travel all over the country photographing horse shows, rodeos, and clinics. I also do a lot of stallion photography and fine art photography—that is, calendar shoots. It only takes a good camera, a special flash and long-life battery, and a good work ethic to get established and become successful.

RESPONDENT: Mara
JOB TITLE: Digital artist (creating art within the computer format with additional mediums incorporated)
PATH TO THE VOCATION: I studied printmaking, photography, graphic design, drafting, and Autocad, and I put them all together with the help of the computer environment.
COMMENTS: Explore many different avenues to express your creativity. Girls often feel self-conscious when they display their ideas, but there is no right or wrong in the creative realm, so all of your expressions are good. Work efficiently so that you always move forward. There are many choices in the visual arts profession; don't limit yourself. (Role-model, 1996)

Job conditions. Whereas the WomensWork web pages describe multiple vocations for which girls can prepare, a web address titled Women in the Professions offers a series of essays describing women's experiences in different workplaces, such as in military settings, computer-science sites, and government offices (Women in the professions, 2008).

Websites are helpful sources of information about nontraditional careers not only for girls but also for boys. In effect, social change over recent decades has opened to males a variety of occupations that earlier had been regarded as appropriate only for females, including such vocations as dental hygienist, dietician, librarian, medical-laboratory technician, nurse, occupational therapist, and preschool teacher.

In summary, the Internet is a valuable resource for teachers and counselors as they seek to expand both girls' and boys' purview of potential careers and of the kinds of studies to pursue in preparing for such careers.

Feeling Comfortable in Class

A problem especially noticeable in secondary schools is that of girls feeling intimidated and out of place in math, science, and technology classes that are dominated by boys who—either intentionally or unwittingly—flaunt their putative superiority in such subjects. One approach to solving this problem has been for school to offer single-sex classes in such subjects. Single-sex classes can be either in single-gender schools or in coeducational schools. The popularity of single-sex classes has increased in recent years, particularly as a result of the U.S. Department of Education's October 2006 regulation permitting the establishment of single-gender classes in public schools that

1. provide a rationale for offering a single-gender class in that subject. A variety of rationales are acceptable, e.g., if very few girls have taken computer science in the past, the school could offer a girls-only computer science class;
2. provide a coeducational class in the same subject at a geographically accessible location. That location may be at the same school, but the school or school district may also elect to offer the coeducational alternative at a different school which is geographically accessible. The term "geographically accessible" is not explicitly defined in the regulations.
3. conduct a review every two years to determine whether single-sex classes are still necessary to remedy whatever inequity prompted the school to offer the single-sex class in the first place. (NASSPE, 2006)

According to publications of the National Association for Single Sex Public Education, there is now

> good evidence that single-sex classrooms can break down gender stereotypes. Girls in single-sex educational settings are more likely to take classes in math, science, and information technology. Boys in single-sex schools are more likely to pursue interests in art, music, drama, and foreign languages. Both girls and boys have more freedom to explore their own interests and abilities in single-gender classrooms. (NASSPE, 2007)

An example of a computer-technology course of study for high-school girls in a single-gender class is the GenYES-GIT curriculum (Generation Youth and Educators Succeeding: Girls' Issues in Technology). The GIT manual explains that the curriculum was built on the following premise:

> You can get young women to develop their confidence, skills, and enthusiasm in using technology by offering a program that focuses on issues that are vitally important to them and that uses a social-learning environment that they find supportive. If they are comfortable in the classroom and vitally interested in the topic, they will be open to learning how to use the tools that enable them to explore the topics. (GenGIT Manual, 1996)

Computer-technology skills are taught during the process of guiding students to investigate issues of particular interest to adolescent girls. The issues are in the form of five study units or modules titled (a) eating disorders, (b) the influence of mass media on your life, (c) choosing a career, (d) women's self-defense skills, and (e) coping with grief and loss.

The technology skills taught as students investigate the five issues include (a) how to operate a computer efficiently; (b) types of software and their functions; (c) the etiquette of computer use; (d) how to search the Internet's World Wide Web; (e) communication tools (e-mail, chat sites, forums, newsgroups, and listservs); (f) how to create CDs, DVDs, PowerPoint presentations, videos, and web pages; and (g) using digital cameras, scanners, photo-editing software, digital-design techniques, and graphics-design software (Generation GIT, 1996).

Redressing Alleged Mistreatment

At a growing rate, schools have established official procedures for coping with apparent violations of students' gender-equity rights. As an example, the following regulation appeared in the 2007–2008 Chippewa Falls (Wisconsin) High School student handbook:

> It is the intention of the Chippewa Falls Area School District to comply with the rules and regulations pertaining to non-discrimination on the basis of sex in all district education programs and activities. To put this policy into action, the following procedure has been established by the Title IX Committee. . . . It is the intention of this committee to encourage the resolution of all sex-equity complaints first upon an informal basis. These procedures are to be used when informal methods are insufficient.
>
> *What is a grievance?* A grievance is an issue related to discrimination within the district on the basis of sex.
>
> *Who may file a grievance?* Any student or employee, full or part-time, who feels that a situation exists which exhibits discrimination on the basis of sex.
>
> *How is a grievance filed?* A grievance is filed according to the instructions below.
>
> *Step 1*: Any person with a sex-equity grievance may first discuss the matter with their building principal or direct supervisor, with the intention of resolving the matter informally. They may be accompanied during this discussion by the Title IX Coordinator or a representative of the Title IX Committee, if they so wish. It is the intention of the committee that all complaints be handled in as informal, low-key a manner as possible at all times. This grievance procedure is to be used only if informal methods have not resolved the situation.
>
> *Step 2*: If the above method proves insufficient, the student or employee fills out the grievance form that can be obtained from the Title IX Coordinator.
>
> *2a*. The Title IX Coordinator investigates the circumstances of the complaint within five working days.
>
> *2b*. Within ten working days of having received the complaint, the Title IX Coordinator will notify all parties named in the grievance of a decision on the complaint, with suggestions for resolution.
>
> *2c*. If either party named in the grievance does not agree with the coordinator's decision, the complaint will be reviewed by the Title IX Committee within ten working days.

2d. If the committee agrees with the coordinator, the matter is resolved.

2e. If the committee disagrees with the coordinator, the matter may be appealed to the Superintendent by the Committee, or by either of the parties named in the grievance. At this point, the Title IX Coordinator shall put the history of the complaint into writing and attach it to the original grievance form.

Step 3: All appeals to the Superintendent will result in a meeting with both parties of the complaint. The Title IX Coordinator and the Superintendent will be present. When the Title IX Committee requests the appeal, a representative from that committee will be present also. All appeals to the Superintendent will result in a decision, which will be put in writing within five working days of the conference and given to all parties attending the meeting.

Step 4: If any further appeals are needed, they can be requested by either of the aggrieved parties present in the meeting in Step 3. This final appeal can be made to the Board of Education at the next monthly meeting. An executive session may be requested. Within five working days after the hearing on the appeal, the Board of Education shall communicate its decision, in writing, together with its supporting reasons to all parties present at the hearing. The Board of Education's decision will be final. (Chippewa Falls, 2007)

Judging Individuals

Finally, it is vitally important for school staff members to realize that information about average differences between the genders in abilities and personality traits is of no help whatsoever when working with individual students. As noted earlier, the distributions of characteristics among boys and girls greatly overlap. Thus, there is no way to estimate what a particular student's aptitude or personality traits will be on the basis of data about average differences between girls and boys as a group. In effect, many girls are superior to "the average boy" in math, science, and spatial relations. Many boys are superior to "the average girl" in reading and verbal skills. Therefore, to understand a given student's cognitive skills, it is necessary to assess that specific student's performance, free from traditional gender stereotypes. The same is true for physical traits—height, weight, strength, agility, endurance, manual dexterity, and the like.

A GAY-RIGHTS POSITION

Every culture's dominant belief system includes notions of how males should differ from females. Table 8.1 has proposed key components of the dominant American belief system that was in vogue during the early decades of the 20th century, a pattern of thought that has carried its influence into the 21st century but has been undergoing significant revision in recent years. The gay-rights movement has played a key role in promoting that change.

A Short History of Homosexual Suppression

The expression *gender-role preference* refers to which lifestyle—masculine or feminine—a person chooses to adopt. Cultures have differed markedly over the centuries in the dominant view held by the populace about what sort—or sorts—of preference are acceptable. For example, the ancient Greeks approved of heterosexuality (erotic attraction to the opposite gender), homosexuality (erotic attraction to one's own gender), and bisexuality (attraction to both one's own and the opposite gender). Furthermore, in traditional Samoan culture, the homosexual male (*fa'afafine*) was—and still is—an acceptable member of society. And when Europeans began settling North America in the 16th century, "American Indian homosexual men were called 'berdaches'—French for 'slave-boys'—used to refer to passive male homosexuals. The name stuck, although its servile connotations were quite inappropriate in the Native American context where *berdaches* were accorded considerable social prestige" (Trewartha, 1989).

In contrast, most Christian European cultures from the Middle Ages forward accorded social approval only to heterosexuals, a tradition carried to the Americas by Christian settlers and widely promoted far into the 20th century, with serious negative sanctions imposed on anyone caught in homosexual or bisexual relationships. Doctrinaire Roman Catholics and evangelical Protestants continue to subscribe to such convictions in the 21st century.

The credit—or blame—for the heterosexual-only dictum has traditionally been assigned to a trio of fourth-century Christian clerics—Augustine (354–430), Ambrose (340–397), and Jerome (342–420). Not only did they condemn homosexuality, but erotic acts other than coitus in marriage were deemed sinful. According to Augustine, even in marriage the aim of intercourse was solely to bear children, and certainly not to experience sensual pleasure. Jerome contended, "The truth is that, in view of the purity of the body of Christ, all sexual intercourse is unclean" (Lim, 1999). And St. Ambrose has been celebrated as "the most eloquent and exhaustive of all the exponents of virginity, and his judgment expresses yet the opinion of the [Roman Catholic] Church" (Loughlin, 1907).

The prevailing attitude toward homosexuality among immigrants during the European colonization of North America was reflected in typical legal sanctions.

1641—Massachusetts makes sodomy a capital crime, but excuses lesbianism as a crime. They cite the biblical verse Leviticus 20:13, which condemns "man lying with mankind as he lies with a woman."
1642—Connecticut includes sodomy in its 12 capital crimes. In Salem, Massachusetts, Elizabeth Johnson receives a whipping for lesbianism.
1646—Jan Creoli, a Negro, is choked to death in New Netherland for supposedly sodomizing a 10-year-old boy named Manuel Congo. Congo receives a flogging for his participation in the crime. William Plaine, one of the original settlers of Guilford, Connecticut, is accused of committing sodomy twice in England and of corrupting "a great part of the youth of Guilford by masturbations." He is executed in New Haven.
1682—Pennsylvania: The Quaker colony is the first state to make sodomy a noncapital offense, limiting punishment to whipping, forfeiture of one-third of one's estate, and 6 months of hard labor. The law was amended in 1700 to life imprisonment or castration.
1718—Pennsylvania revises its laws, making sodomy a capital offense. (*Timeline*, 2008)

Not only were homosexuals and bisexuals subject to official censure and punishment, but they were also scorned by the general populace and ridiculed with such slang labels as:

- For males—*ace queen, ass rider, aunt fancy, bugger, faggot, fairy, gay, lavender boy, lily, queer, Percy pants, sissy queen, yoo-hoo boy*, and dozens more
- For females—*bull dike, butch, dyke, lesbian, manlike, manified, Sapphic, tomboy*, and others
- For bisexuals—*AC-DC, Bi, hoyden, john & joan, switch hitter*, and more

During the latter decades of the 20th century, American homosexuals, bisexuals, and their heterosexual sympathizers responded to such treatment by creating a social movement known variously as the *lesbian-gay-bisexual-transgender protest, gay-rights movement*, and *gay revolution*. (Adopting a traditional heterosexual life style today is commonly referred to as being *straight*.)

Friday evening, June 27, 1969, is often cited as the launching date of the modern-day gay-rights effort. That date marked what is known as the Stonewall riots. However, this was not the first attempt to gain respectable social status for nonheterosexuals. On the day before Christmas in 1924, a World War I veteran, Henry Gerber (1892–1972), founded the Society for Human Rights in Illinois and published a periodical titled *Friendship & Freedom*. But state officials who had approved the society's charter had not realized that the freedom Gerber intended was the right to be homosexual or bisexual. When authorities discovered Gerber's true purpose, they had the Chicago police raid Gerber's office, jail him, stop further publication of *Friendship & Freedom*, and have Gerber fired from his job as a Post Office clerk. Some homosexuals' efforts in later years modestly advanced the gay-rights cause, as when Harry Hay in 1951 founded the first nationwide gay-rights organization—the Mattachine Society—and when in 1956 the Daughters of Bilitis was created as the pioneering national lesbian organization.

However, those early efforts did not ignite the massive efforts of homosexuals and bisexuals to effect significant change in the public treatment of nonheterosexual Americans. Instead, the event that set off the present-day revolution in gender-role preference was the riot that erupted at an illegal singles bar at the Stonewall Inn in New York City's Greenwich Village in June 1969. Seven New York City police officers raided the bar, dragged some patrons to a patrol car, and physically abused others. But in contrast to customers' having submitted meekly to police during raids in the past, this time they resisted, screaming at the officers and pelting them with bottles and debris. Word of the fracas spread quickly through the Village, and dozens of other protesters joined the fray. When police reinforcements arrived, they were met by growing hordes of rioters. The result was a series of intermittent confrontations that lasted 5 days. In such a fashion, the highly aggressive modern-day gay-liberation movement was born.

Over the following decades, groups from the gay community worked to (a) repeal laws prohibiting consensual homosexual acts, (b) pass legislation barring discrimination against gays in housing and employment, and (c) gain acceptance of homosexuals by the general population. With each passing year, thousands of individuals who earlier had kept their erotic inclinations secret now publicly acknowledged their homosexual or bisexual preference. In 1973 the American Psychiatric Association removed homosexuality as an illness from its *Diagnostic and Statistical Manual of Mental Disorders*. By 1999, antisodomy laws in 32 states had been repealed or declared unconstitutional. In 2004 the U.S. Supreme Court overturned all state antisodomy laws and reversed a 1986 decision that had denied the right of privacy for people engaging in consensual sexual acts. By 2008, same-sex marriages were legal in California and Massachusetts.

The term *gay*, which had been used to insult homosexual males in the past, was now embraced by homosexuals as the key identifier of their gender-roles movement. The motto *gay pride* expressed the guiding attitude of the movement's members. Today the word *gay* is used two ways—(a) to label both male and female homosexuals and (b) to identify males in particular, with the word *lesbian* then selected to identify female homosexuals. The movement is now often symbolized by the acronym LGBT (*lesbian-gay-bisexual-transgender*). Furthermore, the gay community has borrowed another former pejorative term—*queer*—and turned it into a symbol of positive self-esteem, as in the expression *queer theory*, which refers to the academic study of gender issues.

Two sets of questions about people's gender-role preferences are especially important for schools:

- What are the causes behind such preferences? To what extent are such preferences inherited?
- What policies do schools adopt regarding heterosexuality, homosexuality, bisexuality, transvestitism, and transsexualism? How do school environments influence students' gender-role preferences?

These two sets of issues are the focus of the following discussion.

Heredity and Environment

The question of what causes people's gender-role preferences is highly complex and far from being settled. Explanations range from (a) citing inherited gene patterns as the exclusive cause to (b) attributing preferences entirely to environmental influences. Between those diametrically opposed views are diverse explanations that propose various combinations of genetic and social factors. Possibly the causes differ from one person to another, thereby rendering the puzzle of gender-role preference infinitely complicated. That is, some people may have inherited a genetic pattern (*queer gene*) that destines them to embrace a particular gender life style—homosexual or bisexual—no matter how the environments they inhabit urge them to do otherwise. In contrast, other people may be easily led by circumstances to engage in acts contrary to the typical behavior expected of their gender in their culture. Such might be true of girls who adopt homosexual acts while attending an all-girls' boarding school or of sailors introduced to homosexuality while on long sea voyages. Furthermore, environments may affect gender-role preferences differently at successive stages of the life span. Experimenting with same-sex engagements is rather common among adolescents who will usually abandon those acts for heterosexual relations in adulthood (Committee on Adolescence, 1993; Harrison, 2003).

It is also the case that there are different degrees to which people adopt a given gender role. For instance, some individuals limit their gender orientation to an occasional homosexual act, but in all other ways—garb, posture, gestures, voice timbre, interests—they adhere to their culture's gender stereotype. Other homosexuals adopt the complete array of their culture's stereotypical attributes of the opposite gender, with such a male homosexual often referred to as a *queen* and a female as a *butch* or *dyke*. Between those extremes are many individuals who assume different degrees of cross-gender traits.

As Bruce Robinson explained, the debate over the cause of gender-role preference is often affected by people's religious convictions.

> Many Christians from fundamentalist, other evangelical, mainline, Roman Catholic, and some other denominations believe that heterosexuality is the only normal, natural, and non-disordered sexual behavior. . . . They believe that homosexuality is ultimately a choice that young people make, although they are often heavily influenced to make this choice by bad parenting and/or sexual molestation during childhood. Being a choice, it can be changed at any time.
>
> Many liberal Christians, progressive Christians, secularists, gays, lesbians, bisexuals, human sexuality researchers, etc. believe that there are three normal, natural, and non-disordered sexual orientations: heterosexuality, homosexuality and bisexuality. . . . They believe that homosexual orientation is fixed early in life, perhaps before birth and perhaps even at conception. Being an orientation, it is rarely if ever changeable. (Robinson, 2008)

In summary, controversies over the nature and cause—or causes—of people's gender orientations may never be resolved to everyone's satisfaction.

Implications for Schools

Because gender-role preferences—and particularly a preference for homosexuality—have become such highly visible and contentious issues, schools find it prudent to establish formal policies for coping with problems of *discussing, behaving, organizing, publicizing,* and *celebrating* preferences. The need for a policy statement is suggested by such incidents as the following:

> In order to "prevent a violent reaction," the principal of Loranger High School in Amite (Louisiana) banned a female student from bringing a female date to a school dance. (Vargas 2008)

> A high-school principal in Webb City (Missouri) sent a student home for wearing a T-shirt that bore the message "I'm gay and I'm proud." When the student was told that "someone might be offended" by the message, he objected by saying that school officials had allowed anti-gay-marriage stickers to be displayed around the school. His objection was ignored. A spokesperson for the American Civil Liberty Union asserted, "This school allows its students to freely express their views on gay and lesbian rights—

but only if they're on the anti-gay side of the issue. . . . This is a classic case of censorship. [The gay student] has the same Constitutional right to political speech and expression that the Supreme Court says all students have." (Kurtenbach, 2004)

A San Diego (California) man, who identified himself as a Christian activist, charged that it was "shocking and demoralizing" to see children and teachers from a charter public elementary school marching in the city's homosexual-pride parade. The activist called the event "an advertisement for the gay pornography industry. . . . [People] can just imagine the depravity that's in this parade." (Brown, 2006)

As a disciplinary measure, a teacher in Lafayette Parish (Louisiana) sent a seven-year-old boy home from school with a note to the child's mother saying that her son had been dismissed because "he explained to another child that you are gay and that gay means . . . when a girl likes a girl." The teacher's note added that such talk was not acceptable in her class. (Vargas, 2008)

Some residents of Lebanon (Missouri) criticized a Lebanon High School group for participating in the national "Day of Silence" during which students chose not to speak all day in honor of the victims of homosexual hate crimes. Reporters from the KSPR television station sought to learn more about public reaction to the event by asking members of the community, "Do you think schools should allow gay-friendly activities?" The range of viewpoints is reflected in these four responses.

"Absolutely no!"

"No way. It's ridiculous. They don't have straight-friendly activities."

"Yes! You live in America with the freedom to choose, to participate or not!"

"Yes. Yes. Yes. It's all about progress. These are real issues and should be addressed as such." (Should schools, 2008)

A federal appeals court ruled that—contrary to a school regulation—a sophomore at Neuqua Valley High School in Naperville (Illinois) could wear to class a T-shirt with an anti-gay message ("Be Happy, Not Gay") in protest to the school's annual Day of Silence. A lawyer for the Alliance Defense Fund, which litigates on behalf of Christian causes, praised the court's decision—"Public school officials cannot censor a message expressing one viewpoint on homosexual behavior and then at the same time allow messages that express another viewpoint." Representatives of the American Civil Liberties Union also supported the court ruling. (Neuqua Valley, 2008)

Controversy erupted among students and faculty members at Kell High School in Marietta (Georgia) after a student wrote an editorial in the school newspaper characterizing homosexuals as products of "reproductive error" and contending that gays should be denied the privilege of marrying. (Anti-gay editorial, 2007)

> During the night, vandals set a small fire and painted graffiti on walls at Oceana High School in Pacifica (California). The graffiti included swastikas, slurs against gays, and "white-power" messages. (Lagos, 2007)

The following paragraphs propose issues that can profitably be addressed in a written school gender-preference policy. Each issue is cast in the form of one or more questions that the policy statement should answer.

Discussing

The term *discussing* in the present context refers to how such matters as heterosexuality, homosexuality, bisexuality, transvestism, and transsexuality are spoken about in regular classroom discourse, forums, and individual or group counseling sessions. (*Transvestism* or *cross-dressing* means wearing the clothing of the opposite gender; a *transvestite* is a person who cross-dresses. *Transsexualism* is a condition in which a person identifies with physical-sex attributes different from the gender he or she was born with. Most transsexual males and females want to permanently assume the status of a member of the gender with which they identify.)

Questions that a policy statement can answer about *discussing* include:

- Will teachers be allowed to: (a) speak about heterosexuality, homosexuality, bisexuality, transvestism, and transsexuality in class, (b) advocate one gender-role preference over another?
- In which kinds of classes (such as biology, health education, social studies) and at which grade levels may gender-role preferences be discussed?
- During classroom sessions, will students be allowed to: (a) speak about heterosexuality, homosexuality, bisexuality, transvestism, and transsexuality, (b) advocate one gender-role preference over another?
- May visitors be invited to class, school forums, or school clubs to: (a) speak about heterosexuality, homosexuality, bisexuality, transvestism, and transsexuality in class, (b) advocate one gender-role preference over another?
- Will school counselors, social workers, or psychologists during small-group or individual sessions with students be allowed to: (a) speak about heterosexuality, homosexuality, bisexuality, transvestism, and transsexuality in class, (b) advocate one gender-role preference over another?
- What sorts of comments by teachers or students about other people's gender-role preferences are acceptable and what sorts are prohibited?
- What sanctions will be imposed on individuals who violate the school's policies about discussing gender-role preferences?

On what rationale or line of reasoning are the school's discussion policies founded?

Behaving

The expression *behaving* refers to overt actions by students or school personnel. Questions about behavior that can suitably be answered in a policy declaration include:

What gestures and kinds of touching between students, between school personnel, or between a school staff member and a student are forbidden, and why?
In what settings does the prohibition against gestures and touching apply?

Organizing

Students, school staff members, or people from outside the school sometimes seek to establish organizations in schools that focus on gender-role preferences. The most prominent example is the series of Gay-Straight Alliances found in many U.S. public high schools. The alliances are student-organized and student-led clubs that support gay, lesbian, bisexual, and transsexual students' efforts to gain rights and nonprejudicial treatment. In contrast to such groups that promote nontraditional gender-role orientations are others that denounce homosexuality, bisexuality, and transsexualism. The antigay groups are sometimes associated with religious denominations whose efforts include strong opposition to nontraditional gender roles.

Are students or school personnel permitted to create, import, or sponsor clubs or social-action groups whose purpose is to promote particular gender-role preferences? If so, what rules govern the establishment and conduct of those organizations?
On what rationale are such policies based?
What sanctions will be imposed on people who violate the rules governing organizations?

Publicizing

Students or school personnel may attempt to advertise their opinions about gender-role preferences via various media, including (a) personal chats with individuals or small groups, (b) speeches at school gatherings (assemblies, graduation exercises, club meetings, athletic events), (c) brochures distributed to individual students or staff members, (d) posters, (e) messages on bulletin boards, (f) editorials in school newspapers or newsletters, (g) Internet e-mails and websites, and (h) public demonstrations (rallies, walk-outs, sit-ins). School policy statements can define how such activities will be controlled by answering such questions as:

Which methods—if any—of distributing messages about gender-role preferences are permitted?

What rules govern the content of such messages, and what line of reasoning supports those rules?

What sanctions will be applied to individuals or groups that violate the rules?

Celebrating

Ceremonies relating to gender-role preferences can assume a variety of forms, with gay and lesbian events often accompanied by the display of the gay community's rainbow-hued flag. As examples of typical modes of celebration, consider the following array of activities:

The San Francisco Unified School District designated April as *Gay Pride Month* to honor the contributions of its "gay, lesbian, bisexual, transgender students, staff, faculty, parents, and families." The celebration was listed as the month's health-awareness event (Gay pride celebration, 2008).

Events at New Hope-Solebury High School (New Hope, Pennsylvania) during the annual Gay Pride Days each May include a League of Our Own Softball Tournament, a songfest (Sing out Loud and Proud), a GLBT film festival, parties, bike tours, and a Rainbow Pride Parade (Collins, 2008).

When a Kalamazoo (Michigan) High School drama group scheduled the production of the play *The Laramie Project,* members of the Westboro Baptist Church in Topeka (Kansas) announced that they would come to Kalamazoo to picket the drama in protest. *The Laramie Project* is a drama based on an actual event—the hate-crime slaying of Matthew Shepard, an openly gay University of Wyoming student who was beaten to death in 1998 in Laramie (Wyoming). The Westboro protestors were well known for picketing gay-pride events (Hugenberg, 2008).

Members of the Gay-Straight Alliance from high schools in the San Francisco Bay area marched in San Francisco's 36th annual gay-pride parade, carrying signs that ranged from the political to the whimsical, including: "Viva la Revolucion Homosexual!" "If you don't want a gay marriage, don't get one," and "My sexual orientation? Horizontal, usually" (Sebastian & Bulwa, 2006).

Schools' policy statements governing gender-role preferences can usefully include answers to such questions as:

What types of ceremonies, rituals, or celebrations relating to gender-role orientations are permitted in school or under school sponsorship in other locations?
What types are not permitted, and why?
What kinds of sanctions will be applied to people who violate school policies regarding ceremonies, rituals, or celebrations?
What process should be followed by people who wish to appeal school officials' decisions about ostensible violations of school policies?

INTERPRETATIONS

As in earlier chapters, six vantage points from which gender traits and role preferences can be viewed in this chapter are those of (a) decision making (by students and school personnel), (b) heredity and environment, (c) *could-be, is,* and *should-be* beliefs, (d) sources of evidence, (e) power and authority, and (f) implications for schools. Because two of the perspectives—heredity/environment and school implications—have already been addressed, the following remarks are limited to the remaining four viewpoints.

Decision Making

Gender Traits

As illustrated in this chapter, Americans' beliefs about the characteristics that distinguish males from females have been changing rather dramatically over the past half century. During this transition period, students have been obliged to decide (a) which traits are "normal" (in the sense of *socially acceptable*) for females and for males, (b) which traits they, themselves, will display in their own lives, and (c) how to treat schoolmates whose traits do not match the ones that they, themselves, accept as "normal."

Teachers, administrators, coaches, counselors, and other staff members face the same three decisions as do students—deciding what is "normal," what gender traits they will exhibit in their own lives, and how to treat students and fellow staff members whose gender characteristics differ from their own. Officials also need to decide in what forms the school's official position about gender traits will be expressed and how rules will be enforced—such forms as student handbooks, written codes of conduct, and dress regulations.

Role Preferences

Students and school personnel face two principal decisions—(a) whether in their own behavior they will adhere to a heterosexual (straight) role preference or else assume a homosexual, bisexual, or transsexual lifestyle and (b) whether they will approve of, or will disapprove of, other people who practice lifestyles other than heterosexual.

Could-be, Is, Should-be

In view of the widespread availability of television and the Internet for people of all ages, there likely is little difference of opinion among students and school personnel about the present-day status (the *is*) of gender traits. American females and males are depicted in so many kinds of garb, occupations, sports, and pastimes that the traditional list of *is* differences in female and male traits has shrunk dramatically. Furthermore, in view of the great diversity of pictured traits in the mass-communication media, there is little debate over what the traits of each gender *could be*. Consequently, the present-day impassioned controversies over gender characteristics are chiefly about what male and female qualities *should be*. In effect, many people appear to believe that even though some folks have adopted—and most folks *could* adopt—traits traditionally indicative of the opposite gender, folks really shouldn't do so—"It's just not right."

Opinions about *should be* usually differ by generation. Younger people are more apt than older people to accept an *androgynous* view of gender characteristics (with *androgynous* meaning "neither distinguishably masculine nor feminine in dress, appearance, or behavior"). As a result, today more male youths than older men wear earrings, and more youthful females than older women are engaged in engineering occupations.

Sources of Evidence

Gender Traits

Four sources of students' beliefs about gender qualities are the family, friends, school, and mass-communication media. The influence of these agents usually varies across the years of childhood and adolescence. Family members are the most significant in early childhood, as parents and siblings dictate children's mode of dress, models of speech, manners, toys, pastimes, and forms of sexual modesty. Second only to young children's family members are the mass media, primarily television. As children enter school, their classmates and teachers exert increasing influence as the young advance into middle school and high school. School rules about garb and behavior affect students' beliefs and actions. The types of classes offered and the manner of teachers' treatment of girls and boys in those classes can also affect youths' beliefs about gender. Yet during adolescence, attentive parents can still be significant in forming students' notions of proper gender traits.

Role Preferences

Students' beliefs about gender orientation (heterosexual, homosexual, bisexual, transsexual) derive not only from parents, friends, television, movies, the Internet, and school but also from religious sources—parents' religious affiliation, students' church attendance, religious clubs, and counseling sessions with priests, ministers, rabbis, or imams. Evangelical, fundamentalist Christian denominations and the Roman Catholic Church have been particularly active in promoting belief in no erotic relationships outside of marriage and in denouncing homosexuality, bisexuality, transvestism, and transsexualism.

Power and Authority

Important sources of power in any society are the culture's statements of values. Examples of such statements from religious traditions are the Judeo Ten Commandments, the Christian Golden Rule, Confucian Analects, Islam's Quran, Scientology's tenets, and dictates in the Book of Mormon. Secular sources of values include national constitutions, states' mottos, and communities' laws. Typically, the originator of the values is identified as an authority whom the populace respects or fears, such as God, Jehovah, Allah, Brahman, or the Buddha.

But in some instances, the values are said to be so self-evident that they require no proof of origin. An example is the Declaration of Independence, issued July 4, 1776, by the 13 colonies that would become the original United States: "We hold these truths to be self-evident, that all men are created equal, that they are endowed by their Creator with certain unalienable Rights, that among these are Life, Liberty, and the pursuit of Happiness." Even the secular Thomas Jefferson, who wrote this passage, sought to buttress the ostensible obviousness of the "truths" by mentioning a divine authority—"their Creator."

It is important to recognize that such statements of values are not descriptions of existing conditions. They do not tell what the society *is* like. Instead, they tell what the society *should be* like. Hence, the values are ideals to be pursued. The statements wield power to the degree that the populace accepts their authoritative nature and will strive to promote the values and endorse punitive sanctions against members of society who fail to abide by the principles.

One way of viewing recent confrontations over gender traits and role preferences is as contests between groups that draw on different authorities for the values they hope will guide American society. Activists who seek to maintain traditional conceptions of gender traits and roles typically appeal to religious authorities, whereas activists who attempt to alter conceptions of traits and roles appeal to the vision of equal rights expressed in the Declaration of Independence and U.S. Constitution.

By way of illustration, advocates of women's customary traits and roles in America's Christian-based culture will often support their position by citing passages from the Bible or declarations of revered theologians.

> And the Lord God said, "It is not good that the man should be alone; I will make him an help [helper] meet [suitable] for him" (Genesis 2:18).
>
> [The Bible's first woman, Eve, is told by God that] "thy desire shall be to thy husband, and he shall rule over thee" (Genesis 3:16).
>
> "As regards the individual nature, woman is defective and misbegotten, for the active power of the male seed tends to the production of a perfect likeness in the masculine sex; while the production of a woman comes from defect in the active power" (St. Thomas Aquinas, cited in Robinson, 2006).

However, religious authorities usually are not invoked by people who credit females with traditional male traits and vice versa. Nor are religious traditions cited during efforts to win respect for nontraditional gender roles (homosexual, bisexual, transsexual). Instead, advocates of such change invoke the Declaration of Independence and the Constitution's Amendments in their effort to attract support. (The 9th Amendment protects rights not specified in the Bill of Rights, the 13th prohibits slavery, and the 19th awards women voting rights.)

So, in such an atmosphere of conflict, confrontations over gender traits and roles continue, with the contending adversaries appealing to different authorities as a means of rallying followers to their cause.

Chapter 9

Sex-Education Programs

Offering sex education in schools has always been a controversial activity. And during the early years of the 21st century, it has continued to be contentious, as this chapter explains. The four aims of the chapter are to (a) offer a brief sketch of the history of sex education in American schools, (b) describe in some detail the nature of recent conflicts over three types of sex-education programs, (c) identify the groups involved in the conflicts, and (d) interpret the chapter's content in terms of the six vantage points introduced in chapter 1.

BACKGROUNDS OF SEX EDUCATION IN AMERICA

Prior to the 20th century, teaching the young about sexual matters had no place in public schools. Instructing youths in "the facts of life" was a family responsibility, assigned primarily to parents, sometimes with the aid and advice of the clergy—a minister, priest, or rabbi. In practice, however, parents often avoided the topic of sex out of their own embarrassment or their lack of knowing how and when to approach the subject. Therefore, much of youngsters' sexual knowledge came from siblings, peers, or older youths and adults who sought to engage the young in sexual activities. Pornography and bawdy songs also contributed to youths' views of what sex was all about. The result was often a distorted understanding of the biological, social, moral, and emotional features of human sexuality. Or, for children who were shielded from such sources, the result was simply a void—little or no knowledge about sexual behavior and its potential consequences.

Jeffrey Moran, in his chronicle of formal sex education in public schools (*Teaching Sex: The Shaping of Adolescence in the 20th Century*), traces the beginning of planned sex education to Chicago, the site of the nation's first formal sex-hygiene program that was

> compelled in part by the city's rampant venereal disease problem, thriving red light districts, and an increasingly permissive sexual culture. When Superintendent Ella Flagg Young led the effort to implement this program in 1913, she encountered breathtaking resistance among local politicians—in a battle that would presage many others to come. (Blount, 2003)

As more schools adopted sex-education programs over the next four decades, they sought to sanitize the erotic aspects of sex behavior by giving instruction a "scientific" flavor. Biological processes were described in technical terms accompanied by depersonalized diagrams, resulting in lessons "too boring to be suggestive" (Moran, 2000, p. 49).

Soon public willingness to openly discuss sexual issues was expanded by the publication of such studies as Alfred Kinsey's *Sexual Behavior in the Human Male* in 1948 and *Sexual Behavior in the Human Female* in 1953. As sexual mores grew more open, high schools in their life-adjustment classes increasingly added topics about dating, choosing a mate, parenting, and avoiding delinquent behavior.

The social revolution in youth culture during the 1960s further liberalized sexual behavior and its discussion. One indicator of this change was the founding of the Sex Information and Education Council of the United States (SIECUS) by Dr. Mary Calderone. SIECUS advocated a scientific approach to such topics as reproduction, responsible sex, and "sexuality as a healthy entity" (Moran, 2000, p. 162). However, a variety of conservative church groups—representing the "Religious Right"—were appalled by SIECUS and succeeded in preventing the introduction of its program into many conservative communities. But such events as the appearance and rapid spread of AIDS in the final decades of the 20th century would heighten popular support for comprehensive sex education in schools.

During the early years of the 21st century, the level of conflict over sex instruction increased, particularly as a result of conservative religious groups strongly influencing the policies of the Republican administration of President George W. Bush. "One could argue that activists—with an interest in sexual morality—fight over the public schools because they know that is where they can seem to make an impact on society's sexual standards" (Moran, 2000).

THREE VARIETIES OF SEX EDUCATION

Particularly in recent decades, proponents of three kinds of programs have sought to have their own preferred type of sex education adopted by schools. The most popular labels for the three have been *abstinence-only*, *abstinence-plus*, and *comprehensive*.

The aim of abstinence-only (*strict-abstinence*) programs is to convince students to postpone sexual acts until they are wed. The aim is pursued by teaching adolescents (a) the virtue of postponing erotic activities, (b) how postponement builds character and earns credit with God, (c) the dangers of sexual diseases and unplanned pregnancy, and (d) techniques for resisting the temptation to engage in erotic acts.

The aim of abstinence-plus programs is to emphasize the desirability of postponing sexual liaisons until marriage and also to inform teenagers of ways to protect themselves from unwelcome pregnancy and infections if they do decide not to wait until they are married.

The aim of comprehensive programs is to offer students an overview of the roles that eroticism can play in their lives, including stages of growth (childhood, puberty, adolescence), choices among ways to respond to sexual urges (including abstinence), dangers of various erotic acts (unplanned pregnancy, disease, guilt, shame), and how to protect themselves from pregnancy and disease.

It may be apparent that these three types of sex education actually represent three points along a scale extending from strict abstinence at one end to broadly inclusive, comprehensive sex education at the other end, with abstinence-plus representing an intermediate position between the two extremes. The following examples of typical abstinence-only, abstinence-plus, and comprehensive programs illustrate those positions along the scale.

Abstinence-Only Programs

The abstinence-only movement has been founded on two main tenets—(a) sexual relations should be postponed until marriage and (b) intercourse should involve a male and a female. In effect, unwed teenagers should not practice any form of erotic acts (vaginal, oral, anal), and they should always limit themselves to a heterosexual relationship (no homosexuality). The principal sponsors of abstinence-only programs have been the Catholic Church and such fundamentalist Protestant denominations as evangelicals, Southern Baptists, and Pentecostals.

The U.S. government first became officially involved with the abstinence-only movement in 1981 when Congress passed the Adolescent Family Life Act (AFLA), which was intended to prevent teen pregnancy by teaching students abstinence and by recommending adoption (as opposed to abortion) as the proper choice for pregnant teens. However, by 1983 the legality of the act was challenged in court by groups that charged (a) the way the act was being administered violated the U.S.

Constitution's First Amendment clause that separated church and state by including programs that were pressing religious views on students, and (b) information presented to students was often factually incorrect. The lawsuit was finally settled out of court in 1993 with an agreement that AFLA-funded sexuality education: (a) could not include religious references, (b) must be medically accurate, (c) must respect teenagers' right to determine for themselves whether to use contraceptives, and (d) must not allow the groups that receive government grants to use church sanctuaries for their programs or to give presentations in parochial schools during school hours (Exclusive purpose, 1997).

The federal government's encouragement of abstinence-only sex education gained strength in 1996 when Christian conservatives in the Republican-controlled Congress passed a welfare bill to which abstinence-only sex-education grants were attached. The bill was endorsed by Democratic President Bill Clinton, then later expanded with increasingly higher budget allocations under Republican President George W. Bush over the period 2001–2008. By 2007, the federal government had spent over $1 billion on abstinence-only school programs, while states had added nearly as much in obligatory matching funds.

The intent of the abstinence-only legislation was explained in a paper written by congressional staff members, who were aided in their task by the conservative Right's Heritage Foundation.

> Regardless of how one feels about the standard of no sex outside marriage, we believe that the statutory language and . . . the intent of Congress [are] clear. This standard was intended to put Congress on the side of social tradition—never mind that some observers now think the tradition outdated—that sex should be confined to married couples. That both the [sex] practices and standards in many communities across the country clash with the standard required by the law is precisely the point. . . . [Thus] the explicit goal of the abstinence-only education program is to change both behavior and community standards for the good of the country. It follows that no program that in any way endorses, supports, or encourages sex outside marriage can receive support from the abstinence-education money. (Boonstra, 2007)

The multitude of abstinence-only curricula on the market appear under such titles as Aspire: Live Your Life—Be Free, Choosing the Best Life, FACTS, Game Plan, Heritage Keepers, Making a Difference, Navigator, Passion and Principles, Sex Respect, and WAIT (Why Am I Tempted) Training.

The typical nature of such curricula can be represented by Choosing the Best Life, a program written by Bruce Cook for eighth-grade students and distributed since 1993 by Choosing the Best, Inc. According to the distributor, Choosing the Best Life was used over the decade 1993–2003 with more than 700,000 students in 2,500 school districts in 50 states (SIECUS curriculum review, 2005).

The sponsors of Choosing the Best Life explain that their curriculum is intended to help middle-school students:

- Understand and protect themselves from very real, damaging, and often overlooked emotional consequences of premarital sexual involvement, such as worry, regret, guilt, declining self-esteem, depression, and distraction from important personal goals.
- Protect themselves from serious and widespread STDs by understanding the nature of these STDs, their prevalence and mode of transmission, and the limitation of condoms to prevent the transmission, even when used consistently. Specific STDs covered include those such as genital herpes, an incurable viral infection, and human papilloma virus (HPV), also an incurable viral infection which can cause genital warts and leads to over 90 percent of all cervical cancer. Also covered are syphilis, gonorrhea, and chlamydia, which left untreated can lead to PID [pelvic inflammatory disease] and infertility.
- Protect themselves from the emotional, social, and economic consequences of teen pregnancy for the teen, the child, and the community.
- [Decide] how to choose healthy relationships, including how to recognize the differences between infatuation and love.
- [Recognize] the benefits of choosing abstinence in terms of providing the best foundation for marriage, freedom to focus on and pursue personal goals, and freedom from worrying about all of the negative emotional and physical effects of premarital sex mentioned above.
- [Understand] how to set boundaries and learn specific methods for keeping those boundaries, including assertiveness skills and strategies for overcoming pressure. These skills are important in achieving abstinence until marriage and in avoiding other high-risk behaviors such as alcohol/drug abuse. (Most frequently asked, 2008)

The program pursues these goals by means of eight lessons titled: (a) Sex, Emotions and Self-Respect, (b) Sex, Alcohol and Respect, (c) Sex, STDs and Honesty, (d) Sex, Pregnancy and Responsibility, (e) Sex, HIV/AIDS and Compassion, (f) Sex, Love and Choices, (g) Sex, Limits and Self-Discipline, and (h) Sex, Saying "No" and Courage. A leader's guidebook directs teachers in how to carry out the five activities that each lesson involves—a short video, a teacher-led discussion of the video, facts and new ideas presented by the teacher, students engaging in activities that require them to apply the lesson's topic to their own lives, and students later discussing the lesson with their parents.

Although the lessons mention the use of condoms as a way to avoid pregnancy and disease, the emphasis is on the likelihood that condoms will fail by leaking or slipping off. In effect, the overriding aim of Choosing the Best Life is to convince students to remain celibate until marriage. For example, when there are sexually active students in a class, the program encourages them "to make a choice to be abstinent from this point forward, teaching that 'renewed virginity' is the best choice they can make for their future. Teachers continually report that teens who have already been sexually active are particularly receptive to the abstinence message. . . . They've experienced first-hand the negative emotional and/or physical consequences of premarital sex and can readily see that choosing abstinence is best for their lives and future" (Most frequently asked, 2008).

No one disputes the claim that abstinence is the best way for teens to avoid pregnancy and sexually transmitted infections. But what opponents of abstinence-only programs do dispute is the claim that students from abstinence-only classes will entirely avoid premarital sex—or at least that they will avoid in larger numbers than do students from other kinds of sex-education programs. Over the years since 1996, growing numbers of empirical studies report that students who have participated in abstinence-only sex education will subsequently engage in premarital erotic ventures as often as students from other types of sex-education programs (Boonstra, 2007). Critics charge that abstinence-only programs not only fail to achieve their aim, but also do damage by leaving students ignorant of how to protect themselves from pregnancy and disease when they do engage in premarital sex.

> The best implemented and evaluated [abstinence-only] programs fail to delay initiation of sexual intercourse or to produce other demonstrable reductions in HIV risk behaviors. A six-year longitudinal study of virginity pledgers found short-term delays in sexual intercourse but no impact on laboratory-verified sexually transmitted infection. A 2004 U.S. Congressional review found that 11 of the 13 most frequently used abstinence-only curricula contained false, misleading, or distorted information—including inaccurate information about contraceptive effectiveness, risks of abortion, and other scientific errors. Another review found that curricula often provide misinformation about condoms and contraception.
>
> Moreover, abstinence-only promotion has undermined comprehensive sexuality education (i.e., complete, age-appropriate education on human sexuality including abstinence and risk reduction) within U.S. public schools, harmed other critical public health efforts such as family planning programs, and created disarray in U.S. efforts to prevent HIV globally. For example, during the period of increasing U.S. emphasis on abstinence, sharp declines have occurred in the percentage of teachers in U.S. public schools who teach

about birth control and the number of students who report receiving such education. (Dworkin & Santelli, 2007)

As one consequence of the questionable effectiveness of abstinence-only sex education, by 2007, 14 states had rejected federal-government abstinence-only funds, with additional states likely to follow (Craig, 2007).

Abstinence-Plus Programs

An abstinence-plus program presents students with a selection of safe-sex methods, with abstinence strongly featured as the most desirable of the choices. However, unlike abstinence-only approaches, the abstinence-plus programs recognize that a substantial number of adolescents will still engage in vaginal, oral, or anal sex, and that those youths deserve to know how to protect themselves without being condemned as wicked and undeserving of respect. Thus, the proper use of condoms and other protective measures is included in such plans, along with a description of such measures' advantages and limitations.

A program titled Safer Choices, published by the nonprofit ETR (Education, Training, Research) organization, illustrates a typical abstinence-plus approach. The objectives of the program are to help students

- Increase their knowledge about HIV and other STDs
- Have more positive attitudes about choosing not to have sex or using condoms if having sex
- Have greater confidence in their ability to refuse sexual intercourse or unprotected intercourse, to use a condom, and to communicate about safer sexual practices
- Perceive fewer barriers to condom use
- Have more accurate perceptions of their risk for HIV and other STDs
- Communicate more with their parents regarding sexual issues
- Use refusal and negotiation skills in sexual situations
- Reduce sexual risk behaviors by choosing not to have sexual intercourse or by increasing condom use and use of other methods of protection if having sex (ETR, 2005)

The Safer Choices curriculum consists of 20 lessons taught over two consecutive years, with the second year's 10 lessons intended to support and expand the content of the first year's 10 lessons. The titles of the first year's sessions reflect a sequence of presentations that favors abstinence in the early lessons (sessions 1–7), then later describes methods of protection for teenagers who choose to engage in erotic encounters (sessions 8–9).

Class 1: Not Everybody's Having Sex
Class 2: The Safest Choice: Deciding Not to Have Sex
Class 3: Saying No to Having Sex
Class 4: Understanding STD and HIV
Class 5: Examining the Risk of Unsafe Choices
Class 6: Teens with HIV: A Reality
Class 7: Practicing the Safest Choice
Class 8: Safer Choices: Using Protection—Part I
Class 9: Safer Choices: Using Protection—Part II
Class 10: Know What You Can Do (ETR, 2005)

Like abstinence-only programs, abstinence-plus curricula have not escaped criticism. The attacks have been launched chiefly by proponents of abstinence-only, such as the Heritage Foundation. After three of the foundation's researchers compared nine abstinence-only curricula to nine "major comprehensive sex-ed / abstinence-plus curricula," they concluded that

> Quantitative analysis revealed that traditional abstinence and comprehensive sex-ed / abstinence-plus curricula differ radically in their contents and messages. It also revealed that the claim that abstinence-plus / comprehensive sex-ed curricula place an emphasis on abstinence is false. On average, authentic or traditional abstinence curricula devote 53.7 percent of their page content to abstinence-related material. In addition, these curricula devote 17.4 percent of their content to the subjects of healthy relationships and benefits of marriage, both of which directly reinforce the main theme of teen abstinence. Authentic abstinence curricula allocate zero percent of their content to promoting contraception.
>
> Comprehensive sex-ed / abstinence-plus curricula take the opposite approach. On average, these curricula devote only 4.7 percent of their page content to the topic of abstinence and zero percent to healthy relationships and marriage. The primary focus of these curricula is on encouraging young people to use contraception. On average, comprehensive sex-ed curricula devote 28.6 percent of their page content to describing contraception and encouraging contraceptive use. Overall comprehensive sex-ed curricula allocate six times more content to the goal of promoting contraception than to the goal of promoting abstinence. (Martin, Rector & Pardue, 2004, p. v)

Proponents of abstinence-plus programs have reacted to the Heritage Foundation's study by complaining that the foundation's authors conflated abstinence-plus and comprehensive sex education. By lumping together abstinence-plus and comprehensive curricula, the authors failed to admit important distinctions between the two. For example, in contrast to the Heritage group's denying that abstinence-plus curricula "place emphasis on abstinence," it is clear that the Safer Choices program does, indeed, strongly favor abstinence.

Comprehensive Programs

The label *comprehensive* is applied to sex-education curricula that inspect many facets of sexual behavior that affect individuals' well-being and the interests of society in general. The following line of reasoning from the Planned Parenthood organization is typical of the arguments that advocates of comprehensive sex education adduce in support of their cause.

> The U.S. has the highest rate of teen pregnancy in the developed world, and American adolescents are contracting HIV faster than almost any other demographic group. The teen pregnancy rate in the U.S. is at least twice that in Canada, England, France, and Sweden, and 10 times that in the Netherlands. Experts cite restrictions on teens' access to comprehensive sexuality education, contraception, and condoms in the U.S., along with the widespread American attitude that a healthy adolescence should exclude sex. By contrast, the "European approach to teenage sexual activity, expressed in the form of widespread provision of confidential and accessible contraceptive services to adolescents, is . . . a central factor in explaining the more rapid declines in teenage childbearing in northern and western European countries." California, the only state [by 2005] that has not accepted federal abstinence-only money, has seen declines in teenage pregnancy similar to those seen in European countries. Over the last decade, the teenage pregnancy rate in California has dropped more than 40 percent. (Planned Parenthood, 2005)

Sex-education programs that subscribe to a comprehensive approach are not all alike. Their components can differ from one school system to another. What they do share in common is their attention to a variety of safe-sex practices beyond abstinence. For an impression of the diversity of topics that comprehensive programs may include, consider the following sampling of items from the SIECUS plan.

The Sexuality Information and Education Council of the United States (SIECUS) has distributed the organization's set of Guidelines for Comprehensive Sexuality Education to more than 100,000 individuals and groups throughout the nation. The guidelines' third edition provides 39 topics that include around 800 *developmental messages* for four age groups—middle childhood (ages 5–8), preadolescence (9–12), early adolescence (12–15), adolescence (15–18). The messages are "brief statements that contain the specific information young people need to learn about each topic" (Guidelines, 2004, p. 17).

The SIECUS plan was originally developed by a task force of 20 professionals in the fields of medicine, education, sexuality, and youth services representing such organizations as the American Medical Association, the March of Dimes Birth Defects Foundation, the Planned Parenthood Federation of America, the National Education Association, the American Social Health Association, the U.S. Centers for Disease Control, and the National School Boards Association.

The guidelines' 39 topics are arranged in groups of six or seven under six *concepts*—human development, relationships, personal skills, sexual behavior, sexual health, and society and culture. The diversity of topics can be suggested by these 10 examples:

- Reproduction and sexual anatomy and physiology
- Sexual orientation [heterosexual, homosexual, bisexual]
- Love
- Romantic relationships and dating
- Sexual abstinence
- Decision making
- Sexuality and the law
- Abortion
- Sexual dysfunction
- HIV and AIDS

The nature of the developmental messages subsumed under topics is illustrated by the following eight points from among the guidelines' 800. Messages define the focus of sex-education lessons.

For ages 9–12:

- Children dealing with [their parents'] separation or divorce may need to talk with an adult about their feelings.
- [The term] *sexual orientation* refers to a person's physical and/or romantic attraction to an individual of the same and/or different gender.
- To make a good decision one must consider all of the possible consequences, good and bad, and choose the action that one believes will have the best outcome.
- Masturbation does not cause physical or mental harm.
- Pregnancy can happen anytime a girl/woman has unprotected vaginal intercourse with a boy/man.
- Some religions and cultures teach that contraception is acceptable while others do not approve of using contraception.
- STDs (sexually transmitted diseases) include such diseases as gonorrhea, syphilis, HIV infection, Chlamydia, genital warts, and herpes.

- Families might need outside help to deal with problems involving alcohol, drugs, money, violence, health, and abuse.

The SIECUS topics and messages are founded on a set of 19 convictions about values, such as:

- Sexuality is a natural and healthy part of living.
- Families should provide children's first education about sexuality.
- Young people explore their sexuality as a natural process in achieving sexual maturity.
- Abstaining from sexual intercourse is the most effective way of preventing pregnancy and STD/HIV.
- Individuals can express their sexuality in varied ways.

The SIECUS guidelines are intended to serve as a resource on which curriculum planners can draw in fashioning a comprehensive sex-education program suited to their particular school's student population, time allotment for sexual matters, teachers' talents, and attitudes of the surrounding community.

> Ideally, all sexuality education programs would cover all of the concepts, topics, and developmental messages included in the *Guidelines*. SIECUS realizes, however, that due to constraints on time, staff, and other resources, many programs will not be able to tackle every topic in the *Guidelines*. . . . Educators can use the key concepts and topics as a jumping off point and then work with staff, parents, and/or young people to narrow down and prioritize this list. Many educators prioritize topics based on their personal observations of the needs of the young people they work with. For example, after hearing young people spread misinformation about reproduction or demonstrate a lack of information about anatomy, an educator may choose to focus a program or lesson on *Key Concept 1: Human Development*. It can also be helpful to ask young people directly for their input in determining which topics will be covered. (*Guidelines*, 2004, p. 81)

In summary, comprehensive sex-education programs are designed to provide a many-sided view of sexual relationships—physical, emotional, intellectual, societal—as adjusted to the maturity level of children at different age stages.

THE CONTENDING CONSTITUENCIES

A convenient way to classify the groups that support different approaches to sex education is to place them in three categories—(a) conservatives, (b) centrists and liberals, and (c) parents in general.

Conservatives

In the main, people who qualify as conservatives favor sex education that teaches abstinence. Stricter conservatives advocate abstinence-only programs. More lenient conservatives accept abstinence-plus alternatives that stress the desirability of abstinence over the "plus" options that are included in the curriculum (condoms, birth-control pills, masturbation, and the like).

Two influential Christian groups that qualify as sex-education conservatives are right-wing Protestants and Roman Catholics. Furthermore, an important political body that has promoted conservatives' interests has been President George W. Bush's administration as supported mainly by Republicans in both houses of Congress.

Right-Wing Protestants

Perhaps the most influential Christian Protestant group is the Southern Baptist Convention because of its size—16.3 million members—and vigorous political activity. At the organization's 2005 annual conference, delegates urged parents to "demand discontinuation" of public school programs that were morally offensive. One vocal branch of the membership recommended withdrawing children from public schools in order to home-school pupils or enroll them in private schools. However, the public statement that the conference issued did not go that far. It only advised parents to "fully embrace their responsibility to make prayerful and informed decisions regarding where and how they educate their children, whether they choose public, private, or home schooling . . . [and] hold accountable schools, institutions and industries for their moral influence on our children" (Vara, 2005).

Officially, Southern Baptists subscribe to abstinence-only sex education. As a means of judging the success of that policy, a researcher at Baptist-affiliated Baylor University in Texas interviewed young married couples from Baptist churches in order to learn about their premarital sexual experience. The results showed that

> The majority [64 percent] of the couples surveyed admitted to having sexual intercourse prior to marriage. However, the study was consistent with previous findings in its suggestion that Baptist couples were more likely to save sex for their wedding night if they took a formal abstinence pledge. . . . Six out of ten who made purity commitments did not have sexual intercourse until marriage, while only three of ten who did not pledge purity remained abstinent. . . . Only 27 percent of the young people surveyed entered marriage "chaste," having refrained not only from intercourse but also from other sexual practices such as oral sex. (Apparently, 2006)

Thus, a religious denomination's official endorsement of a sex-education policy does not mean that all congregates agree with the policy, so that a substantial number of Baptists could be expected to hold a view different from the church's position, preferring instead some version of abstinence-plus or comprehensive sex instruction.

It is also the case that a faith identified by a broad label—Baptist, Presbyterian, Methodist—can actually be divided into more than one branch, with each branch advocating a different sort of sex education. For instance, American Lutherans in the mid-1970s split into two factions—the Lutheran Church Missouri Synod (LCMS) with a nationwide membership of 2.6 million members (10th largest Christian denomination in the United States) and the Evangelical Lutheran Church of America (ELCA) with 5.1 million members. Usually the word *evangelical* is associated with faiths that are dedicated to a literal interpretation of the Bible and conservative social policies, such as abstinence-only sex education. But in the case of Lutherans, the two groups' titles are misleading. The Missouri-Synod branch is the conservative wing that approves of abstinence-only instruction (Lutheran church, 2006). In contrast, the Evangelical branch is liberal, endorsing an expanded version of sex education.

Roman Catholics

The official position of the Vatican in Rome is that abstinence-only should be taught in sex-education programs. As Pope John Paul II wrote in his 1981 apostolic exhortation (The Role of the Christian Family in the Modern World), sex education is "education in love as self-giving" that is not "solely with the body and with selfish pleasure" but must be "education for chastity, for it is a virtue which develops a person's authentic maturity and makes him or her capable of respecting and fostering the 'nuptial meaning' of the body" (Whitehead, 1993). Hence, like popes before and after him, John Paul II agreed with St. Augustine's conviction that sexual behavior should be solely for the purpose of producing offspring in a marriage.

As is true in other Christian faiths, Catholics—including Catholic educators—are not all of one mind about what should be included in sex education. This point has been illustrated in Walter Feinberg's book *For Goodness Sake* (2006) in which he describes religious-education classes in four Catholic schools he visited, classes that revealed the extent of pedagogical variation that can be found within a single faith. Feinberg applied the label *traditionalist* to a class in which the instructor taught students "the fixed nature of doctrine as defined by the authorities in Rome" (p. 47). Feinberg called two other classes *modernist* because the teachers presented traditional doctrine but modified its application as they tried to protect the self-esteem of individual students, such as homosexuals, children of divorced parents, and ones who were sexually active. Feinberg dubbed a fourth class *postmodernist,* because its teacher (a nun in an all-girls school) subscribed to feminism and liberation theology. She used historical analysis to show how church doctrine changed over the centuries from what she viewed as a gender-equality position in Jesus' time to a present-day male-dominated church, a patriarchy that she believed could be reversed in the future. Thus, in Catholic schools, "teachers will differ from one another in their view of the moral authority of the Church hierarchy and the emphasis they place on critical thinking" (Feinberg, 2006, p. 47).

Not only do some priests and nuns who teach in parochial schools deviate in practice from the strict abstinence policy of the church, but there are also splinter groups, such as Catholics for a Free Choice, that openly advocate comprehensive sex education.

In a modern-day American society that increasingly strays from traditional Christian sexual values, orthodox Catholics and like-minded conservatives face a daunting challenge in promoting abstinence among the young. Christian educators' appeal to youths frequently involves recommending intensive religious study in order to reap the reward of self-fulfillment that is earned by chastity. Consider, for example, Stafford's (1993) advice about what Catholic teens need to know about sex.

> Parents, catechists, and parish youth leaders should stress the importance of Bible reading, prayer, and frequent reception of the sacraments of Reconciliation and the Eucharist in forming a close relationship with Christ. As God becomes increasingly important in their lives, teens will find it much easier to say no to illicit sex. Today's Catholic teens also need to know about the lives of saints such as Maria Goretti, who died a martyr's death to preserve her purity, and Augustine, who turned from a life of immorality to become one of the greatest bishops and saints in the Church's history. Teens should be encouraged to read about the lives of these saints and other famous saints who overcame sexual temptations so that they will realize chastity is a realistic and attainable goal.
>
> One outstanding Catholic who has high expectations for today's teens is Mother Teresa of Calcutta, whom many consider a living saint. In a speech she gave in Assisi, Italy, on June 6, 1982 she said: "It is very beautiful for a young man to love a young woman and for a young woman to love a young man, but make sure that on the day you get married you have a pure heart, a virgin heart, a heart full of love; purity, and virginity." (Stafford, 1993)

Federal and State Governments

During the presidency of George W. Bush (2001–2008), when the executive branch of the federal government distributed millions of dollars in tax money to organizations that promoted abstinence-only sex education, most recipients of funds were church-related groups. By 2005, more than $1 billion had been granted to faith-based abstinence programs.

Tax money from individual states has also been given to churches' abstinence efforts. For instance, the Catholic diocese of Helena (Montana) received $14,000 from that state's Department of Health and Human Services to conduct "Assets for Abstinence" classes. The Louisiana governor's "Program on Abstinence" furnished money for the same purpose to such religious groups as the Baptist Collegiate Ministries, Diocese of Lafayette, Revolution Ministries, All Saints Crusade Foundation, Concerned Christian Women of Livingston, and Catholic Charities (Planned Parenthood, 2005).

The most widely publicized Christian just-say-no-to-sex program has been the Silver Ring Thing (SRT), created in 1995 by Denny Pattyn, executive director of the John Guest Evangelistic Team in Sewickley (Pennsylvania). The aim of the Silver Ring Thing has been to convince young people to avoid sexual contacts until they are wed. Each youth who pledges abstinence is entitled to wear a silver ring. The way the SRT sponsors recruit teenagers is by conducting performances in cities around the nation, often in convention halls or on college campuses. The typical performance is a 3-hour show in which the first 90 minutes consist of live music, skits, and lectures informing the audience about the dangers of HIV/AIDS and the emotional distress that accompanies risky sexual behavior. During the second 90 minutes, youths choose which of two discussion groups they wish to join—one religious (a strong Christian theme) and the other secular (no religious content). Members of both groups are pressed to make an abstinence pledge and publicly attest to the pledge by wearing a silver ring. The actual number of young people who have accepted rings over the past decade is unclear. However, in 2003 Pattyn said his goal was to have rings on the fingers of 2 million youths by 2010 (Saltzman, 2005).

Initially, the Silver Ring Thing was funded entirely by private sources, but in 2003 the organization began receiving funds from the federal government's faith-based-initiatives program.

In May 2005, the American Civil Liberties Union (ACLU) filed a lawsuit against the U.S. Department of Health and Human Services, charging that the department had granted the Silver Ring Thing over $1 million, a violation of the U.S. Constitution's traditional separation of church and state. The ACLU, to support its claim that the SRT promoted religion, noted that the group's typical show featured passages from the Bible and included testimonials about accepting Jesus Christ. In addition, the silver rings youths bought for $15 were inscribed with a reference to a New Testament verse: "God wants you to be holy, so you should keep clear of all sexual sin." Teenagers who bought a ring also received a Bible (Saltzman, 2005).

In response to the ACLU lawsuit, the government suspended further grants to SRT, and Silver Ring Thing officials immediately altered their public performances, removing all religious matter from the first 90 minutes, thereby limiting Christian content to the faith-related discussion section, which officials said was financed from private sources. The ACLU then dropped the suit after being assured that tax money would no longer be used to fund any faith-related SRT activities. In effect, the federal government could give money to faith-based groups that performed social services, but it could not bankroll activities that explicitly promoted a religion.

During the first decade of the 21st century, the U.S. government not only funded abstinence programs, but in 2002—at the urging of conservative church groups—members of the Bush administration pressed the United Nations to adopt a just-say-no approach to family planning around the world. The United Nations rejected the abstinence-only proposal on the ground that a wide range of birth-control measures was required to cope with the world's health and population-growth problems.

> [W]omen's health experts, inside and outside the United Nations . . . say Washington's campaign can only hurt girls in the poorest nations. . . . [More than] 82 million girls between the ages of 10 and 17 living in developing countries will be married before their 18th birthdays. Young women ages 15 to 19 are twice as likely to die in childbirth than are women in their 20s, and those under 15 are five times as likely not to survive pregnancy. . . . Sex education is not a moral question but often a matter of life or death, especially now that AIDS has begun to affect girls and women in sharply rising numbers in Africa and Asia, outstripping the spread of the disease among men. (Crossette, 2002)

Centrists and Liberals

The word *centrist* refers to people who favor sex education that features abstinence but also includes a substantial amount of information about other health-protection and birth-control methods. Thus, centrists advocate abstinence-plus programs.

The label *liberal* identifies proponents of comprehensive sex education that includes a wide diversity of topics, such as the array of subject matter found in the SIECUS *Guidelines*.

Two types of centrist and liberal constituencies are nonevangelical mainline religious denominations and secular organizations that subscribe to the separation of church and state.

Mainline Religious Denominations

Religious groups with policies supporting comprehensive sex education in public schools include the Central Conference of American Rabbis,

Church of the Brethren, Episcopal Church, Evangelical Lutheran Church of America, Presbyterian Church (U.S.A), Unitarian Universalist Association, United Church of Christ, and United Methodist Church. In addition, more than 2,400 religious leaders signed a Religious Declaration on Sexual Morality, Justice, and Healing, which advocates lifelong, age-appropriate sexuality education in schools, seminaries, and community settings. A statement by Planned Parenthood Federation of America, calling for comprehensive sexuality education in schools and opposing abstinence-only education, was endorsed by more than 1,600 members of the clergy.

Secular Organizations

The website for the National Coalition to Support Sexuality Education lists 140 national, nonprofit organizations and associations that advocate comprehensive sex education in schools. The groups on the list range from Advocates for Youth and the AIDS Alliance to YAI/National Institute for People with Disabilities and the Young Women's Project.

A typical sex-education policy of such organizations can be illustrated with a resolution of the National Education Association, the country's largest teachers union with 2.8 million members.

> The Association urges its affiliates and members to support appropriately established sex education programs, including information on sexual abstinence, birth control and family planning, diversity of culture, diversity of sexual orientation, parenting skills, prenatal care, sexually transmitted diseases, incest, sexual abuse, sexual harassment. To facilitate the realization of human potential, it is the right of every individual to live in an environment of freely available information, knowledge, and wisdom about sexuality. (Sex education, 1995)

Parents in General

Obviously such a category as *parents nationwide* overlaps with *conservatives* and *centrists and liberals*. But I include it here to show how general public opinion compares with the positions of specific religious and secular organizations that have issued sex-education policies.

A nationwide public survey in 2004 found that only 7 percent of respondents believed there should be no sex education in schools. Among those who approved of sex education, 15 percent advocated abstinence-only, 46 percent preferred abstinence-plus, and 36 percent said abstinence was not the most important thing; rather, it was more important to teach teens how to make responsible decisions about sex.

> In spite of the fact that only 15 percent of Americans say they want abstinence-only sex education in the schools, 30 percent of the principals

> of public middle schools and high schools where sex education is taught report that their schools taught abstinence-only. Forty-seven percent of their schools taught abstinence-plus, while 20 percent taught that making responsible decisions about sex was more important than abstinence. (Middle schools were more likely to teach abstinence-only than high schools. High schools were more likely than middle schools to teach abstinence-plus. High schools and middle schools were equally likely to teach that abstinence is not the most important thing.)
>
> The most controversial topic—"that teens can obtain birth control pills from family planning clinics and doctors without permission from a parent"—was found to be inappropriate by 28 percent of the public, but even there, seven out of 10 (71 percent) thought it was appropriate. The other most controversial topics were oral sex (27 percent found it inappropriate) and homosexuality (25 percent). (NPR, 2004)

A Planned Parenthood analysis of national sex-education polls reported that 81 percent of Americans and 75 percent of parents wanted school children to receive a range of information about sexual behavior, including "contraception and condom use, sexually transmitted infection, sexual orientation, safer sex practices, abortion, communications and coping skills, and the emotional aspects of sexual relationships." In the survey, 56 percent of respondents did not believe that abstinence-only programs would prevent sexually transmitted infections or unintended pregnancies (Planned Parenthood, 2005).

INTERPRETATIONS

As in previous chapters, the six perspectives used for interpreting the contents of this chapter are those of (a) decision making (by students and school personnel), (b) heredity and environment, (c) *could-be, is,* and *should-be* beliefs, (d) sources of evidence, (e) power and authority, and (f) implications for schools.

Decision Making

Students are obliged to decide how they will use the information and advice they receive in their school's sex-education program. As illustrated in this chapter, such information and advice can differ from one kind of sex education to another. For example, in abstinence-only programs, participants are often urged to openly adopt an abstinence or virginity pledge. Whereas participants in abstinence-plus classes are taught to favor abstinence, they are also given information to guide their decisions about protecting themselves if they do engage in sex. Students in comprehensive programs are typically told the advantages and disadvantages of various types of sexual activities and then are encouraged to use that information in choosing their own sexual behavior.

Different types of school personnel also face sex-education decisions. Administrators (superintendents, curriculum planners, principals) decide which commercial curriculum to adopt or what the contents will be in a school's self-prepared plan. School-board members have the power to accept or reject the content of a proposed curriculum. The teachers who are assigned to teach sex education decide which topics in an adopted curriculum to skip and which new ones to add.

Heredity and Environment

One way that heredity affects sex education is by helping determine how closely a sex-information program's topics match the stages of students' sexual development. The best match results when a topic is addressed slightly before students experience a particular developmental change. For example, an explanation of menarche and menstruation is most helpful for girls who are about to experience those changes. If teachers offer such topics far earlier than the advent of the changes in girls' lives, the girls are less likely to be interested or to understand what the topics are all about. And if the topics are offered well after girls have experienced the menarche and menstruation, it is too late to assuage any puzzlement or fear that girls might have felt when those events occurred without warning in their own lives. Timing is also important for explaining to boys wet dreams and penis erections. For both genders, the causes of pregnancy and the transmission of diseases can appropriately be taught somewhat before the time that the danger of such events is likely to threaten youngsters' welfare. However, as explained in chapter 2, the significant variations in young people's rates of sexual development make it difficult for program planners to choose the best grade level in which to introduce particular eroticism issues.

Next, consider typical environmental conditions that interact with children's genetic sexual-development timing to influence the kinds of topics that can effectively be included in a school's sex-education offerings. Illustrative conditions include

- Parents' beliefs about which topics are appropriate, the age at which the young should encounter each topic, who should teach sex education, and which kinds of sexual acts should be approved or condemned
- The type of sex education (abstinence-only, abstinence-plus, comprehensive) that school authorities adopt and the reasons for adopting

that type (religious convictions, government funding, results of public-opinion surveys, incidence of venereal disease)

- What a community's youth believe about eroticism
- The portrayal of eroticism by the mass communication media—movies, television, magazines, the Internet

Could-Be, Is, Should-Be

As proposed in chapter 1, *could-be* beliefs are a person's idea of what is genetically and environmentally possible for a young person's eroticism and gender development at a given time of life. *Is* beliefs are descriptions (apparently factual) of a youngster's present sexual characteristics—the youngster's appearance, feelings, thoughts, and actions relating to eroticism and gender matters. *Should-be* beliefs are convictions about what a particular person's sexual characteristics and behavior *ought to be* at present and in the future. In effect, *should-be* is a set of values that guides people in distinguishing between good and bad or proper and improper erotic thoughts, feelings, and actions.

I think it's important for people to recognize the differences among *could-be, is,* and *should-be* and to understand how those three perspectives can interact. Although the three are separate beliefs, they often are not independent. For example, people frequently hold strong opinions about what *should be* when they describe the type of sex education they prefer. Those *should-be* opinions may then influence people's expressed beliefs about what teenagers' eroticism behavior *is*. This phenomenon of *should-be* beliefs affecting people's *is* beliefs can occur whenever proponents of abstinence-only programs support their position by (a) citing only those empirical studies (*is*) that show students delaying intercourse until they are wed and (b) dismissing studies that show students have broken their pledge to remain celibate. The same sort of influence (*should-be* infecting *is*) occurs whenever supporters of comprehensive sex education reject the results of empirical studies (*is*) that show that students from high-school abstinence-only programs often delay erotic encounters until their 20s, even if they do not wait until they are married.

Sources of Evidence

What people believe about *could-be, is,* and *should-be* depends heavily on the sources of evidence on which they base their convictions. Common sources are family members (parents, grandparents, siblings, uncles, aunts), friends, religious leaders (priests, ministers, rabbis, imams), Sunday school teachers, public-school classes, movies, television, radio, books, newspapers, tabloid weeklies, academic journals, and the Internet (pornographic, scientific, philosophical, and religious websites and blogs).

Two conditions that determine the sources of evidence on which individuals base their beliefs are (a) the availability of different information sources and (b) which sources individuals regard as most trustworthy. Sex-education programs in schools can influence these two conditions by limiting the availability of certain sources and by praising some sources while denigrating others. For example, proponents of abstinence-plus may (a) focus students' attention on abstinence-only and abstinence-plus approaches, leaving students unaware of comprehensive approaches, and then (b) laud strengths of abstinence-plus while emphasizing supposed weaknesses of abstinence-only.

The kinds of reasoning that advocates of sex-education approaches offer to convince school administrators, teachers, and parents that their programs are superior can be illustrated with the following quotations from proponents of two competing sex-education approaches. The first example praises abstinence-only and disparages both abstinence-plus and comprehensive plans. The second example endorses comprehensive programs and devalues abstinence-only.

> *Example 1.* To call these curricula "abstinence plus" is simply misleading. A more accurate term would be "safe sex-plus," meaning that such courses focus predominantly on contraceptive use with only minor reference to abstinence. The term "comprehensive sexuality education" is also misleading, because there is nothing "comprehensive" about these curricula. In reality, there is a lot more to sex than avoiding STDs and pregnancy. Indeed, most of what is important about human sexuality is missing from these courses. . . . [For example,] authentic abstinence courses instruct teens about the differences between lust, infatuation, and real love. Their curricula teach that teen sexual relationships generally involve large elements of self-delusion and that, despite expectations that they will last, nearly all such relationships are unstable and short-term. (Martin, Rector & Pardue, 2004, p. 57)

> *Example 2.* Both comprehensive sex education and abstinence-only programs delay the onset of sexual activity. However, only comprehensive sex education is effective in protecting adolescents from pregnancy and sexually transmitted illnesses at first intercourse and during later sexual activity. In contrast, scientifically sound studies of abstinence-only programs show an unintended consequence of unprotected sex at first intercourse and during later sexual activity. In this way, abstinence-only programs increase the risk of these adolescents for pregnancy and sexually transmitted illnesses, including HIV/AIDS. (Lyon in Willenz, 2005)

Power and Authority

Authority (the official right to make decisions) is a highly significant factor in determining the kind of sex education offered in a school. The amount of power and how it is wielded can vary from one source of authority to another. Consider, for example, the authority of different levels of educational control—federal, state, school district, school, and teacher—in relation to sex education.

The federal government's three branches consist of (a) Congress, which passes legislation bearing on sex education throughout the nation, (b) the U.S. president and all of the bureaus and departments that comprise the executive branch, which carries out the laws, and (c) the federal courts as the judicial branch that decides which laws are acceptable under the U.S. Constitution. Because the Constitution assigns responsibility for education to the states rather than to the national government, federal officials cannot require states to abide by laws passed by Congress. But the president and executive-branch bureaucrats can seek to convince states to follow congressional dictates by offering states money for adopting abstinence-only programs.

States exert their authority by passing laws that public school systems are obligated to follow. Some states (such as Arkansas, Mississippi, and Texas) have required schools to teach abstinence only, whereas others (such as California, Maine, New Jersey, and Virginia) have promoted comprehensive or abstinence-plus programs.

If a state does not require a particular type of sex education, it is the local school district, through its board of education, that determines which form of sex education (if any at all) will be offered. Or sometimes the decision about the form of sex education is left to the principals and curriculum planners of individual schools. Ultimately, the kind of eroticism information and advice students receive depends on the teacher in charge of a class. Teachers can emphasize certain topics, delete others, insert ones of their own choosing, and reflect their own value judgments in the lessons they offer. Finally, parents—although they are outside the government and schools—exert power by dint of the authority society gives them as their children's immediate guardians.

So it is that one way to view the determinants of sex education in a school is in terms of power interactions among different authorities—federal, state, school district, individual school, teacher, and parental.

Implications for Schools

An obvious implication of this chapter's contents is that school personnel are likely to receive complaints from some students or parents about the school's sex-education plan. Administrators can prepare to cope with such complaints by

- Making available a written explanation of the purposes of the sex-education aspects of the curriculum, including the grade levels at which different topics are addressed;
- Inviting students, parents, or members of the community to discuss the school's sex-education offerings with such individuals as the principal, curriculum coordinator, counselors, or teachers; and
- Adopting a policy that allows students to avoid, without penalty, sex-education class sessions or instructional materials (books, videos) that students or their parents find objectionable.

Chapter 10

Retrospect and Prospect

This final chapter focuses on eight sex-related topics that were featured in chapters 2 through 9. The discussion of each topic is divided into a pair of opposing viewpoints, with the first glancing into the past (retrospect) and the second peering into the years ahead (prospect). The purpose of such a presentation is to summarize dominant trends from the past and then speculate about the likely future by extending the trends into the coming decades.

THE EIGHT TOPICS

Physical Development

Past

From the early 19th century until the middle of the 20th, American children matured physically at increasingly early ages, primarily as a result of improved environments (cleaner air, cleaner water), better nutrition, and better health care. Such maturation was illustrated in youngsters displaying greater height and the earlier onset of puberty as the decades advanced. Although experts generally agree that this trend ended around 1950, recent studies have suggested that, at least in certain localities, some slight increase has occurred in the early arrival of puberty and such physical accompaniments as height (Freedman et al., 2000).

Over the decades, students' weight followed the same trend until, in recent years, weight increases accelerated to levels that seriously threatened youngsters' welfare. By the early 21st century, overweight issues among children and teenagers were judged a critical problem that required immediate attention. Schools responded by replacing junk foods in lunch programs and vending machines with nutritious edibles and by reinstituting physical education classes that had been eliminated in earlier times.

Future

It seems unlikely that puberty and its observable indicators (increased height, body hair, sex organ growth, and the like) will arrive any earlier in children's development than has been true in recent decades. Improved environments and health care have apparently reached their limits for the child population in general—except for the matter of excess weight. On the brink of the 21st century's second decade, childhood and adolescent obesity continued to be a critical problem. Given youngsters' taste for junk food, their sedentary habits (television, computer games, the Internet), and the vigorous advertising by the junk-food industry, there appears to be little likelihood of significant early progress toward getting America's youth into the physical shape typically considered sexually attractive.

Psychological Development

Past

As suggested in chapter 2, four psychological phenomena often associated with people's eroticism are their sexual self-concept, erotic satisfaction, guilt, and fear. I estimated that changes in societal attitudes about sex over the past half century, coupled with developments in mass-communication media, had likely affected children's and adolescents' psychological development by:

- Influencing their sexual self-concepts by offering far more opportunities to estimate other people's erotic prowess through the revealing displays of erotic acts in public communication media—television, movies, videos, magazines, and the Internet
- The mass media offering a host of examples of other people's sexual satisfaction with which youths might compare the level of their own satisfaction (frequency of sex acts, types of sex acts, intensity of emotion)
- Diminishing young people's sense of guilt and shame over their sexual thoughts and acts by showing how public standards of acceptable sexual thoughts and behavior have been changing in recent decades from traditional Judeo-Christian standards of the past

- Increasing youths' fear of infection by informing them about the kinds and incidences of sexually transmitted diseases
- Diminishing young people's fear of pregnancy and disease by informing them of methods for protecting themselves from infections when engaging in sex acts

Future

I imagine that these trends of recent years will continue and intensify in the years ahead. Controversies over the trends are bound to continue, especially pitting the more conservative older generation against more progressive younger people. However, the societal and technological forces that stimulated change in public attitudes in the recent past will likely continue to grow.

Students' Sexual Acts

Past

The types of sexual acts described in chapter 3 are nothing new. Without doubt, they have been practiced since prehistoric times. But what is new is how readily children and adolescents can view all manner of acts via present-day mass media, especially the Internet.

Future

The rate of annual increase in sexually explicit movies, videos, and Internet websites over the past decade portends an accelerating increase in visual pornographic fare in the years to come. That trend places greater responsibility on parents and school personnel to (a) monitor children's and teenagers' access to videos and websites and (b) teach students how to cope with such material in ways that guard them from physical, psychological, and social damage.

Methods of Protection

Past

The last half of the 20th century witnessed both (a) a growing need for ways to prevent unwanted pregnancy and sexually transmitted infections (especially HIV/AIDS) and (b) improved ways to prevent and treat sexually related diseases. The era also was marked by increased efforts by schools to warn students against pregnancy and infections. However, the federal government's sponsorship of abstinence as the only means of protection kept many students from learning about ways to protect themselves if they did, indeed, engage in vaginal, oral, or anal intercourse.

Future

The development and spread of effective protective measures and treatments for venereal diseases will undoubtedly continue in years to come. The effectiveness of campaigns to reduce teen pregnancy rates and sexually acquired infections will improve as more health-education programs extend their information about protection beyond abstinence.

Sexual Abuse

Past

As illustrated in chapter 5, sexual abuse can assume diverse forms, including harassment and bullying, seduction, statutory rape, forcible rape, and date rape. Over the past several decades, schools and criminal-justice agencies have taken incidents of abuse far more seriously than in the past. Many acts that previously had been dismissed as "boys will be boys" and "just kidding" were no longer taken lightly. New regulations that outlawed abusive behavior were established, and sanctions were imposed on people who breached the rules.

Future

The recent measures that schools adopted to protect students from abuse are bound to continue in force. And school personnel will continue to face problems of distinguishing between true abuse and the harmless teasing and flirting that so often mark girls' and boys' attempts at social interaction.

Gender Traits

Past

At an accelerating pace, public perceptions of suitable gender traits changed during the 20th century. Females were no longer considered physically too delicate to engage in vigorous sports, nor were they viewed as lacking logic when coping with difficult decisions or as too incompetent to succeed in a variety of occupations that traditionally had been reserved for men. By the early 21st century, controversies continued over whether females and males, on the average, were equally apt in math, science, verbal skills, and the arts. Debates also continued over questions of whether girls and boys differed in emotional sensitivity, control, and expression as a result of their genetic inheritance.

Future

Increasing respect for girls' physical and intellectual abilities will undoubtedly continue in the years ahead, with such respect accompanied by richer opportunities for females to succeed in academic and occupational fields that were formerly reserved for males.

One harbinger of the progress to be expected in the public's regard for females' traits has been the recent trend in college-attendance and graduation rates. In 2005 there were more men than women ages 18 to 24 in the United States (15 million men, 14.2 million women), but 57 percent of college students were female and only 43 percent male, a reversal from the late 1960s when men outnumbered women on campuses. In 2005, woman earned 58 percent of all bachelor degrees, compared to 35 percent in 1960 (Marklein, 2005). Among students graduating in 2008, more women than men earned doctorates, master degrees, and bachelor degrees.

> Armed with college degrees, large numbers of women have entered fields once dominated by men. Nearly half of new doctors today are women, up from just 10 percent in the early 1970s. In all, the average inflation-adjusted weekly pay of women has jumped 26 percent since 1980. (Leonhardt, 2008)

Gender-Role Preferences

Past

Over the past half century, legislation about—and public attitudes toward—individuals' sex-role choices have undergone a remarkable transformation. By 2009, people who chose a homosexual or bisexual life style increasingly enjoyed the rights and respect that previously had been available only to heterosexuals. This transformation extended to the schools, which became battlegrounds for pro-homosexuality and anti-homosexuality activists.

Future

I expect that confrontations in schools over gender-role preferences will persist, but that anti-homosexuality and anti-bisexuality proponents will—at a growing pace—lose influence over school policy and practice.

Sex Education

Past

Sex education in schools increased in frequency over the last half of the 20th century and into the 21st century. The three kinds of programs that competed for acceptance featured (a) strict abstinence from sexual acts until marriage, (b) emphasis on abstinence, but inclusion of protective measures (abstinence-plus) for students who did engage in intercourse, and (c) comprehensive information about all facets of sexual behavior. In the mid-1990s, abstinence-only programs grew rapidly after federal-government legislation provided funds to schools that taught strict abstinence. However, as research on sex education revealed in the early years of the 21st century, students who completed abstinence-only programs engaged in premarital sex as often as those who did not. Thus, disenchantment with the success of strict-abstinence plans caused a growing number of schools to adopt abstinence-plus or comprehensive approaches.

Future

I imagine that the disappointing results of abstinence-only programs will encourage more schools to develop abstinence-plus or comprehensive approaches to sex education. The move away from abstinence-only will be hastened if the new federal administration following the George W. Bush years abandons or significantly reduces the funding of strict abstinence plans.

CONCLUSION

On the brink of the 21st century's second decade, American schools still confronted diverse sexual issues to resolve, such as:

- *Erotic acts*. What kinds of erotic acts or displays of affection should our school permit—where, when, and why? What kinds should be forbidden—where, when, and why? In what form should policies about such matter be cast—unwritten understandings, written rules? What sanctions should be imposed on students and staff members who violate the policies?
- *Sex education*. Should our school offer sex education? If so, at what grade levels? What should be the scope and focus of sex education—abstinence-only, abstinence-plus, comprehensive? What qualifications should be required of persons who teach sex education? Should stu-

dents be required to participate in sex education or should participation be voluntary?

- *Protection.* Should our school offer services to protect students from pregnancy and disease? If so, what should be the nature of such services—advice, physical examinations, supplies (condoms, diaphragms, pills, dental dams)? Should parental permission be required before students are furnished services?
- *Pregnant and parenting students.* What services, if any, should be provided for pregnant girls, expectant fathers, and students who are already parents? What should be the nature of the services—personal advice, classes in child-rearing practices, daycare for students' children?
- *Gender traits.* How should boys and girls in our school be treated differently because of their gender, and what is the reason for such differentiated treatment—the two genders' different developmental rates, physical traits, intellectual aptitudes, emotional tendencies, social skills?
- *Gender-role preference.* What policies should our school adopt about students' and staff members' displayed gender orientation (heterosexual, homosexual, bisexual, transsexual)? Should students or staff members be permitted to discuss matters of gender-role preference in class? Should school personnel (teachers, administrators, counselors) be allowed to propose unconventional sexual orientations (homosexuality, bisexuality, transvestism, transsexualism) as acceptable lifestyles? Should students and staff members be permitted to wear the garb and accoutrements that are usually associated with the opposite gender (transvestism)? In what form should the school's gender-preference policies be cast—unwritten expectations, written rules? What sanctions should be applied to individuals who fail to abide by the school's gender-orientation policies?

References

Abel, D. (2004, October 26). Bishop attacks school condom plan. *Boston Globe*. Retrieved October 6, 2008, from www.boston.com/news/local/articles/2004/10/26/bishop_attacks_school_condom_plan/.

Abstinence students still having sex. (2007, April 16). *MSNBC*. Retrieved October 6, 2008, from www.msnbc.msn.com/id/18093769/.

Ackard, D., & Neumark-Sztainer, D. (2001, August 26). One out of ten female adolescents experience date violence or rape. *American Psychological Association online*. Retrieved October 6, 2008, from www.apa.org/releases/dateviolence.html.

Adler, N. E., & Tschann, J. M. (1993). Conscious and preconscious motivation in pregnancy among female adolescents. In A. Lawson & D. L. Rhodes (Eds.), *The politics of pregnancy: Adolescent sexuality and public policy* (pp. 144–158). New Haven, CT: Yale University Press.

Age-of-consent criminal, victim. (2006, January 3). *Free Market News Network*. Retrieved October 6, 2008, from www.freemarketnews.com/WorldNews.asp?nid=4620.

American Academy of Child and Adolescent Psychiatry. (2004, July). *When children have children*. Retrieved October 6, 2008, from www.aacap.org/cs/root/facts_for_families/when_children_have_children.

American Association of University Women. (2001). *Hostile hallways: Bullying, teasing, and sexual harassment in school*. Retrieved October 6, 2008, from www.aauw.org/research/hostile.cfm.

American Bar Association. (2008). *Sexual harassment*. Retrieved March 17, 2008, from www.abanet.org/publiced/practical/sexualharassment_defined.html.

Ampersand. (2005, September 22). For many poor black girls, teen pregnancy is a rational choice. *Alas*. Retrieved October 6, 2008, from www.amptoons.com/blog/archives/2005/09/22/for-many-poor-black-girls-teen-pregnancy-is-a-rational-choice/.

Anderson, S. (1999). The safe schools act protects Missouri students. *Mobar—Missouri state bar*. Retrieved October 6, 2008, from www.mobar.org/journal/1999/sepoct/anderson.htm.

Anorexic teens. (2005). *Troubled teens 101*. Retrieved October 31, 2008, from www.troubledteen101.com/articles40.

Another Tampa student-teacher sex bust. (2005). *The Smoking Gun*. Retrieved October 6, 2008, from www.thesmokinggun.com/archive/1102051teach1.html.

Apparently true love doesn't always wait. (2006, March 29). *Agape Press*. Retrieved October 6, 2008, from headlines.agapepress.org/archive/3/292006d.asp.

Ausilio sentenced to 8–10 months in juvenile facility. (2003, December 16). *San Juan Islander*. Retrieved October 6, 2008, from www.sanjuanislander.com/county/juvenile-court/trial-10-03.shtml.

Bailey, C. E., & Piercy, F. P. (1997). Enhancing ethical decision making in sexuality and AIDS education. *Adolescence, 32*(Winter), 989–998.

Bloom, P. (2008). *Married people & masturbation: Catholic perspective*. Retrieved February 17, 2008, from www.geocities.com/Heartland/2964/masturbation2.html.

Blount, J. (2003). The history of teaching and talking about sex in schools [Electronic version]. *History of Education Quarterly, 4*(4). Retrieved from www.historycooperative.org/journals/heq/43.4/ess_1.html.

Boonstra, H. D. (2007, Spring). The case for a new approach to sex education mounts; will policymakers heed the message? [Electronic version]. *Guttmacher Policy Review, 10*(2). Retrieved October 6, 2008, from www.guttmacher.org/pubs/gpr/10/2/gpr100202.html.

Bosman, J. (2007, May 24). New York's schools for pregnant girls will close. *New York Times*. Retrieved October 6, 2008, from www.nytimes.com/2007/05/24/education/24educ.html?_r=1&oref=slogin.

Brasier, L. L. (2008, March 12). 2nd boy gives details in teacher sex-assault trial. *Detroit Free Press*. Retrieved October 6, 2008, from www.freep.com/apps/pbcs.dll/article?AID=/20080312/NEWS03/803120399/1005/NEWS03.

Brennan, W. (1982, June 25). *Board of education v. Pico*. Retrieved October 6, 2008, from caselaw.lp.findlaw.com/scripts/getcase.pl?court=US&vol=457&invol=853.

Brianne. (2008). Girls who aborted. *Teen Breaks*. Retrieved April 19, 2008, from www.teenbreaks.com/abortion/girlswhoaborted.cfm?start=35.

Brown, J. (2006, August 22). CA teachers take elementary students to "gay pride" parade. *Agape Press*. Retrieved October 6, 2008, from familypolicy.net/ca/?p=513

Burner, J. A. (2003, February 6). Review of: 101 questions about sex and sexuality. *School Library Journal Newsletter*.

Bush, B. (2005, April 6). Mifflin High principal fired. *Columbus Dispatch*. Retrieved October 6, 2008, from www.dispatch.com/live/content/local_news/stories/schools/mifflin/040605_story.html.

Buss, D. E. (1995). Psychological sex differences. Origins through sexual selection. *American Psychologist, 50*(3), 164–168.

Caldwell, D. (2007, November 8). Trial begins for teacher in rape case. *Harlan Daily Enterprise*. Retrieved October 6, 2008, from www.harlandaily.com/articles/2007/11/08/news/local_news/news8620.txt.

Centers for Disease Control and Prevention. (2004, May 12). Washington: Number of Chlamydia cases jumps 12 percent. Retrieved October 6, 2008, from www.thebody.com/content/prev/art26361.html.

Centers for Disease Control and Prevention. (2005). STD surveillance 2004—Syphilis. Retrieved October 6, 2008, from www.cdc.gov/STD/stats04/syphilis3.htm.

Centers for Disease Control and Prevention. (2006). Genital warts—Treatment guidelines. Retrieved October 6, 2008, from www.cdc.gov/STD/treatment/2006/genital-warts.htm#warts1.

Centers for Disease Control and Prevention. (2007, November 13). STD surveillance 2006—Racial and ethnic minorities. Retrieved October 6, 2008, from www.cdc.gov/std/stats/minorities.htm.

Centers for Disease Control and Prevention. (2008a, January 4). Genital herpes—CDC fact sheet. Retrieved October 6, 2008, from www.cdc.gov/STD/herpes/STDFact-Herpes.htm.

Centers for Disease Control and Prevention. (2008b, March). HIV/AIDS in the United States. Retrieved October 6, 2008, from www.cdc.gov/hiv/resources/factsheets/us.htm.

Centers for Disease Control and Prevention. (2008c). Syphilis—CDC fact sheet. Retrieved May 6, 2008, from www. cdc.gov/std/syphilis/STDFact-Syphilis.htm.

Cervical cap, Fem cap, and Lea's shield. (2008). *Brown University health education.* Retrieved February 2, 2008, from www.brown.edu/Student_Services/Health_Services/Health_Education/sexual_health/ssc/cervicalcap.htm.

Chesterton, G. K. (2008). On sex. Quote DB. Retrieved February 7, 2008, from www.quotedb.com/category/sex/author/gk-chesterton.

Child pornography. (2005). *Wikipedia.* Retrieved October 6, 2008, from en.wikipedia.org/wiki/Child_pornography.

Chippewa Falls Senior High School. (2007). *Student handbook 2007–2008.* Retrieved October 6, 2008, from cfsd.chipfalls.k12.wi.us/includes/documents/studenthandbook.pdf.

Choosing the Best Life. (2005). *SIECUS Curriculum Review.* Retrieved October 6, 2008, from www.communityactionkit.org/reviews/ChoosingTheBestLife.html.

Cianciolo, A. T., & Sternberg, R. J. (2004). *Intelligence: A brief history.* New York: Wiley-Blackwell.

Citizens for Literary Standards in Schools. (2007). *I Know Why the Caged Bird Sings.* Retrieved August 27, 2007, from www.abffe.com/bbw-classkc-angelou.htm.

Cohen, J. (2000, January 30). Date-rape drug trial to start. *Detroit News.* Retrieved from www.detnews.com/2000/metro/0001/30/01300014.htm.

Colavecchio-Van Sickler, S. (2005, November 1). Police: Teacher had an affair with student. *St. Petersburg Times.* Retrieved October 6, 2008, from www.sptimes.com/2005/11/01/Hillsborough/Police__Teacher_had_a.shtml.

Collins, A. (2008). New Hope gay pride. *About.com.* Retrieved October 31, 2008, from gaytravel.about.com/odpreviewsofpridefestivals/qt/NewHopePride.htm.

Collins, R., Elliott, M. N., Berry, S. H., Kanouse, D. E., Kunkel, D., Hunter, S. B., et al. (2004, September). Watching sex on television predicts adolescent initiation into sexual behavior [Electronic version]. *Pediatrics, 114*(3), 280–289. Retrieved

October 6, 2008, from pediatrics.aappublications.org/cgi/content/full/114/3/e280.

Committee on Adolescence, American Academy of Pediatrics. (1993, October). Homosexuality and adolescence [Electronic version]. *Pediatrics, 92*(4), 631–634. Retrieved October 6, 2008, from www.medem.com/MedLB/article_detaillb_for_printer.cfm?article_ID=ZZZUHJP3KAC&sub_cat=269.

Condoms. (2008). *Brown University health education*. Retrieved February 2, 2008, from www.brown.edu/Student_Services/Health_Services/Health_Education/sexual_health/ssc/condoms.htm.

Condoms do not promote sex in schools—study. (2003, May 29). *ABC News*. Retrieved October 6, 2008, from www.abc.net.au/science/news/stories/s866400.htm.

Corcoran, K. (2005, September 22). Fired teacher gets 1 year in sex case. *Indianapolis Star*. Retrieved October 6, 2008, from www.indystar.com/apps/pbcs.dll/article?AID=/20050922/NEWS01/509220438.

Coulter sentenced to 79 to 120 weeks. (2004, March 15). *San Juan Islander*. Retrieved October 6, 2008, from www.sanjuanislander.com/county/juvenile-court/trial-11-18-03.shtml.

Couple gets prison time in Internet teen sex sting. (2007, October 1). *WPBF-TV*. Retrieved October 6, 2008, from www.wpbf.com/news/14051704/detail.html.

Craig, T. (2007, November 13). Abstinence-only sex-ed funds cut off by Kaine. *Washington Post*. Retrieved October 6, 2008, from www.washingtonpost.com/wp-dyn/content/article/2007/11/12/AR2007111201716.html.

Crossette, B. (2002, May 20). U.S. tells teen girls worldwide to just say no. *Women'sENews*. Retrieved October 6, 2008, from www.womensenews.org/article.cfm/dyn/aid/914/context/archive.

Cunningham, E. (2006, December 20). School accuses 5-year-old of sex harassment. *The Herald-Mail*. Retrieved October 6, 2008, from www.herald-mail.com/?module=displaystory&story_id=154557.

Date rape drugs. (2005). *Women's Health*. Retrieved October 6, 2008, from www.4woman.gov/faq/rohypnol.htm.

A deadly trip. (2000, April 11). *PBS News Hour*. Retrieved October 16, 2008, from www.pbs.org/newshour/extra/ features/jan-june00/ghb.html.

DeNoon, D. (2007, February 5). Internet porn reaches most teens. *WebMD Medical News*. Retrieved October 6, 2008, from www.medicinenet.com/script/main/art.asp?articlekey=79320.

Dirks, T. (2008). Sex in cinema: The greatest and most influential erotic/sexual films and scenes. Retrieved October 30, 2008, from www.filmsite.org/sexinfilms.html.

deVise, D. (2007, January 10). Board of education approves new sex-ed curriculum. *Washington Post*. Retrieved October 6, 2008, from www.washingtonpost.com/wp-dyn/content/article/2007/01/09/AR2007010901707.html.

DeWeerdt, S. E. (2003, January 15). What's a Genome? *Genome News Network*. Retrieved October 6, 2008, from www.genomenewsnetwork.org/resources/whats_a_genome/Chp1_4_1.shtml.

Diaphragms. (2008). *Brown University health education*. Retrieved February 2, 2008, from www.brown.edu/Student_Services/Health_Services/Health_Education/sexual_health/ssc/diaphragm.htm.

Division of Parasitic Diseases. (2008, February 4). Pubic lice infestation. Retrieved October 6, 2008, from www.cdc.gov/NCIDOD/dpd/parasites/lice/factsht_pubic_lice.htm.

Dobson, J. (2008, February 11). Masturbation. *Boys Under Attack*. Retrieved October 6, 2008, from boysunderattack.com/masturbation.html#concerns.

Dougherty, T., & Kurosaka, L. (1996, October 11). *Study finds teen pregnancy and crime levels are higher among kids from fatherless homes*. Retrieved October 6, 2008, from patriot.net/~crouch/adc/jds.html.

Dress code. (2005, May 24). *Pinellas County Schools Code of Student Conduct*. Retrieved October 6, 2008, from www.pinellas.k12.fl.us/forParents/2005-2006dresscode.html.

Dworkin, S. L., & Santelli, J. (2007, September 18). Do abstinence-plus interventions reduce sexual risk behavior among youth? *PloS Medicine Perspectives*. Retrieved November 30, 2007, from www.medicine.plosjournals.org/perlserv/?request=getdocument&doi=10.1371%2Fjournal.pmed.0040276&ct=1d.0040276&ct=1.

Eisenberg, M. E., Bearringer, L. H., Sieving, R. E., Swain, C., & Resnick, M. D. (2004, April). Parents' beliefs about condoms and oral contraceptives: Are they medically accurate? *Perspectives on Sexual and Reproductive Health*. Retrieved October 6, 2008, from findarticles.com/p/articles/mi_m0NNR.

Eisenberg, N. (2006, July). Genital herpes. *Teen Health*. Retrieved October 6, 2008, from www.teensource.org/pages/3024/Genital_Warts_HPV.htm.

Equal Rights Advocates. (2008). *Sexual harassment at school: Know your rights*. Retrieved March 17, 2008, from www.equalrights.org/publications/kyr/shschool.asp.

Ertelt, S. (2007, November 26). Coach in abortion-rape coverup was banned from sports, not arrested. *LifeNews.com*. Retrieved October 6, 2008, from www.lifenews.com/state2623.html.

Essig, M. G. (2007, June 6). Human immunodeficiency virus (HIV) infection—Symptoms. *Yahoo Health*. Retrieved October 6, 2008, health.yahoo.com/hiv-symptoms/human-immunodeficiency-virus-hiv-infection-symptoms/healthwise--hw151445.html.

ETR (Education, Training, Research). (2005). *Safer Choices*. Retrieved October 6, 2008, from www.etr.org/recapp/programs/saferchoices.htm.

Everett, S. A., Warren, C. W., Santelli, J. S., Kann, L, Collins J. L., & Kolbe, L. J. (2002, August). Use of birth control pills, condoms, and withdrawal among U.S. high school students [Electronic version]. *Adolescent Health, 27*(2), 112–118. Retrieved October 6, 2008, from www.ncbi.nlm.nih.gov/pubmed/10899471.

Exclusive purpose: Abstinence-only proponents create federal entitlement in welfare reform. (1997). *Policy & Advocacy, 24*(4). Retrieved September 7, 2007, from www.siecus.org/policy/SReport/srep0001.html.

Facts and statistics: Sexual health and Canadian youth condom use. (2008). *Sexuality and U.ca*. Retrieved October 6, 2008, from www.sexualityandu.ca/teachers/data-5.aspx.

Fair game? The battle over Title IX—women in sports. (2003, January 24). *Current Events*. Retrieved October 6, 2008, from findarticles.com/p/articles/mi_m0EPF/is_16_102/ai_96892095.

Feinberg, W. (2006). *For goodness sake*. New York: Routledge.

Ferrara, L. A. (2007, September 4). *Since when is seduction legal?* Retrieved October 6, 2008, from www.nyrealestatelawblog.com/2007/09/since_when_is_seduction_legal.html.

Fertig, B. (2004, January 6). High school for pregnant teens and young mothers. *WNYC*. Retrieved October 6, 2008, from www.wnyc.org/news/articles/39194.

Field, F. (2006, May 12). Best on the subject. *Amazon.com/books*. Retrieved November 2, 2007, from www.amazon.com.review/R2GRF9MMORV70T/ref=cm_cr_pr_viewpnt#R2GRF9MMORV70T.

First trimester abortion: A comparison of procedures. (2008). *National Abortion Federation*. Retrieved October 6, 2008, from www.prochoice.org/about_abortion/facts/first_trimester.html.

Former Middleboro teacher charged with raping student. (2004, January 7). *Boston Globe*. Retrieved October 6, 2008, from www.boston.com/news/local/massachusetts/articles/ 2004/01/07/former_middleboro_teacher_charged_with_raping_student/.

Former private school coach charged with statutory rape. (2008, February 14). *WATE-Channel 6*. Retrieved October 6, 2008, from www.wate.com/Global/story.asp?S=7876385.

Fowler, B. (2007, November 5). Oak Ridge teacher pleads guilty to statutory rape charges. *Knoxville News Central*. Retrieved October 6, 2008, from www.knoxnews.com/news/2007/nov/05/oakridge-teacher-pleads-guilty-statutory-rape-cha/.

Freedman, D. S., et al. (2000). Secular trends in height among children during 2 decades. *Archives of Pediatric Adolescent Medicine, 154*, 1155–1161. Retrieved November 3, 2008, from www.archpedi.ama-assn.org/cgi/content/abstract/154/2/155.

Friends' school achievement influences high school girls' interest in math. (2008, February 7). *Science Daily*. Retrieved October 6, 2008, from www.sciencedaily.com/releases/2008/02/080207085618.htm.

Garcia, N. (2008, February 7). Boy wants to return to school as a girl. *Channel 9 News*. Retrieved October 6, 2008, from www.9news.com/news/article.aspx?storyid=85989.

Gardiner, B. (2007, May 22). Teacher accused of repeated sex acts with student. *Times Union*. Retrieved October 6, 2008, from timesunion.com/AspStories/story.asp?storyID=591461&category=FRONTPG&BCCode=HOME&newsdate=5/22/2007.

Gavin, M. L. (2005, August). Overweight and obesity. *Kids Health*. Retrieved October 30, 2008, from www.kidshealth.org/parent/general/body/overweight obesity.html.

Gay boy in a dress barred from school prom. (2006, May 25). *The Advocate*. Retrieved October 6, 2008, from www.advocate.com/news_detail.asp?id=31327.

Gay pride celebration. (2008). *Annual SFUSD Gay Pride Celebration*. Retrieved October 6, 2008, from www.healthiersf.org/News/HealthAwarenessMonths/Gay%20Pride%20WAD%202008.pdf.

Gebser v. Lago Vista Independent School District. (2008). *National Organization for Women*. Retrieved March 31, 2008, from www.now.org/issues/harass/gebser.html.

Gehrke-White, D. (2001). Dangerous liaisons: Date rape soaring among teens. *Miami Herald*. Retrieved October 6, 2008, from www.elon.edu/e-web/pendulum/Issues/2004/2_12/onlinefeatures/daterape1.xhtml.

Generation GIT—Technology skills taught. (1996). *Generation Yes*. Retrieved October 6, 2008, from www.genyes.org/programs/gengit/skills.

Generation Yes. (1996). *Generation GIT manual*. Olympia, WA: Generation Yes.

Georgia court frees man in teen sex case. (2007, October 26). *Newsvine.com*. Retrieved October 6, 2008, from www.newsvine.com/_news/2007/10/26/1051481-georgia-court-frees-man-in-teen-sex-case.

Gilbert, A., & Olsen, S. (2006, January 24). Do Web filters protect your child? *CNET News.com*. Retrieved October 6, 2008, from news.com.com/Do+Web+filters+protect+your+child/2100-1032_ 3-6030200.html.

Gonorrhea. (2005). *The microbial world*. Retrieved October 6, 2008, from www.bact.wisc.edu/themicrobialworld/gonorrhea.html.

Guidelines for comprehensive sexuality education (3rd ed.). (2004). SIECUS. Retrieved October 6, 2008, from www.siecus.org/data/global/images/guidelines.pdf.

Guido, M. (2003, January 6). State court defines rape. *San Jose Mercury News*. Retrieved October 6, 2008, from www.bayarea.com/mld/mercurynews/4889062.htm.

Gutierrez, S. (2006, September 18). If there's a sex offender student, schools will know. *Seattle Post Intelligencer*. Retrieved October 6, 2008, from seattlepi.nwsource.com/local/285484_offenders18.html.

Guttmacher Institute. (2006, September). Pregnancy. *Facts on American teens' sexual and reproductive health*. Retrieved October 6, 2008, from www.guttmacher.org/pubs/fb_ATSRH.html.

A guy's perspective on paternity. (2006, December). *American Pregnancy Hotline*. Retrieved October 6, 2008, from teenadvice.about.com/gi/dynamic/offsite.htm?zi=1/XJ/Ya&sdn=teenadvice&cdn=people&tm=30&f=21&tt=14&bt=1&bts=1&zu=http%3A//www.thehelpline.org/guys-corner/.

Hardcastle, M. (2008). Teen fatherhood FAQ. *About.com*. Retrieved April 15, 2008, from teenadvice.about.com/od/teenfathers/a/teenfathersFAQ.htm.

Harris, R. A. (1996). *It's perfectly normal*. New York: Publishers Weekly.

Harrison, T. W. (2003, March 1). Adolescent homosexuality and concerns regarding disclosure. *Journal of School Health*. Retrieved October 6, 2008, from goliath.ecnext.com/coms2/gi_0199-2638877/Adolescent-homosexuality-and-concerns-regarding.html.

Heatherc. (2007, October 26). Holly Hatcher statutory rape case. *Associated Content*. Retrieved October 6, 2008, from www.associatedcontent.com/article/428869/holly_hatcher_statutory_rape_case.html.

Hedges, L. V., & Nowell, A. (1995). Differences in mental test scores, variability, and numbers of high-scoring individuals. *Science, 269*(5220), 41–45.

Heins, M. (2003, June 24). Ignoring the irrationality of Internet filters, the Supreme Court upholds CIPA. *Free Expression Policy Project*. Retrieved October 6, 2008, from www.fepproject.org/commentaries/cipadecision.html.

Hirsch, L. (2007a, February). Birth control patch. *Teens' Health*. Retrieved November 1, 2008, from www.kidshealth.org/teen/sexual_health/contraception/contraception_patch.htm.

Hirsch, L. (2007b, August). Public lice. *Kids' Health*. Retrieved October 6, 2008, from www.kidshealth.org/parent/infections/parasitic/pubic_lice.html.

Hitti, M. (2005, September 16). CDC: Oral sex common among U.S. teens. *WebMd*. Retrieved October 6, 2008, from www.foxnews.com/story/0,2933,169602,00.html.

HIV, STD, and pregnancy prevention education. (2007, September 5). *State level school health policies—Mississippi*. Retrieved October 6, 2008, from www.nasbe.org/HealthySchools/States/states.asp?Name=Mississippi.

Holy Bible. (King James authorized version). New York: American Bible Society.

Homeier, B. P. (2005, August). When your teen is having a baby. *The Children's Hospital*. Retrieved October 6, 2008, from www.thechildrenshospital.org/wellness/info/parents/27941.aspx.

Hsuan, A., Navas, M., & Graves, B. (2008, February 18). Schools cut secret deals with abusive teachers. *The Oregonian*. Retrieved October 6, 2008, from www.oregonlive.com/special/index.ssf/2008/02/schools_cut_secret_deals_with.html.

Hugenberg, J. (2008, February 14). Gay-themed high school play draws protest, support. *Kalamazoo Gazette*. Retrieved October 6, 2008, from www.mlive.com/news/index.ssf/2008/02/kalamazoo_a_group_has.html.

Hyde, J. S., & Linn, M. C. (1988). Gender differences in verbal ability: A meta-analysis. *Psychological Bulletin, 104*, 53–69.

Hyde, J. S., & McKinley, N. M. (1997). Gender differences in cognition: Results from meta-analyses. In P. J. Caplan, M. Crawford, J. S. Hyde & J. R. E. Richardson (Eds.), Gender differences in human cognition (pp. 30–51). New York: Oxford University Press.

I know why the caged bird sings. (2007). *Spark Notes*. Retrieved October 6, 2008, from www.sparknotes.com/lit/cagedbird/.

Impregnable defences. (2007, July 19). *Snopes.com*. Retrieved October 6, 2008, from www.snopes.com/pregnant/conceive.asp.

Internet filter report. (2007). *Internet Filter Review*. Retrieved October 6, 2008, from internet-filter-review.toptenreviews.com/?ttreng=1&ttrkey=internet+filter&gclid=CLOsqbXKk40CFQEyYQodZy7pkA.

Intrauterine device. (2008). *Brown University Health Education*. Retrieved February 2, 2008, from www.brown.edu/Student_Services/Health_Services/Health_Education/sexual_health/ssc/iud.htm.

Jackson, D. N., & Rushton, J. P. (2006). Males have greater *g*: Sex differences in general mental ability from 100,000 17- to 18-year-olds on the Scholastic Assessment Test [Electronic version]. *Intelligence, 34*, 479–486. Retrieved October 16, 2008, from www.ssc.uwo.ca/psychology/faculty/rushton_pubs.htm.

Jackson, F. W. (2006). *Hepatitis*. Retrieved January 8, 2008, from www.gicare.com/jos0001.htm.

Joyce, J., III. (2008, April 20). Davis, Stanton offer child care so parents can stay in school. *Yakima Herald-Republic*. Retrieved October 16, 2008, from www.yakima-herald.com/stories/3356.

Kaiser Family Foundation. (2005, January). *U.S. teen sexual activity*. Retrieved October 16, 2008, from www.kff.org/youthhivstds/upload/U-S-Teen-Sexual-Activity-Fact-Sheet.pdf.

Kalfrin, V., & Poltilove, J. (2007, October 24). Stakeout leads to teacher-student sex charge. *Tampa Tribune*. Retrieved December 5, 2007, from www.newstin.com/sim/us/28530895/en-005-005852397.

Kallen, L. (1998, September 1). Men don't cry, women don't fume. *Psychology Today*. Retrieved October 31, 2008, from www.medicinenet.com/script/main/art.asp?articlekey=35801.

Kansas school district settles sexual harassment case for $45K. (2008, February 4). *Title IX Blog*. Retrieved October 6, 2008, from title-ix.blogspot.com/2008/02/kansas-school-district-settles-sexual.html.

Kaplan, D. (2007, February 28). Connecticut teacher convicted on school porn charge a victim of spyware, says BigFix CTO. *SC Magazine*. Retrieved October 16, 2008, from www.scmagazine.com/asia/news/article/636255/connecticut-teacher-convicted-school-porn-charge-victim-spyware-says-bigfix-cto/.

Karcher, P. (2008). *GRADS Teen Parent Program*. Retrieved October 6, 2008, from www.opt.bham.wednet.edu/grads/.

Kelly, J. R., & Hutson-Comeaux, S. L. (January, 1999). Gender-emotion stereotypes are context specific. *Sex Roles: A Journal of Research*. Retrieved October 31, 2008, from www.findarticles.com/p/articles/mi_m2294/is_1_40/ai_54250822.

Kocieniewski, D. (2006, October 10). A history of sex with students, unchallenged. *New York Times*. Retrieved October 16, 2008, from www.nytimes.com/2006/10/10/nyregion/10teacher.html?_r=1&ex=1161748800&en=c590f144e2fe6c49&ei=5070&oref=slogin.

Kurtenbach, D. (2004, October 29). ACLU scolds Missouri high school for censoring gay student. *American Civil Liberties Union*. Retrieved October 6, 2008, from www.aclu.org/lgbt/youth/12418prs20041029.html.

LaFontaine, T. (2008). Physical activity: The epidemic of obesity and overweight among youth: Trends, consequences, and interventions [Electronic version]. *American Journal of Lifestyle Medicine, 2*(1), 30–36. Retrieved October 6, 2008, from ajl.sagepub.com/cgi/content/abstract/2/1/30.

Lagos, M. (2007, April 25). Racist graffiti defiles Oceana High School. *San Francisco Chronicle*. Retrieved October 6, 2008, from www.sfgate.com/cgi-bin/article.cgi?f=/c/a/2007/04/25/BAGLGPET 8B1.DTL&hw=gay&sn=015&sc=101.

Lamb, A. (2003, November 25). Police investigate alleged sexual assault at Raleigh High School. *Local Tech Wire*. Retrieved October 6, 2008, from www.localtechwire.com/news/local/story/107835/.

Larsen, D. (2005). Schools can take action against date-rape. *About*. Retrieved July 6, 2007, from incestabuse.about.com/od/daterape/a/daterape.htm.

Laureano, B. (2003, February). Children's voice article. *Child Welfare League of America*. Retrieved October 6, 2008, www.cwla.org/programs/r2p/cvarticleslat.htm.

Lawson, A., & Rhode, D. L. (1993). *The politics of pregnancy: Adolescent sexuality and public policy*. New Haven, CT: Yale University Press.

Leonhardt, D. (2008, May 21). Does a college degree pay off? Ask women. *International Herald Tribune*. Retrieved October 30, 2008, from www.iht.com/articles/2008/05/21/business/ leonhardt.php.

Libby, R. (2006, August 12). Just another irrelevant abstinence book intended for today's teenagers. *Amazon.com/books*. Retrieved July 6, 2007, from www

.amazon.com.review/R2GRF9MMORV70T/ref=cm_cr_pr_viewpnt#R2GRF9M MORV70T.

Lickona, T., Lickona, J., & Boudreau, W. (2003, March). *Sex, love and you: Making the right decision*. Notre Dame, IN: Ave Maria Press.

Lim, I. (1999, May). Jerome on marriage and sex. *Patriarchy Website*. Retrieved October 6, 2008, from www. patriarchywebsite.com/bib-patriarchy/deception-jerome-marriage-sex.htm.

Litigating morality II. (1997, January–March). *Lincoln legal briefs*. Retrieved October 6, 2008, from www.papersofabrahamlincoln.org/Briefs/briefs41.htm.

Loughlin, J. (1907). St. Ambrose. *The Catholic Encyclopedia*. New York: Robert Appleton Company. Retrieved July 9, 2008, from www.newadvent.org/cathen/01383c.htm.

Luna, K. (2007, December 3). Teen pregnancies: Rocky day care helps keep teen parents in school. *Quad City Times*. Retrieved October 6, 2008, from www.qctimes.com/articles/2007/12/03/news/local/doc4753a1e759ddb983023655.txt.

Lutheran Church Missouri Synod. (2006). *Abortion and the gospel*. Retrieved October 6, 2008, from www.lcms.org/pages/internal.asp?NavID= 8174.

Lynn, R. (1999). Sex differences in intelligence and brain size: A developmental theory. *Intelligence*, *27*(1), 1–12.

MacDonald, H. (2006, Autumn). Hispanic Family Values? *City Journal*. Retrieved October 6, 2008, from www.city-journal.org/html/16_4_hispanic_family_values.html.

Maine middle school to offer birth control. (2007, October 18). *CNN*. Retrieved October 6, 2008, from www.cnn.com/2007/HEALTH/10/18/middleschool.contraception.ap/.

Manning, M. L. (1998, Spring). Gender differences in young adolescents' mathematics and science achievement. *Childhood Education*. Retrieved October 6, 2008, from findarticles.com/p/articles/mi_qa3614/is_199804/ai_n8803458.

Marklein, M. B. (2005, October 19). College gender gap widens: 57% are women. *USA Today*. Retrieved October 30, 2008, from www.usatoday.com/news/education/2005-10-19-male-college-cover_x.htm.

Marston, C., & King, E. (2006, November 4). Factors that shape young people's sexual behaviour: A systematic review. *The Lancet*, *358*, 1581–1586.

Martin, S., Rector, R., & Pardue, M. G. (2004). *Comprehensive sex education vs. authentic abstinence*. Washington, DC: Heritage Foundation. Retrieved October 6, 2008, from www.heritage.org/Research/Abstinence/abstinencereport.cfm.

Martindale, M. (2008, April 1). Perry case declared a mistrial. *Detroit News*. Retrieved October 6, 2008, from detnews.com/apps/pbcs.dll/article?AID=/20080401/METRO/804010436/1409/METRO.

Masturbation. (2005, November 10). *InteliHealth*. Retrieved October 6, 2008, from www.intelihealth.com/IH/ihtIH/E/9103/23888/266765.html?d=dmtContent.

Masturbation. (2008). *CoolNurse.com*. Retrieved February 16, 2008, from www.coolnurse.com/masturbation.htm.

Mathias, M. J. (2006, November 27). Fond du Lac should let the caged bird sing. *Pundit Nation*. Retrieved October 6, 2008, from punditnation.blogspot.com/2006/11/fond-du-lac-should-let-caged-bird-sing.html.

Maxwell, L. A. (2007, November 14). Digital age adds new dimension to incidents of staff-student sex. *Education Week, 27*(13), 1, 14.

McGrath, M. J. (2008). Profile of a pedophile. *Pittsburgh Post-Gazette*. Retrieved February 27, 2008, from www.post-gazette.com/newslinks/19991102profile.asp.

McKie, R. (2005, November 6). Who has the bigger brain? *The Observer*. Retrieved October 6, 2008, from education.guardian.co.uk/higher/news/story/0,,1635507,00.html.

Meeker, M. (2002, October). How teen sex is killing our kids. *Epidemic*. Retrieved October 6, 2008, from www.regnery.com/lifeline/020715_epidemic.html.

Millner-Fairbanks, A. (2007, December 4). Girls make history by sweeping top honors at a science contest. *New York Times*. Retrieved October 6, 2008, from www.nytimes.com/2007/12/04/nyregion/04siemens.html?ref=education.

Miscarriage. (2006, November). *Bupa*. Retrieved October 6, 2008, from hcd2.bupa.co.uk/fact_sheets/html/miscarriage.html.

Moran, J. P. (2000). *Teaching sex: The shaping of adolescence in the 20th century*. Cambridge, MA: Harvard University Press.

Morris, D. W. (2006, February 28). Man with foot fetish accused of making obscene calls to teens. *CNHI*. Retrieved March 18, 2007, from www.cnhins.com/crime/cnhinscrime_story_059140627.html.

Most frequently asked questions about *Choosing the Best*. (2008). *Choosing the Best*. Retrieved May 23, 2008, from www.choosingthebest.com/faqs/faq_print.html.

Muir, M. (2004, January 19). Research brief: School-based child care. *The Principal's Partnership*. Retrieved October 6, 2008, from www.principalspartnership.com/schoolbasedchildcare.pdf.

Mulvihill, M., & Bergantino, J. (2007, September 24). Questions surround kids' sexual harassment charges. *WBZTV*. Retrieved October 6, 2008, from wbztv.com/local/sexual.harrassment.in.2.590041.html.

Nagourney, E. (2006, May 9). Patterns of deceit raise concerns about teenage sex surveys. *New York Times*. Retrieved October 6, 2008, from www.nytimes.com/2006/05/09/health/09virg.html?r=1&oref=slogin.

NASSPE. (2006). *Legal status of single-sex education*. National Association for Single Sex Public Education. Retrieved October 6, 2008, from www.singlesexschools.org/legal.html.

NASSPE. (2007). *Single-sex education*. National Association for Single Sex Public Education. Retrieved October 6, 2008, from www.singlesexschools.org/home-introduction.htm.

National Campaign to Prevent Teen and Unplanned Pregnancy. (2006a, October). *Teen pregnancy—so what?* Retrieved October 6, 2008, from www.teenpregnancy.org/whycare/sowhat.asp.

National Campaign to Prevent Teen and Unplanned Pregnancy. (2006b, November). *General facts and stats*. Retrieved October 6, 2008, from www.teenpregnancy.org/resources/data/genlfact.asp.

National Campaign to Prevent Teen and Unplanned Pregnancy. (2007). *Teens tell all about . . . the reality of being a teen parent*. Retrieved October 6, 2008, from www.teenpregnancy.org/resources/teens/voices/teenrent.asp.

National Center for HIV/AIDS, Viral Hepatitis, STD, and TB Prevention. (2008, February 21). *Hepatitis B: Frequently asked questions*. Retrieved October 6, 2008, from www.cdc.gov/NCIDOD/DISEASES/HEPATITIS/b/faqb.htm.

National Coalition for the Protection of Children and Families. (2008). Sex and media statistics. Retrieved January 21, 2008, from www.nationalcoalition.org/parenting/mediastats.html.

National Institute of Allergy and Infectious Diseases. (2008). *Human papillomavirus and genital warts*. Retrieved May 10, 2008, from www3.niaid.nih.gov/healthscience/healthtopics/human_papillomavirus/overview.htm.

Neuqua Valley High School student can wear anti-gay T-shirt to school, appeals court rules. (2008, April 24). *Chicago Tribune*. Retrieved from www.chicago tribune.com/news/local/chi-naper-t-shirt-25-both-apr25,0,898199.story.

Nicholson, K. (2008, February 8). Douglas County school employee charged in sex case. *Denver Post*. Retrieved October 6, 2008, from www.denverpost.com/headlines/ci_8202792.

Norman-Eddy, S., Reinhart, C., & Martino, P. (2003, April 14). *Statutory rape laws by state*. Retrieved October 6, 2008, from www.cga.ct.gov/2003/olrdata/jud/rpt/2003-R-0376.htm.

North Carolina battling sexual predators on MySpace. (2007, May 24). *Vindy.com*. Retrieved October 6, 2008, from www.vindy.com/content/national_world/333331756220859.php.

Nowell, A., & Hedges, L. V. (1998, July). Trends in gender differences in academic achievement from 1960 to 1994: An analysis of differences in mean, variance, and extreme scores [Electronic version]. *Sex Roles: A Journal of Research*. Retrieved October 6, 2008, from findarticles.com/p/articles/mi_m2294/is_n1-2_v39/ai_21136459.

NPR—National Public Radio. (2004, February 24). *Sex education in America*. Retrieved October 6, 2008, from www.npr.org/templates/story/story.php?storyId=1622610.

O'Conner, S. D. (1998, June 22). *Gebser v. Lago Vista Independent School District*. Retrieved October 6, 2008, from www.law.cornell.edu/supct/html/96-1866.ZS.html.

O'Conner, S. D. (1999, May 24). *Davis v. Monroe County Board of Education*. Retrieved October 6, 2008, from supct.law.cornell.edu/supct/html/97-843.ZS.html.

Office for Civil Rights, U.S. Department of Education. (2008). *Sexual harassment: It's not academic*. Retrieved March 17, 2008, from www.ed.gov/about/offices/list/ocr/docs/ocrshpam.html.

One million Chlamydia cases in U.S. sets record. (2007, November 13). *MSNBC*. Retrieved October 6, 2008, from www.msnbc.msn.com/id/21772732/.

Onishi, N. (1994, June 29). School guard is charged with statutory rape of student. *New York Times*. Retrieved October 6, 2008, from query.nytimes.com/gst/fullpage.html?res=9B02E1DA143CF93AA15755C0A962958260.

Others not likely to follow school's contraception move. (2007, October 19). *USA Today*. Retrieved October 6, 2008, from www.usatoday.com/news/health/2007-10-17-middle-school-birth-control_N.htm.

Paraphilia. (2002). *Discovery Health*. Retrieved October 6, 2008, from health.discovery.com/centers/sex/sexpedia/paraphilia_04.html.

Pardini, P. (2003, summer). A supportive place for teen parents. *Rethinking Schools*. Retrieved October 16, 2008, from www.rethinkingschools.org/sex/teen174.shtml.

Peacefire. (2007). *Wikipedia*. Retrieved October 6, 2008, from en.wikipedia.org/wiki/Peacefire.

Planned Parenthood. (2005). *Abstinence-only "sex" education*. Retrieved October 6, 2008, from www.plannedparenthood.org/pp2/portal/files/portal/medicalinfo/teensexualhealth/fact-abstinence-education.xml.

Police: Exhibitionist ruins field trip. (2008, February 22). *WBBM-News Radio*. Retrieved October 6, 2008, from www.wbbm780.com/pages/1702539.php?.

Pölling-Vocke, B. (2003, September). *Women basketball in the United States*. Retrieved October 6, 2008, from hockeyarenas.com/womenbasketballintheus.htm.

Pope, D. (2007). *Math is for boys?* Retrieved May 25, 2008, from marketing.wharton.upenn.edu/news/dp_colloquia/Fall%202007/Pope-MathisforBoys-Abstract.pdf.

Pregnancy choices: Raising the baby, adoption, and abortion. (2005). *Medical Library*. Retrieved October 6, 2008, from www.medem.com/medlb/article_detaillb.cfm?article_ID=ZZZ24GBS89F&sub_cat=2005.

Pryor, D. (2006). Teenage sex and pregnancy. *Black Women's Health*. Retrieved October 6, 2008, from www.blackwomenshealth.com/2006/articles.php?id=91.

Ramirez, E. (2007, March 9). Students say bus driver ignored sexual behavior. *St. Petersburg Times*. Retrieved October 6, 2008, from www.sptimes.com/2007/03/09/Citrus/Students_say_bus_driv.shtml.

Ranalli, R., & Mischa, R. (2006, February 6). Boy's suspension in harassment case outrages mother. *Boston Globe*. Retrieved October 6, 2008, from www.boston.com/news/local/massachusetts/articles/2006/02/08/boys_suspension_in_harassment_case_outrages_mother/.

Report: Fewer soft drinks in school. (2007, September 17). *MSNBC*. Retrieved October 30, 2008, from www.msnbc.msn.com/id/20820091/.

A resource guide of best practices for pregnant and parenting teen programs—Teen father services. (2008). *Pregnant and Parenting Teen Initiative*. Retrieved April 8, 2008, from www.center-school.org/education/ppt/pptfather.htm#practices.

Rickert, V. J., & Weinmann, C. M. (2000, September). Date rape among adolescents and young adults. *Resource Center for Adolescent Pregnancy Prevention*. Retrieved October 6, 2008, from www.etr.org/recapp/about.htm.

Rivers, C., & Barnett, R. C. (October 28, 2007). The difference myth. *Boston Globe*. Retrieved October 31, 2008, from www.boston.com/news/globe/ideas/articles/2007/10/28/the_difference_myth/.

Robinson, B. A. (2006, May 7). The status of women in the Bible in early Christianity. *Religious Tolerance*. Retrieved October 6, 2008, from www.religioustolerance.org/fem_bibl.htm.

Robinson, B. A. (2008, June 17). What causes sexual orientation? Nature, nurture, both or neither. *Ontario consultants on religious tolerance*. Retrieved October 6, 2008, from www.religioustolerance.org/hom_caus.htm.

Role-model project: Professional women's careers. (1996). *Women's professions*. Retrieved October 6, 2008, from www.womenswork.org/girls/careers.html.

Ropelato, J. (2006). Internet pornography statistics. *Internet Filter Review*. Retrieved October 6, 2008, from internet-filter-review.toptenreviews.com/internet-pornography-statistics.html#anchor1.

Ropelato, J. (2008). Internet pornography statistics. *Top Ten Reviews*. Retrieved January 23, 2008, from internet-filter-review.toptenreviews.com/internet-pornography-statistics.html#anchor4.

Sadker, D. (2008). *What is title IX?* Retrieved July 1, 2008, from www.american.edu/sadker/titleix.htm.

Saltzman, J. (2005, May 17). ACLU suit sees religious content in abstinence plan. *Boston Globe*. Retrieved October 6, 2008, from www.boston.com/news/education/k_12/articles/2005/05/17/aclu_suit_sees_religious_content_in_abstinence_plan?pg=2.

School sex predators a persistent worry here. (2007, October 21). *Arizona Daily Star*. Retrieved October 6, 2008, from www.azstarnet.com/sn/printDS/207410.

School systems across U.S. challenge books on reading lists. (2001, August 15). *Freedom Forum*. Retrieved October 6, 2008, from www.freedomforum.org/templates/document.asp?documentID=14624.

Schuster, M. A., Bell, R. M., Berry, S. H., & Kanouse, D. E. (1998). Impact of a high school condom availability program on sexual attitudes and behaviors. *Family Planning Perspectives*, *30*(2), 67–72, 88.

Sebastian, S., & Bulwa, D. (2006, June 26). 36th S.F. gay parade—Huge celebration of pride. *San Francisco Chronicle*. Retrieved October 6, 2008, from www.sfgate.com/cgi-bin/article.cgi?f=/c/a/2006/06/25/MNpride25.DTL.

Seiler, S. (1996). *Gender differences in endurance performance and training*. Retrieved October 6, 2008, from home.hia.no/~stephens/gender.htm.

Sex education in the public schools. (1995, November). *The Message, 20* (5), 28–29. Retrieved October 6, 2008, from www.missionislam.com/homed/sexeducation.htm.

Sexual abstinence. (2008). *Wikipedia*. Retrieved March 3, 2008, from en.wikipedia.org/wiki/Sexual_abstinence.

Sexual harassment. (2007). *Norton high school student handbook 2007–2008*. Retrieved November 2, 2008, from www.nortonschools.org/highschool/handbk.pdf.

Sexual harassment policy. (2005). *Mount Miguel high school student handbook*. Retrieved October 6, 2008, from mmhs.guhsd.net/MMStudentHandbook.htm.

Sexual intercourse. (2008). *Massachusetts General Hospital for Children*. Retrieved February 22, 2008, from www.massgeneral.org/children/adolescenthealth/articles/aa_sexual_intercourse.aspx.

Should schools allow gay-friendly activities? (2008, June 4). *KSPR News*. Retrieved October 6, 2008, from www.kspr.com/news/talkback/19546474.html.

SIECUS curriculum review—Choosing the Best Life. (2005). Retrieved October 6, 2008, from communityactionkit.org/reviews/ChoosingTheBestLifeSummary.html.

Slack, D. (2005, March 7). School sex case probe extended. *Boston Globe*. Retrieved October 6, 2008, from www.boston.com/news/local/new_hampshire/articles/2005/03/07/school_sex_case_probe_extended/.

Stafford, G. (1993, October). What Catholic teens need to know about sex. *The Homiletic & Pastoral Review*. Retrieved March 20, 2005, from mafg.home .isp-direct.com / sexedu01.htm. Available at Apache / 1.3.34 Server at mafg .home.isp-direct.com Port 80.

Staten, C. (1996, January 6). "Roofies," the new "date rape" drug of choice. *Emergency Net News*. Retrieved October 6, 2008, from www.emergency.com / roofies .htm.

STD / AIDS Prevention Branch. (2003). *Syphilis*. Retrieved October 6, 2008, from hawaii.gov / health / healthy-lifestyles / std-aids / data-statistics / more-stds.html.

Steele, R. (2008). Masturbation: Is this normal for preschoolers? *iVillage*. Retrieved July 20, 2008, from parenting.ivillage.com / tp / tpdevelopment / 0,,3q9m,00 .html.

Strauss, S. (1994, September). Sexual harassment at an early age. *Principal*. Retrieved October 6, 2008, from www.straussconsulting.net / article3.htm.

Student dress code. (2005, July). *Stafford County Public Schools*. Retrieved October 6, 2008, from www.pen.k12.va.us / Div / Stafford / dresscode.html.

Study confirms males / females use different parts of brain in language and visuospatial tasks. (2006, July 18). *Science Daily*. Retrieved October 6, 2008, from www.sciencedaily.com / releases / 2006 / 07 / 060718180450.htm.

Study finds smaller girl-boy math gap in countries with gender equality. (May 30, 2008). *Jerusalem Post*. Retrieved October 31, 2008, from www.jpost.com / servlet / Satellite?pagename=JPost / JPArticle / ShowFull&cid=1212041432648.

Study of language use in children suggests sex influences how brain processes words. (2006, November 28). *Science Daily*. Retrieved October 6, 2008, from www.sciencedaily.com / releases / 2006 / 11 / 061127210527.htm.

Suit challenges school book ban. (1987, May 14). *New York Times*. Retrieved October 6, 2008, from query.nytimes.com / gst / fullpage.html?res=9B0DE4D9173EF9 37A25756C0A961948260.

Surveillance Summaries. (2006, June). Centers for Disease Control and Prevention. MMWR 2006:55 (No. SS-5). Retrieved October 6, 2008, from www.teen pregnancy.org / resources / data / pdf / TeenSexActivityOnePagerJune06.pdf.

Teen abortion laws. (2008). *Cool Nurse*. Retrieved October 6, 2008, from www .coolnurse.com / abortion_laws.htm.

Teen father services—a resource guide of best practices for pregnant and parenting teen programs. (2008). *Pregnant and parenting teen initiative*. Retrieved April 8, 2008, from www.center-school.org / education / ppt / pptfather.htm#practices.

Teen found guilty of two counts of rape. (2003, October 16). *San Juan Islander*. Retrieved October 6, 2008, from www.sanjuanislander.com / county / juvenile-court / trial-10-03.shtml.

Teen parents: Red Lake High School Daycare Center. (2008). Retrieved April 22, 2008, from www.rlnn.com / 2008All / ArtJan08 / TeenParentsRLHSDayCareCenter .html.

Third girl involved in school porn case. (2008, January 25). *Midstate News*. Retrieved October 6, 2008, from www.pennlive.com / midstate / index.ssf / 2008 / 01 / third_ girl_involved_in_allento.html.

Thompson, K., & Yokota, F. (2004, July 13). Study finds "ratings creep": Movie ratings categories contain more violence, sex, profanity than decade ago. *Medscape*

General Medicine. Retrieved October 6, 2008, from www.hsph.harvard.edu/news/press-releases/archives/2004-releases/press07132004.html.

Thornburg, D., & Lin, H. S. (Eds.). (2002). *Youth, pornography, and the Internet*. Washington, DC: National Academies Press. Retrieved October 6, 2008, from www.nap.edu/openbook.php?isbn=0309082749.

Three high school students accused of rape of girl, 15, in school bathroom. (2004, April 17). *WUSA9*. Retrieved October 6, 2008, from www.wusa9.com/news/news_article.aspx?storyid=28527.

Timeline of Homosexual History. (2008). Retrieved July 7, 2008, from www.geocities.com/WestHollywood/Park/2609/timeline2.htm.

Trewartha, R. (1989, November). What your dreams make you. *New Internationalist*. Retrieved October 6, 2008, from www.newint.org/issue201/dreams.htm.

Trichomoniasis. (2005, May). *Women's Health*. Retrieved October 6, 2008, from www.4woman.gov/faq/stdtrich.htm.

Tucker, N. (2006, December 18). Absentee Black Fathers. *Washington Post*. Retrieved October 6, 2008, from www.washingtonpost.com/wp-dyn/content/discussion/2006/12/15/DI2006121501107.html.

Underhill, H. C. (1910). *A treatise on the law of criminal evidence*. Indianapolis: Hollenback Press (Original work published 1898).

Vanderheyden, T. (2006, March 23). *TV promotes promiscuity in children*. Retrieved October 6, 2008, from www.lifesite.net/ldn/2006/mar/06032304.html.

Van Vranken, M. (2006a, April). Chlamydia. *Teens Health*. Retrieved October 6, 2008, from www.kidshealth.org/teen/infections/stds/std_chlamydia.html.

Van Vranken, M. (2006b, April). Gonorrhea. *Teens Health*. Retrieved November 2, 2008, from www.teen source.org/pages/3018/Gonorrhea.htm.

Vara, R. (2005, June 22). Baptists agree to hold schools accountable. *Houston Chronicle*. Retrieved October 6, 2008, from www.chron.com/cs/CDA/ssistory.mpl/nation/3237327.

Vargas, R. A. (2008, June 27). ACLU participates in gay pride fest, on heels of public school disputes. *Times-Picayune*. Retrieved from www.nola.com/news/index.ssf/2008/06/aclu_participates_in_weekend_g.html.

Ventura, S. (2007, December 5). Teen birth rate rises for first time in 15 years. *National Center for Health Statistics*. Retrieved October 6, 2008, from www.cdc.gov/NCHS/pressroom/07newsreleases/teenbirth.htm.

Voyeurism. (2008). *Encyclopedia of Mental Disorders*. Retrieved July 20, 2008, from www.minddisorders.com/Py-Z/Voyeurism.html.

Warren Township schools superintendent's letter to parents. (2007, March 14). *WTHR*. Retrieved October 30, 2008, from www.wthr.com/Global/story.asp?S=6180780.

Washkuch, F. (2007, June 6). Judge grants Amero new trial in school-porn case. *SC Magazine*. Retrieved October 6, 2008, from www.scmagazine.com/asia/news/article/662775/judge-grants-amero-new-trial-school-porn-case/.

Web server survey. (2007, December). *Netcraft*. Retrieved October 6, 2008, from news.netcraft.com/archives/web_server_survey.html.

Weigl, A. (2007, May 23). State Senate approves MySpace bill. *Raleigh News & Observer*. Retrieved from www.newsobserver.com/news/story/577639.html.

Weiss, R. E. (2008). Teen pregnancy. *Pregnancy and Childbirth*. Retrieved April 15, 2008, from pregnancy.about.com/cs/teenpregnancy/a/teenpreg.htm.

What is medical abortion? (2008). *National Abortion Federation*. Retrieved October 6, 2008, from www.prochoice.org/about_abortion/facts/medical_abortion.html.

Whitehead, M. M. (1993, May). Sex education: The Catholic scene. *Voices*. Retrieved October 6, 2008, from www.wf-f.org/Whitehead-SexEdintro.html.

Willenz, P. (2005, February 23). Based on the research, comprehensive sex education is more effective at stopping the spread of HIV infections, says APA committee. *American Psychological Association Press Release*. Retrieved March 7, 2006, from www.apa.org/releases/sexeducation.html.

Williams, E. G., & Sadler, L. S. (2001, February). Effects of an urban high-school-based child care center on self-selected adolescent parents and their children. *Journal of School Health, 71*(2), 47–52.

Williamson, E., & Aratani, L. (2005, June 14). As school bus sexual assaults rise, danger often overlooked. *Washington Post*. Retrieved October 6, 2008, from www.washingtonpost.com/wp-dyn/content/article/2005/06/13/AR2005061301642.html.

Winn, P. (2008, March 10). High school offers homosexual porn, parents complain. *CNS News.com*. Retrieved May 7, 2008, from www.cnsnews.com/ViewCulture.asp?Page=/Culture/archive/200803/CUL20080310a.html.

Withdrawal. (2008). *Brown University Health Education*. Retrieved February 2, 2008, from www.brown.edu/Student_Services/Health_Services/Health_Education/sexual_health/ssc/withdrawal.htm.

Women and the marathon. (2008). *Hickok Sports*. Retrieved June 17, 2008, from www.hickoksports.com/history/marathonw.shtml.

Women in the professions. (2008). *Feminism and Women's Studies*. Retrieved July 5, 2008, from feminism.eserver.org/workplace/professionals.

World Health Organization. (2008). Women and HIV/AIDS. *Gender, women, and health*. Retrieved May 16, 2008, from www.who.int/gender/hiv_aids/en/.

Zwillich, T. (2005, November 9). More sex content on teens' TV shows. *WebMD Medical News*. Retrieved November 2, 2008, from www.medicinenet.com/script/main/art.asp?articlekey=55266.

Index

About the Author

R. Murray Thomas is professor emeritus at the University of California, Santa Barbara. He retired in 1991 after 50 years of teaching, first in high schools, then in universities. His last 30 years were at the University of California, Santa Barbara, where he taught educational psychology and headed the program in international education.